Boswelliana

The Commonplace Book of James Boswell, with a Memoir and Annotations

James Boswell

Alpha Editions

This edition published in 2021

ISBN : 9789355750068

Design and Setting By
Alpha Editions
www.alphaedis.com
Email - info@alphaedis.com

As per information held with us this book is in Public Domain. This book is a reproduction of an important historical work. Alpha Editions uses the best technology to reproduce historical work in the same manner it was first published to preserve its original nature. Any marks or number seen are left intentionally to preserve its true form.

Contents

PREFACE.	- 1 -
INTRODUCTORY REMARKS	- 3 -
MEMOIR OF JAMES BOSWELL.	- 8 -
BOSWELLIANA.	- 151 -
UXORIANA.	- 222 -
APPENDIX.	- 223 -
FOOTNOTES:	- 226 -

PREFACE.

JAMES BOSWELL had not, by publishing his great work, the Life of Dr. Samuel Johnson, completed his literary plans. He preserved the letters he received from notable persons, and retained copies of his own. For many years he kept a journal, in which he recorded not merely his conversations with Dr. Johnson, but the diurnal occurrences of his own life. Respecting his journal, in a letter to his friend Mr. Temple, dated 22nd May, 1789, he writes:—"You have often told me that I was the most thinking man you ever knew; it is certainly so as to my own life. I am continually conscious, continually looking back or looking forward, and wondering how I shall feel in situations which I anticipate in fancy. My journal will afford materials for a very curious narrative. I assure you I do not now live with a view to have surprising incidents, though I own I am desirous that my life should tell." Boswell evidently intended to adapt the contents of his journal to an autobiography; his early death precluded the intention.

Besides a journal, Boswell kept in a portfolio a quantity of loose quarto sheets, inscribed on each page BOSWELLIANA. In certain of these sheets the pages are denoted by numerals in the ordinary fashion; another portion is numbered by the folios; while a further portion consists of loose leaves and letterbacks. The greater part of the entries are made so carefully as to justify the belief that the author intended to embody the whole in a volume of literary anecdotes.

At Boswell's death his portfolio was sold along with the books contained in his house in London. It came into the possession of John Hugh Smyth Pigott, Esq., of Brockley Hall, Somersetshire, an indefatigable book collector. On Mr. Pigott's death in 1861 the volume, bound in russia, was sold along with the stores of the Brockley library. Purchased by Mr. Thomas Kerslake, bookseller in Bristol, it was afterwards sold by him to Lord Houghton. By his lordship it was lately handed to the Grampian Club, with a view to publication.

Boswell's commonplace-book exhibits some of the author's weaknesses, but is on the whole a valuable repertory. The social talk of leading persons during the latter part of the century is graphically depicted. Considerable light is thrown on the character of individuals respecting whom every fragment of authentic information is treasured with interest. In preparing the commonplace-book for the press the Editor has omitted a few entries which transgressed on decorum. He has generally retained the author's orthography.

The Memoir has been prepared with a desire to depict the author's history in his own words. Letters to correspondents have been copiously introduced. Of these a most interesting portion have been obtained from the volume of Boswell's Letters to Mr. Temple, published by Mr. Bentley, under the care of Mr. Francis. It is curious to remark that these letters, like the commonplace-book, left the family of the owner, and were accidentally discovered in the shop of a trader at Boulogne.

The Editor cannot venture to enumerate all the kind friends who have aided his inquiries. He has been indebted to Lord Houghton for important particulars. The representatives of Thomas David Boswell, the biographer's brother, and of his uncle, Dr. John Boswell, have been most polite and obliging in their communications. The Rev. W. H. Wylie has kindly furnished Boswell's address to the Ayrshire constituency.

GRAMPIAN LODGE,

FOREST HILL, SURREY,

May, 1874.

INTRODUCTORY REMARKS

By Lord Houghton.

There is no word of vindication or appreciation to be added to Mr. Carlyle's estimate of the character and merits of James Boswell. That judgment places him so high that the most fantastic dream of his own self-importance would have been fully realized, and yet there is no disguise of his follies or condonation of his vices. We understand at once the justice and the injustice of his contemporaries, and while we are amused at the thought of their astonishment could the future fame of the object of so much banter and rude criticism have been revealed to them, we doubt whether, had we been in their place, our misapprehension and depreciation would not have been still greater than theirs.

It was the object of Boswell's life to connect his own name with that of Dr. Johnson; the one is now identified with the other. He aspired to transmit to future time the more transitory and evanescent forms of Johnson's genius; he has become the repository of all that is most significant and permanent. The great "Dictionary" is superseded by wider and more accurate linguistic knowledge; the succinct and sententious biographies are replaced, where their subjects are sufficiently important, by closer criticisms and by antiquarian details, while in the majority of his subjects the Lives and Works of the writers are alike forgotten. The "Rambler" and the "Idler" stand among the British Essayists, dust-worn and silent; and though a well-informed Englishman would recognise a quotation from "Rasselas" or "London," he would hardly be expected to remember the context.[1] But the "Johnsoniad" keeps fresh among us the noble image of the moralist and the man, and when a philosopher of our time says pleasantly of Boswell what Heinrich Heine said gravely of Goethe, that he measures the literary faculty of his friends by the extent of their appreciation of his idol, it is to a composite creation of the genius of the master and of the sympathetic talent of the disciple that is paid this singular homage. For it was assuredly a certain analogy of character that fitted Boswell to be the friendly devotee and intellectual servitor of Dr. Johnson, and the resemblances of style and manner which are visible even in the fragments brought together in this volume cannot be regarded as parodies or conscious imitations, but rather as illustrations of the mental harmony which enabled the reporter to produce with such signal fidelity, in the words of another, his own ideal of all that was good and great.

"Elia," with his charming othersidedness, writes, in one place, "I love to lose myself in other men's minds," and in another, "the habit of too constant intercourse with spirits above you instead of raising you, keeps you down;

too frequent doses of original thinking from others restrains what lesser portion of that faculty you may possess in your own. You get entangled in another man's mind, even as you lose yourself in another man's ground; you are walking with a tall varlet, whose strides outpace yours to lassitude." Both observations are true, and instances are not wanting of the spirit of reverence and the habit of waiting on the words and thoughts of those who are regarded as the spokesmen of authority, emasculating the self-reliance and thralling the free action of superior men. This is especially observable in political life, where a certain surrender of independence is indispensable to success, but where, if carried too far, it tends to dwarf the stature and plane down the beneficial varieties of public characters. But there will always be many forces that militate against this courtliness in the Republic of Letters; leading men will have their clique, and too often like to be kings of their company, but more damage is done to themselves than to those who serve them, and there is little fear of too rapid a succession of Boswells or Eckermanns.

In these days of ready and abundant writing the value of Conversation, as the oral tradition of social intercourse, is not what it was in times when speech was almost the exclusive communicator of intelligence between man and man. Yet there will ever be an appreciation of the peculiar talent which reproduces with vivacity those fabrics of the hour, and gives to the passing lights and shades of thought an artistic and picturesque coherence. This is the product of a genial spirit itself delighting in the verbal fray, and of a society at once familiar and intellectual. We have from other sources abundant details of the vivacity of the upper classes of the Scottish community in the latter half of the last century and the beginning of the present. It had the gaiety which is the due relaxation of stern and solid temperaments, and the humour which is the genuine reverse of a deep sense of realities and an inflexible logic. It was intemperate, not with the intemperance of other northern nations, to whom intoxication is either a diversion to the torpor of the senses, or a narcotic applied by a benevolent nature to an anxious and painful existence, but with a conviviality which physical soundness and moral determination enabled them to reconcile with the sharpest attention to their material interests and with the hardest professional work.

FAC-SIMILE OF A PAGE OF BOSWELL'S COMMONPLACE BOOK
IN THE POSSESSION OF LORD HOUGHTON.

Scotland had had the remarkable destiny in its earlier history of assimilating to itself the elements of a finer civilisation without losing its independence or national character; and it had even interchanged with the continent of Europe various influences of manners and speech. It had thus retained a certain intellectual self-sufficiency, especially in its relations with English society and literature, which never showed itself more distinctly than in its estimate of Dr. Johnson and of his connection with Boswell. In the pamphlets, and verses, and pictures of the time, Boswell appears as a monomaniac, and Johnson as an impostor. The oblong quarto of Caricatures which followed their journey to the Hebrides shows that Boswell not only did not gain any favour from his countrymen, by introducing among them the writer, who, however little understood in his entire worth, nevertheless held a high place among English wits and men of letters, but brought abundant ridicule on himself, his family, and his friend. It required all

Boswell's invincible good humour to withstand the sarcasm that assailed him. Dr. Johnson certainly repaid with interest the prejudice and ill-will he encountered, but it remains surprising that so good and intelligent a company did not better recognise so great a man. We did not so receive Burns and Walter Scott. The agreeable reminiscences of Lord Cockburn and Dean Ramsay have given us the evening lights of the long day of social brightness which Scotland, and especially Edinburgh, enjoyed; and if this pleasantness is now a thing of the past, the citizens of the modern Athens have only shared the lot of other sections of mankind, even of France, *par excellence*, the country of Conversation.[2]

This decadence in the art and practice of the communication of ideas, and in the cultivation of facile and coloured language, is commonly attributed to the wide extension of literature and the press, which give to every man all the knowledge of matters of interest which he can require without the intervention of a fellow-creature. It may be that men may now read and think too much to talk, but the change is, perhaps, rather the effect of certain alterations in the structure of society itself, accompanied by the fastidiousness that tries to make up by silence and seclusion for the arbitrary distinctions and recognised barriers, which limited and defined the game of life, but admitted so much pleasant freedom within the rules. We can however, still acknowledge the value of such records as those of the late Mr. Nassau, Senior, whose "Conversations" with the most eminent politicians and men of action of his time, especially in France, afford trustworthy and interesting materials for the future historian, and where a legal mind and well-trained observation take the place of vivid representation and literary skill. "Quand un bon mot," writes Monsieur L.'Enfant in one of his prefaces to his "Poggiana" "est en même temps un trait d'Histoire, on fait aisèment grace à'ce qui peut lui manquer du côté de la force et du sel."

The title of "Boswelliana," which the editor has taken from the original manuscript, is hardly correct. This is, in fact, one of the note-books of the anecdotes and *facetiæ* of the society in which Boswell lived; and though such a use of the termination may find some analogy in the Luculliana,—cherries that Lucullus brought from Pontus—and the Appiana—apples introduced into Rome by him of the Appian way,—yet the term "Ana," in its most important applications, has always referred not to the collector, but to the personage or at any rate to the subject-matter of the book. Some vindication for its use on the present occasion may, however, be found in those instances in which Boswell acts as Bozzy to himself, and where the opinions and the mode of enunciating them are so thoroughly Boswellian that they give a characteristic flavour to the whole. What can be more delightfully his own than the prefixes "Uxoriana," and "My son Alexander?"

There is some mystery in the insertion of certain occasional Johnsoniana, which could hardly have found their way into this collection, if Boswell had at the time been keeping special memoranda of his great Oracle. They are not very numerous nor consecutive, nor do they imply that at the time they were taken down they were intended as portions of the *magnum opus*. Most of them, however, are incorporated in it, and are only repeated here to preserve the integrity of the manuscript. The few omissions, such as they are, are of the same character as the *lacunæ* in the Temple letters.

The historical and biographical annotation of these anecdotes has been a work requiring considerable local knowledge and antiquarian research. Executed, as it is, by Dr. Rogers, it affords an interesting social picture of the Scotland of the day, and there are many families still living, who will here gladly recognise and welcome the words and thoughts of their ancestors.

MEMOIR OF
JAMES BOSWELL.

AS Dr. Johnson's biographer, and the chronicler of his conversations, James Boswell is entitled to remembrance. On the publication of his "Life of Johnson,"—though seven years had elapsed since the moralist's decease, and two memoirs had in the interval appeared,—a deep interest was excited; and the author, whose peculiarities had hitherto subjected him to ridicule, at once attained a first place as a biographer. Time, which effects many changes in literary popularity, has borne in an even current the "Life of Johnson," and therewith in every home of lettered Britons has rendered familiar the name of Boswell.

Representing a landed branch of a Norman House, James Boswell inherited no small share of family pride, a point of character which under proper regulation might have proved salutary. Sieur de Bosville accompanied William of Normandy into England, and held a considerable command at the battle of Hastings. His descendants migrated into Scotland during the reign of David I., and there acquired lands in the county of Berwick. Robert Bosville obtained the lands of Oxmuir, in Berwickshire, under William the Lion; he witnessed many charters in the reign of that monarch. He was father of Adam de Bosville de Oxmuir, whose name appears in an obligation of Philip de Lochore in 1235, during the reign of Alexander II. In the lands of Oxmuir he was succeeded by his son Roger, and his grandson William de Bosville, the latter of whom was compelled with other barons to swear fealty to Edward I. in 1296. Richard, son of William, obtained from King Robert the Bruce, lands near Ardrossan, in Ayrshire, in addition to his estates in Berwickshire.

Roger de Boswell, second son of Richard of Oxmuir, married in the reign of David II., Mariota, daughter and co-heiress of Sir William Lochore of that ilk, with whom he obtained half the barony of Auchterderran, in Fife. In this barony he was succeeded by his son John de Boswell, who espoused Margaret, daughter of Sir Robert Melville, of Carnbee. Their son, Sir William Boswell, was judge in a perambulation of the lands of Kirkness and Lochore. He married Elizabeth, daughter and heiress of Alexander Gordon, with whom he got some lands in the constabulary of Kinghorn. His son, Sir John Boswell, designed of Balgregie, married, early in the fifteenth century, Mariota, daughter of Sir John Glen, and with her obtained the barony of Balmuto, in Fife.

Sir John Boswell, of Balmuto, was succeeded by his son David, who married first Elizabeth, daughter of Sir John Melville, of Raith, and secondly, Isabel, daughter of Sir Thomas Wemyss, of Rires, relict of David Hay, of

Naughton. Robert, younger son by the first marriage, became parson of Auchterderran, and was much esteemed for his piety and learning: he attained his hundredth year. David, the elder son, obtained, in 1458, from James II., by a charter under the great seal, the lands of Glasmont, in Fife. He married first Grizel, daughter of Sir John Wemyss of that ilk; and secondly, in 1430, Lady Margaret Sinclair, daughter of William, Earl of Orkney and Caithness. Thomas, eldest son of the second marriage, obtained from James IV., as a signal mark of royal favour, the estate of Auchinleck,[3] in Ayrshire. He was slain at Flodden on the 9th September, 1513. By his wife Annabella, daughter of Sir Hugh Campbell, of Loudoun, he had an only son David, who, succeeding to the paternal estate, espoused Lady Janet Hamilton, daughter of James, first Earl of Arran. David was succeeded by his son John, whose first wife was Christian, daughter of Sir Robert Dalzell, of Glenae, progenitor of the Earls of Carnwath. Of this marriage, James, the eldest son, succeeded to Auchinleck. He died in 1618, leaving by his wife, Marion Crawford, of Kerse, six sons, three of whom entered the service of Gustavus Adolphus, and ultimately settled in Sweden. David Boswell, the eldest, succeeded to Auchinleck; he was an ardent supporter of Charles I., and was fined ten thousand marks for refusing to subscribe the Covenant. He married Isabel, daughter of Sir John Wallace, of Cairnhill, but having no male issue, he was at his death in 1661 succeeded by his nephew David, son of his next brother James by his wife, a daughter of Sir James Cunninghame, of Glengarnock.

David Boswell of Auchinleck espoused Anne, daughter of James Hamilton of Dalziel, by whom, besides three daughters, he had two sons, James and Robert. The latter settled in Edinburgh as a Writer to the Signet, and acquiring a handsome fortune, purchased from his kinsman, Andrew Boswell, the estate of Balmuto, which had belonged to his ancestors. His son, Claude James Boswell, born in 1742, passed advocate in 1766, and after serving eighteen years as sheriff of Fife, was in 1798 raised to the bench, under the judicial title of Lord Balmuto.[4] His lordship died on the 22nd July, 1824.

James Boswell, elder son of David Boswell of Auchinleck, succeeded to the paternal estate: he practised as an advocate, and attained considerable eminence in his profession. By his wife, Lady Elizabeth Bruce, daughter of Alexander, second Earl of Kincardine, he had two sons and a daughter, Veronica; she married David Montgomerie, of Lainshaw, and his daughter Margaret espoused James Boswell, the subject of this memoir. John, younger son of James Boswell of Auchinleck, studied medicine, and became censor of the Royal College of Physicians, Edinburgh. Alexander, the elder son, succeeded to Auchinleck on his father's death in 1748.

Through his father, Alexander Boswell was attracted to legal studies; he passed advocate 29th December, 1729, and after a period of successful practice at the bar, was in 1743 appointed sheriff of Wigtonshire. He was raised to the bench in 1754, when he assumed the title of Lord Auchinleck;[5] he was appointed a Lord of Justiciary in the following year.

About the year 1739, Alexander Boswell married his cousin[6] Euphemia Erskine, descended of the ennobled House of Erskine of Mar. Her father, Colonel John Erskine, was a younger son of the Hon. Sir Charles Erskine, first baronet of Alva, and her mother was Euphemia, one of the four daughters of William Cochrane of Ochiltree, a scion of the noble House of Dundonald by his wife Lady Mary Bruce, eldest daughter of Alexander, second Earl of Kincardine. Of the marriage of Alexander Boswell and Euphemia Erskine were born three sons: John, the second son, became a military officer and died unmarried; David, the youngest, entered a house of business, and at the close of his apprenticeship in 1768 joined partnership with Charles Herries, a Scotsman, and Honorius Dalliol, a Frenchman, in establishing a mercantile house at Valencia in Spain. On account of the Spaniards being prejudiced against the name of David, as of Jewish origin, he assumed the Christian name of Thomas. On account of the war he left Spain in 1780, when he settled in London, and commenced business as a merchant and banker. He afterwards accepted a post in the Navy Office, where he became the head of the Prize Department. He purchased the estate of Crawley Grange, Buckinghamshire, and died in 1826. A man of grave deportment and correct morals, he was esteemed for his discretion, urbanity, and intelligence. By his marriage with Anne Catherine, sister of General Sir Charles Green, Bart., he became father of one child, Thomas David, who was born 24th September, 1800. This gentleman succeeded his father in the estate of Crawley Grange; he married in 1841 Jane, daughter of John Barker, Esq. Having died without issue, his estate passed to another branch of the Boswell family.

James Boswell, eldest son of Lord Auchinleck, was born at Edinburgh on the 29th October, 1740. He received his rudimentary training from a private tutor, Mr. John Dun, a native of Eskdale, and who, on the presentation of his father, was, in 1752, ordained minister of Auchinleck. He was afterwards sent to a school at Edinburgh, taught by Mr. James Mundell, a teacher of eminence. Afterwards he was enrolled as a pupil in the High School, under Mr. John Gilchrist, one of the masters, a celebrated classical scholar.[7]

Possessed of strong religious and political convictions, Lord Auchinleck sought to imbue his children with a love of Presbyterianism and a loyal attachment to the House of Hanover. In those aims he was assisted by his wife, a woman of vigorous sagacity and most exemplary piety. To her affectionate counsel rather than to the wishes of his father, the eldest son was disposed to yield some reverence. But he early affected to despise the simple ritual of the Presbyterian Church, and in direct antagonism to his father's commands he declared himself a Jacobite and a warm adherent of the exiled House. He related to Dr. Johnson, that when his father prayed for King George, he proceeded to pray for King James, till one day his uncle, General Cochrane, gave him a shilling on condition that he would pray for the Hanoverian monarch. The bribe overcame his scruples, and he did as he was asked.

With a view to his becoming an advocate at the Scottish Bar, Boswell entered the University of Edinburgh. There he formed the acquaintance of Mr. William Johnson Temple, from Allardine in Northumberland, a young gentleman preparing in the literary classes for orders in the English Church. Mr. Temple was Boswell's senior, and much surpassed him in general knowledge. He belonged to an old and respectable, if not an affluent family, and he was of a pleasing and gentlemanly deportment. The exiled king being forsaken, he became Boswell's next hero. In parting from him at the close of their first college session, Boswell begged that their friendship might be maintained by correspondence; and letters actually passed between them for thirty-seven years. To Boswell's share of that correspondence we are indebted for many materials illustrative of his life.

It will be convenient at this point to present a few particulars of Mr. Temple's career, closely associated as that gentleman was with the subject of our history. After leaving Edinburgh he sustained the loss of a considerable fortune through the embarrassments of his father. Proceeding to the University of Cambridge, he took the degree of LL.B., and soon afterwards entered into orders. In 1767 he was preferred to the Rectory of Mamhead, Devonshire, which, added to the Vicarage of St. Gluvias, Cornwall, brought him, with the remains of his private fortune, an income of £500 a year. In youth he afforded proof of original power; he was a considerable politician, and an excellent classical scholar. He composed neatly; his character of the poet Gray, with whom he was acquainted, has been quoted approvingly by Dr. Mason, his biographer, and likewise by Dr. Johnson. He published an essay on the studies of the clergy, another "On the Abuse of Unrestrained Power," and "A Selection of Historical and Political Memoirs;" but none of these compositions were much sought after. He died on the 8th August, 1796, surviving our author little more than a year. He was oppressed by an habitual melancholy, which the untoward temper of his wife served materially to intensify. He has been described as "Boswell's faithful monitor;" he was scarcely so, for his remonstrances were feeble. Had he reproved sternly he might have been of some service.

In a letter to Mr. Temple dated 29th July, 1758, Boswell informs him that he had been introduced to Mr. Hume, whom he thus describes:—"He is a most discreet, affable man, as ever I met with, and has really a great deal of learning, and a choice collection of books. He is indeed an extraordinary man,—few such people are to be met with now-a-days. We talk a great deal of genius, fine language, improving our style, &c., but I am afraid solid learning is much wore out. Mr. Hume, I think, is a very proper person for a young man to cultivate an acquaintance with. Though he has not perhaps the most delicate taste, yet he has applied himself with great attention to the study of the ancients, and is likewise a great historian, so that you are not only entertained in his company, but may reap a great deal of useful instruction."

When Mr. Temple proceeded to Cambridge he reported to his Edinburgh friend that he was studying in earnest. In his reply, dated 16th December, 1758, Boswell describes his own studies:—"I can assure you," he writes, "the study of the law here is a most laborious task.... From nine to ten I attend the law class; from ten to eleven study at home; and from one to two attend a college [class] upon Roman antiquities; the afternoon and evening I always spend in study. I never walk except on Saturdays." Thanking his friend for the perusal of a MS. poem he adds, "To encourage you I have enclosed a few trifles of my own.... I have published now and then the production of a leisure hour in the magazines. If any of these essays can give entertainment to my friend, I shall be extremely happy."

On the importance of religion Boswell reciprocated his friend's sentiments. After informing him that the continuance of his friendship made him "almost weep with joy," he proceeds, "May indulgent Heaven grant a continuance of our friendship! As our minds improve in knowledge may the sacred flame still increase, until at last we reach the glorious world above when we shall never be separated, but enjoy an everlasting society of bliss. Such thoughts as these employ my happy moments, and make me—

'Feel a secret joy

Spring o'er my heart, beyond the pride of kings.'"

After a reference to companionship he adds, "I hope by Divine assistance, you shall still preserve your amiable character amidst all the deceitful blandishments of vice and folly."

In the same letter Boswell informed Mr. Temple that he had fallen desperately in love. The object of his affection was a Miss W—— t, for so he disguises her name—a reticence in matters of the heart which he does not evince subsequently. After expatiating on the lady's charms and angelic qualities, especially her "just regard for true piety and religion," he remarks that "she *is* a fortune of thirty thousand pounds." With so large a dowry, he feels that she might be difficult to win, but he conceives that "a youth of *his* turn has a better chance to gain the affections of a lady of her character than of any other." He adds complacently, "As I told you before, my mind is in such an agreeable situation, that being refused would not be so fatal as to drive me to despair." He sums up by assuring his correspondent that he had entrusted the secret of his passion only to another whose name was "Love."

Mr. Love was one of Boswell's early heroes. A native of England, he was originally connected with Drury Lane Theatre, but for some cause he left London and sojourned at Edinburgh. There he at first practised private theatricals, but afterwards became a teacher of elocution. He read with Miss W—— t, and also with Boswell, though at different hours, and advised the latter to look after the pretty heiress. Boswell took the hint; but the dream soon passed away, for the name of the rich beauty does not reappear.

To his young friend Mr. Love administered more useful counsel by advising him to cultivate an easy style of composition. To accomplish this he recommended him to keep a journal or commonplace-book, and daily to record in it notes of conversations, and of more remarkable occurrences. Boswell acted on Mr. Love's suggestion. Writing to Mr. Temple, he reports that having gone with his father to the Northern Circuit, he travelled in a chaise with Sir David Dalrymple the whole way, and that he kept an exact journal at the particular desire of his friend Mr. Love, and sent it to him in sheets, by every post. Such was Boswell's first effort in journal-making; it was next to be practised on Paoli, and latterly, with unprecedented success, on Dr. Johnson. As to Mr. Love, it may be remarked that he compensated himself for his early counsel by sponging his pupil. "Love is to breakfast with me to-morrow," wrote Boswell to Mr. Temple in July 1763. "I hope I shall get him to pay me up some more of what he owes me. Pray, is *pay up* an English phrase, I know *pay down* is?"

Sir David Dalrymple, Bart., better known by his judicial title of Lord Hailes, was now an Advocate Depute,[8] one of the faculty specially retained by the Crown for arraigning offenders in the Justiciary Court. An able lawyer, he had already afforded evidence of his ability and accurate scholarship in several separate publications and in various contributions to the periodicals. Possessing a fund of information which he communicated with much suavity of manner, Boswell hailed him as his Mæcenas. Having enrolled him among his divinities, he was disposed to idolize likewise all those whom he approved. Of these the most conspicuous was Dr. Samuel Johnson, whose existence was first made known to him in a post-chaise conversation. He was delighted to learn that he still lived, was the centre of a literary circle, had composed a literary medley styled the *Rambler*, and had edited a dictionary.

As Sir David expatiated on his learning and his virtues, Boswell resolved that one day Johnson should have a place among his gods.

In November, 1759, Boswell entered the University of Glasgow as a student of civil law; he also attended the lectures of Dr. Adam Smith on moral philosophy and rhetoric. His evenings were spent in places of public amusement. From Mr. Love he had contracted a fancy for dramatic art, which in the absence of a licensed theatre he could not gratify in the capital. With more enlightened views the merchants of Glasgow tolerated theatrical representations, obtaining on their boards such talent as their provincial situation could afford. Among those who sought a livelihood at the Glasgow theatre was Francis Gentleman, a native of Ireland, and originally an officer in the army. This amiable gentleman sold his commission in the hope of obtaining fame and opulence as a dramatic author; but disappointed in obtaining a patron, he attempted to subsist as an actor. He was entertained by Boswell, who encouraged him to publish an edition of Southern's tragedy of "Oroonoco," himself accepting the poetical dedication. The dedicatory verses closed thus:—

"But, where, with honest pleasure, she can find
Sense, taste, religion, and good nature joined,
There gladly will she raise her feeble voice,
Nor fear to tell that Boswell is her choice."

Boswell's patronage did not avail the unfortunate player. He was compelled to leave Glasgow; thereafter he removed from place to place, "experiencing all the hardships of a wandering actor, and all the disappointments of a friendless author." He died in September, 1784.

At Glasgow, while spending his week-day evenings in places of amusement, Boswell began to frequent on Sundays the services of the Church of Rome. Before the end of the College session he had resolved to embrace the Catholic faith, and to qualify himself for orders in the Romish Church. These vagaries were so distressing to his parents that he was recalled to Edinburgh. He consented to abandon his sacerdotal aspirations, provided he was allowed to substitute for the law the profession of arms. In March 1760 his father accompanied him to London in order to procure him a commission in the Guards. They waited on the Duke of Argyll, who, according to Boswell's narrative, keenly discommended the military proposal. "My lord," said the Duke, "I like your son; this boy must not be shot at for three shillings and sixpence a day." Lord Auchinleck soon after returned to Edinburgh.

Boswell was allowed to remain in London. His religious views were opposed to his interests in the North, and it was evident that he would not be restrained from avowing his belief in public. It was therefore advisable that he should meanwhile reside in London. At the request of his father, Lord Hailes introduced him to Dr. Jortin, in the hope that that eminent divine would lead him to conform to the doctrines of the English Church. The following letter from Dr. Jortin to Lord Hailes, dated 27th April, 1760, would imply that Boswell had already, amidst the gaieties of London, ceased to concern himself with ecclesiastical questions:—

> "Your young gentleman[9] called at my house on Thursday noon, April 3. I was gone out for the day, and he seemed to be concerned at the disappointment, and proposed to come the day following. My daughter told him that I should be engaged at church, it being Good Friday. He then left your letter, and a note with it for me, promising to be with me on Saturday morning. But from that time to this I have heard nothing of him. He began, I suppose, to suspect some design upon him, and his new friends and fathers may have represented me to him as an heretic and an infidel, whom he ought to avoid as he would the plague. I should gladly have used my best endeavours upon this melancholy occasion, but, to tell you the truth, my hopes of success would have been small. Nothing is more intractable than a fanatic. I heartily pity your good friend. If his son be really sincere in his new superstition, and sober in his morals, there is some comfort in that, for surely a man may be a papist and an honest man. It is not to be expected that the son should feel much for his father's sorrows. Religious bigotry eats up natural affection, and tears asunder the dearest bonds. Yet, if I had an opportunity I should have touched that string, and tried whether there remained in his breast any of the *veteris vestigia flammæ*."

To his early attachment to the Romish Church, Boswell afterwards refers only once. In a letter addressed to Mr. Temple in November, 1789, he remarks that his "Popish imagination induces him to regard his correspondent's friendship as a kind of *credit* on which he may in part repose."

With his father Boswell was not candid in his professed military ardour. In seeking a commission in the Guards, he informed Mr. Temple[10] his desire was "to be about court, enjoying the happiness of the *beau monde* and the company of men of genius." As to military zeal he afterwards announced in a pamphlet,[11] that he was troubled with a natural timidity of personal danger, which cost him some philosophy to overcome.

He protracted his residence in London for a whole year. For some time he resided with Alexander, tenth Earl of Eglinton, a warm friend of the

Auchinleck family. By his lordship he was introduced "into the circle of the great, the gay, and the ingenious." Having been presented to the Jockey Club, and carried to Newmarket, he was deeply moved by the events of the racecourse. Retiring to the coffee-room he composed a poem, making himself the theme, though in styling himself "The Cub at Newmarket" he gratified his egotism by the forfeiture of dignity. Presented by Lord Eglinton to the Duke of York, he invited his Royal Highness to listen to his poem, and ventured to offer him the dedication. The Duke accepted what it would have been ungracious to refuse, and Boswell printed his poem with an epistle dedicatory, in which he "let the world know that this same Cub has been laughed at by the Duke of York, had been read to his Royal Highness by the genius himself, and warmed by the immediate beams of his kind indulgence." Boswell thus describes himself:—

"Lord * * * * n, who has, you know,
A little dash of whim or so;
Who through a thousand scenes will range,
To pick up anything that's strange,
By chance a curious cub had got,
On Scotia's mountains newly caught;
And after driving him about
Through London, many a diff'rent route,
The comic episodes of which
Would tire your lordship's patience much;
Newmarket Meeting being near,
He thought 'twas best to have him there.
*   *   *   *   *
He was not of the iron race
Which sometimes Caledonia grace;
Though he to combat could advance,
Plumpness shone in his countenance;
And belly prominent declared
That he for beef and pudding cared;
He had a large and pond'rous head,
That seemed to be composed of lead;
From which hung down such stiff, lank hair,
As might the crows in autumn scare."

For some time Lord Eglinton was amused by the juvenile ardour and vivacity of his guest. At length, overcome by his odd ways, he checked in plain terms his visitor's vanity and recklessness. The admonition was probably unheeded, for his Lordship seems to have withdrawn his patronage. His own career was cut short by a sad and memorable occurrence; he was shot on his own estate by a poacher, whose firelock he had forcibly seized. He died on the 25th October, 1769.

In London, Boswell got acquainted with the poet Derrick, who became his companion and guide. Derrick was in his thirty-sixth year. A native of Dublin, he had been apprenticed to a linendraper, but speedily relinquished the concerns of trade. In 1751 he proceeded to London and tried his fortune on the stage. He next sought distinction as a poet. Introduced to Dr. Johnson, he obtained a share of the lexicographer's regard; but, while entertaining affection for him as a man, the moralist reproved his muse and condemned his levity. Writing to Mr. Temple, Boswell refers to some of Derrick's verses as "infamously bad." When Nash died, Derrick succeeded him as master of ceremonies at Bath. He died there about the year 1770.

In April, 1761, Boswell, in reluctant obedience to his father's wishes, returned to Edinburgh. Writing to Mr. Temple on the 1st May, he implores his friend's commiseration. "Consider this poor fellow [meaning himself] hauled away to the town of Edinburgh, obliged to conform to every Scotch custom, or be laughed at—'Will you hae some jeel? oh, fie! oh, fie!'—his flighty imagination quite cramped, and he obliged to study '*Corpus Juris Civilis*;' and live in his father's strict family; is there any wonder, sir, that the unlucky dog should be somewhat fretful? Yoke a Newmarket courser to a dung-cart, and I'll lay my life on't he'll either caper or kick most confoundedly, or be as stupid and restive as an old battered post-horse." In the same letter Boswell acknowledges that his behaviour in London had been the reverse of creditable. On his return to Edinburgh, he contributed to a local periodical some notes on London life. This narrative attracted the notice of John, thirteenth Lord Somerville, a nobleman of singular urbanity and considerable literary culture. His lordship invited the author to his table, commended his composition, and urged him to perseverance. Lord Somerville died in 1765. Boswell cherished his memory with affection.

At Edinburgh, Boswell was admitted into the literary circles. He dined familiarly with Lord Kames, was the disciple and friend of Sir David Dalrymple, and passed long evenings with Dr. Robertson and David Hume. His passion for the drama gained force. At this period there was no licensed theatre in Edinburgh, and among religious families playgoing was proscribed. Just five years had elapsed since the Rev. John Home, minister of Athelstaneford, had, on account of taking part in the private representation of his tragedy of "Douglas," been constrained to resign his parochial charge. The popular prejudice against theatricals was a sufficient cause for our author falling into the opposite extreme; he threw his whole energies into a movement which led six years afterwards to a theatre being licensed in the capital.

Boswell's chief associate in theatrical concerns was Mr. David Ross, a tragedian who sometime practised on the London boards, but who, like our author's friends, Messrs. Love and Gentleman, had been driven northward by misfortune. A native of London, Mr. Ross was of Scottish parentage. His father had practised in Edinburgh as a Writer to the Signet; he settled in London in 1722 as a Solicitor of Appeals. Born in 1728, David, his only son, was sent to Westminster School. There he committed some indiscretion, which led to his expulsion and his father's implacable resentment. For some years he earned subsistence as a commercial clerk, but obtaining from Quin lessons in the dramatic art, he came on Covent Garden stage in 1753, where he acquired a second rank as a tragedian. Irregular habits interfered with his advancement, and he proceeded to Edinburgh, in the hope of obtaining professional support. He became Master of Revels, and gave private entertainments which were appreciated and patronized. At length, on the 9th December, 1767, he was privileged to open the first licensed theatre in the capital. Boswell, at his request, composed the 'prologue;' the verses, now unhappily irrecoverable, were described by Lord Mansfield as "witty and conciliating." The theatre proved a success, and the player soon afterwards acquired by marriage considerable emolument. He accepted as his wife Fanny Murray, who had in a less honourable connexion been associated with a deceased nobleman, receiving with her an annuity of two hundred pounds. Ross obtained a further advance of fortune in a manner singularly unexpected. On his death-bed his father made a will, excluding him from any share of his property, and cruelly stipulating that his sister "should pay him one shilling annually, on the first day of May, his birthday, to remind him of his misfortune in being born"! On the plea that by the law of Scotland, a person could not bequeath an estate by mere words of exclusion without an express conveyance of inheritance, Ross obtained a reduction of the settlement, and on a decision by the House of Lords got possession of six thousand pounds. He now retired from the Edinburgh theatre, and renewed his engagements at Covent Garden; but he soon became a victim to reckless improvidence. To the close Boswell cherished his society, though he did not venture to introduce him into literary circles. He died in September, 1790. The following extract from Boswell's letter to Mr. Temple, dated 16th September, 1790, will close the narrative of his career:—

> "My old friend Ross, the player, died suddenly yesterday morning. I was sent for, as his most particular friend in town, and have been so busy in arranging his funeral, at which I am to be chief mourner, that I have left myself very little time— only about ten minutes. Poor Ross! he was an unfortunate man

in some respects; but he was a true *bon vivant*, a most social man, and never was without good eating and drinking, and hearty companions. He had schoolfellows and friends who stood by him wonderfully. I have discovered that Admiral Barrington once sent him £100, and allowed him an annuity of £60 a year."

Among those of his own age and standing who supported Boswell in managing theatricals at Edinburgh was the Honourable Andrew Erskine, youngest son of Alexander, fifth Earl of Kellie. This young gentleman, then a lieutenant in the 71st regiment, was abundantly facetious, and composed respectable verses. Replying to a letter from Boswell, dated at Auchinleck on the 25th August, Erskine expressed himself in verse, and letters were exchanged on both sides for a considerable period. Boswell meanwhile resolved to lay further claim to the poet's bays. In November he issued a poem in sixteen Spenserian stanzas, covering a like number of printed pages, entitled "An Ode to Tragedy, by a Gentleman of Scotland." It was characteristically inscribed to himself—the epistle dedicatory proceeding thus:—

"The following ode which courts your acceptance is on a subject grave and solemn, and therefore may be considered by many people as not so well suited to your volatile disposition. But I, sir, who enjoy the pleasure of your intimate acquaintance, know that many of your hours of retirement are devoted to thought, and that you can as strongly relish the productions of a serious muse as the most brilliant sallies of sportive fancy."

Writing to Erskine on the 17th December, Boswell further enlarges on his own personal qualities. "The author of 'The Ode to Tragedy,'" he proceeds, "is a most excellent man; he is of an ancient family in the west of Scotland, upon which he values himself not a little. At his nativity appeared omens of his future greatness. His parts are bright, and his education has been good. He has travelled in post-chaises miles without number. He eats of every good dish, especially apple pie. He drinks old hock. He has a very fine temper. He is somewhat of a humourist, and a little tinctured with pride. He has a good manly countenance, and owns himself to be amorous. He has infinite vivacity, yet is observed at times to have a melancholy cast. He is rather fat than lean, rather short than tall, rather young than old. His shoes are neatly made, and he never wears spectacles."

In 1760, Mr. Erskine edited the first volume of a work in duodecimo, entitled "A Collection of Original Poems, by the Rev. Mr. Blacklock and other Scotch gentlemen." This publication contained compositions by Mr.

Blacklock, Dr. Beattie, Mr. Gordon of Dumfries, and others; it was published by Alexander Donaldson,[12] an Edinburgh bookseller, and was intended as the first of a series of three volumes. The second volume was considerably delayed, owing to Mr. Erskine's absence with his regiment, and on Boswell were latterly imposed the editorial labours. As contributors Erskine and Boswell were associated with Mr. Home, author of Douglas, Mr. Macpherson, editor of Ossian, and others. Of twenty-eight pieces from Boswell's pen one is subjoined, eminently characteristic of its author.

"B——, of Soapers[13] the king,

On Tuesdays at Tom's does[14] appear,

And when he does talk, or does sing,

To him ne'er a one can come near

For he talks with such ease and such grace,

That all charm'd to attention we sit,

And he sings with so comic a face,

That our sides are just ready to split.

"B—— is modest enough,

Himself not quite Ph[oe]bus he thinks,

He never does flourish with snuff,

And hock is the liquor he drinks.

And he owns that Ned C——t,[15] the priest,

May to something of honour pretend,

And he swears that he is not in jest,

When he calls this same C——t his friend.

"B—— is pleasant and gay,

For frolic by nature design'd;

He heedlessly rattles away

When the company is to his mind.

'This maxim,' he says, 'you may see,

We can never have corn without chaff;'

So not a bent sixpence cares he,

Whether *with* him or *at* him you laugh.

"B—— does women adore,

And never once means to deceive,

He's in love with at least half a score;

If they're serious he smiles in his sleeve.

He has all the bright fancy of youth,

With the judgment of forty and five.

In short, to declare the plain truth,

There is no better fellow alive."

Writing to Erskine on the 8th December, 1761, Boswell remarks that the second volume of the "Collection" was about to appear, adding that his friend would "make a very good figure, and himself a decent one." But the public, while not disapproving the strain of the known authors, condemned the levity of the anonymous contributors, and thrust aside the book. The publishing enterprise was ruined, and the projected third volume did not appear.

Boswell determined to leave Edinburgh, assuring his father that a military life was alone suited to his tastes. In a letter to Erskine, dated the 4th of May, he proceeds:—

> "My fondness for the Guards must appear very strange to you, who have a rooted antipathy at the glare of scarlet. But I must inform you that there is a city called London, for which I have as violent an affection as the most romantic lover ever had for his mistress. There a man may indeed soap his own beard, and enjoy whatever is to be had in this transitory state of things. Every agreeable whim may be fully indulged without censure. I, however, you will not impute my living in England to the same cause for which Hamlet was advised to go there, because the people were all as mad as himself."[16]

Paternal remonstrances having proved unavailing, Boswell was permitted to return to the metropolis. From Parliament Place, Edinburgh, writing to Erskine on the 10th November, he informs him that "on Monday next he is to set out for London." On the 20th November he writes from London, "If I can get into the Guards, it will please me much; if not, I can't help it."

Boswell brought from Scotland a recommendation to Charles, Duke of Queensberry, the patron of Gay, but that nobleman took no part in his concerns. He again sought the field of authorship. He and Erskine had corresponded on a variety of topics, and he fancied that their letters might attract attention. The letters were printed in an octavo volume,[17] Boswell remarking in the preface, that he and his correspondent "have made themselves laugh, and hope they will have the same effect upon other people." Erskine and Boswell were afterwards associated in writing "Critical Strictures" on Mallet's tragedy of "Elvira," acted at Drury Lane in the winter of 1762-3. In 1764, Erskine published a drama entitled "She's not Him, and He's not Her; a Farce in Two Acts, as it is performed in the Theatre in the Canongate." In 1773 he issued "Town Eclogues," a poem of twenty-two quarto pages, intended "to expose the false taste for florid description which prevails in modern poetry."

From the 71st Erskine in 1763 exchanged into the 24th Regiment, in which he became Captain. Retiring from the army, he settled at Edinburgh. There he resided after 1790 with his sister, Lady Colville, at Drumsheugh, near the Dean Bridge. He was an extraordinary pedestrian, and walked nearly every morning to Queensferry, about ten miles distant, where he breakfasted at Hall's Inn. He dispensed with attendance, and when he had finished his repast, left payment under a plate. He was of a tall, portly form, and to the last wore gaiters and a flapped vest. Though satirical with his pen, he was genial and humorous in conversation. He was an early admirer and occasional correspondent of the poet Burns. Like his brother, "the musical Earl of Kellie," he was a lover of Scottish melodies, and was one of a party of amateurs who associated with Mr. George Thomson in designing his "Collection of Scottish Airs." He actively assisted Mr. Thomson in the earlier stages of his undertaking. Several songs from his pen, Burns, in a letter to Mr. Thomson, written in June, 1793, described as "pretty," adding, his "Love song is divine." The composition so described beginning "How sweet this lone vale," became widely popular; but the opening stanza only was composed by him. He was one of the early friends of Archibald Constable, the eminent publisher, who, in an autobiographical fragment has described him as having "an excellent taste in the fine arts," and being "the most unassuming man he had ever met."[18] His habits were regular, but he indulged occasionally at cards, and was partial to the game of whist. Having sustained a serious loss at his favourite pastime he became frantic, and threw himself into the Forth, and perished. This sad event took place in September, 1793. In a letter to Mr. Thomson, dated October, 1791, Burns writes that the tidings of Erskine's death had distressed and "scared" him.

From the day Sir David Dalrymple first named Dr. Samuel Johnson in the post-chaise, Boswell entertained a hope of forming the lexicographer's acquaintance. On his former visit to London he had exerted some effort to procure an introduction. Derrick promised it, but lacked opportunity. During the summer of 1761, Thomas Sheridan lectured at Edinburgh on the practice of elocution, and charmed Boswell by descanting on Dr. Johnson's virtues. Through Sheridan an introduction seemed easy, but Boswell on visiting him found that he and the lexicographer had differed. Boswell did not despair. He obtained leave to occupy his friend Mr. Temple's chambers in the Inner Temple, near Dr. Johnson's residence, and adjoining his well-known haunts.

A further effort was necessary. Boswell ingratiated himself with Mr. Thomas Davies, bookseller, of No. 8, Russell Street, Covent Garden, formerly a player. Mr. Davies knew Dr. Johnson well, saw him frequently in his shop, and was privileged to entertain him at his table. To meet Boswell, the lexicographer was invited more than once, but as our author puts it, "he was by some unlucky accident or other prevented from coming to us." In an unexpected manner Boswell at length attained his wishes. The occurrence must be described in his own words:—"At last, on Monday, the 16th of May, when I was sitting in Mr. Davies' back parlour, after having drunk tea with him and Mrs. Davies,[19] Johnson unexpectedly came into the shop; and Mr. Davies having perceived him through the glass door in the room in which we were sitting advancing towards us, he announced his awful approach to me something in the manner of an actor in the part of Horatio, when he addresses Hamlet on the appearance of his father's ghost,—'Look, my lord, it comes!' * * * Mr. Davies mentioned my name, and respectfully introduced me to him. I was much agitated; and recollecting his prejudice against the Scotch, of which I had heard much, I said to Davies, 'Don't tell where I come from.' 'From Scotland,' cried Davies, roguishly. 'Mr. Johnson,' said I, 'I do indeed come from Scotland, but I cannot help it.' I am willing to flatter myself that I meant this as light pleasantry to soothe and conciliate him, and not as a humiliating abasement at the expense of my country. But however that might be, this speech was somewhat unlucky; for with that quickness of wit for which he was so remarkable he seized the expression "come from Scotland," which I used in the sense of being of that country; and as if I had said I had come away from it or left it, retorted, 'That, sir, I find, is what a very great many of your countrymen cannot help.' This stroke stunned me a good deal; and when we had sat down I felt myself not a little embarrassed, and apprehensive of what might come next. He then addressed himself to Davies: 'What do you think of Garrick? He has refused me an order for the play for Miss Williams, because he knows the house will be full, and that an order would be worth three shillings.' Eager to take any opening to get into conversation with him, I ventured to say, 'Oh, sir, I cannot think Mr. Garrick would grudge such a trifle to you.' 'Sir,' said he, with a stern look, 'I have known David Garrick longer than you have done, and I know no right you have to talk to me on this subject.' Perhaps I deserved this check; for it was rather presumptuous in me, an entire stranger, to express any doubt of the justice of his animadversion upon his old acquaintance and pupil. I now felt myself much mortified, and began to think that the hope which I had long indulged of obtaining his acquaintance was blasted. And in truth, had not my ardour been uncommonly strong, and my resolution uncommonly persevering, so rough a reception might have deterred me for ever from making any further attempts. Fortunately, however, I remained upon the field not wholly discomfited, and was soon rewarded by hearing some of his conversation." Boswell closes his narrative thus:—"I had for a part of the evening been left alone with him, and had ventured to make an observation now and then, which he received very civilly, so that I was satisfied that though there was a roughness in his manner, there was no ill-nature in his disposition. Davies followed me to the door, and when I complained to him a little of the hard blows which the great man had given me, he kindly took upon him to console me by saying, 'Don't be uneasy. I can see he likes you very well.'"

Dr. Johnson regarded Boswell as an adventurer, who had come to London in quest of literary employment. Davies perceiving this, privately explained to him that Boswell was the son of a Scottish judge and heir to a good estate. "A few days afterwards," writes Boswell, "I called on Davies, and asked him if he thought I might take the liberty of waiting on Mr. Johnson at his chambers in the Temple. He said I certainly might, and that *Mr. Johnson would take it as a compliment.* So upon Tuesday, the 24th of May, after having been enlivened by the witty sallies of Messieurs Thornton, Wilkes, Churchill, and Lloyd, with whom I had passed the morning, I boldly repaired to Johnson. His chambers were on the first floor of No. 1, Inner Temple Lane, and I entered them with an impression given me by the Rev. Dr. Blair, of Edinburgh, who had been introduced to me not long before and described his having 'found the giant in his den,' an expression which, when I came to be pretty well acquainted with Johnson, I repeated to him, and he was diverted at this picturesque account of himself. * * * He received me very courteously; but it must be confessed that his apartment and furniture and morning dress were sufficiently uncouth. His brown suit of clothes looked very rusty; he had on a little old shrivelled unpowdered wig, which was too small for his head; his shirt-neck and knees of his breeches were loose; his black worsted stockings ill drawn up, and he had a pair of unbuckled shoes by way of slippers. But all these slovenly particularities were forgotten the moment that he began to talk. Some gentlemen, whom I do not recollect, were sitting with him; and when they went away I also rose, but he said to me, 'Nay, don't go.' 'Sir,' said I, 'I am afraid that I intrude upon you. It is benevolent to allow me to sit and hear you.' He seemed pleased with this compliment, which I sincerely paid him, and answered, 'Sir, I am obliged to any man who visits me.' * * * Before we parted he was so good as to promise to favour me with his company one evening at my lodgings; and as I took my leave, shook me cordially by the hand. It is almost needless to add that I felt no little elation at having now so happily established an acquaintance of which I had been so long ambitious."

The evident sincerity of Boswell's respect pleased and flattered Dr. Johnson. He listened to details of literary life in Edinburgh, and was gratified to learn that certain Scotsmen appreciated his learning. He visited Boswell in his chambers, and invited him to the Mitre Tavern, where afterwards they frequently supped, and drank port till long after midnight. At one of these festive meetings Boswell related the story of the post-chaise, and expatiated on the merits of Sir David Dalrymple with the ardour of a hero worshipper. Dr. Johnson toasted Sir David in a bumper as "a man of worth, a scholar, and a wit." He added, "I have, however, never heard of him except from you; but let him know my opinion of him, for as he does not show himself much in the world, he should know the praise of the few who hear of him." On the 2nd of July, Boswell communicated with Sir David Dalrymple in these terms:[20]—

> "I am now upon a very good footing with Mr. Johnson. His conversation is instructive and entertaining. He has a most extensive fund of knowledge, a very clear expression, and much strong humour. I am often with him. Some nights ago we supped by ourselves at the Mitre Tavern, and sat over a sober bottle till between one and two in the morning. We talked a good deal of you. We drank your health, and he desired me to tell you so. When I am in his company I am rationally happy, I am attentive and eager to learn, and I would hope that I may receive advantage from such society."

To Boswell's letter, in its allusion to Dr. Johnson, Sir David Dalrymple made the following answer:—[21]

> "It gives me pleasure to think that you have obtained the friendship of Mr. Samuel Johnson. He is one of the best moral writers which England has produced. At the same time I envy you the free and undisguised converse with such a man. May I beg you to present my best respects to him, and to assure him of the veneration which I entertain for the author of the 'Rambler' and of 'Rasselas.'"

On the 15th July Boswell thus communicated with Mr. Temple:—

> "I had the honour of supping *tête-à-tête* with Mr. Johnson last night; by-the-bye, I need not have used a French phrase. We sat till between two and three. He took me by the hand

cordially, and said, 'My dear Boswell, I love you very much.' Now, Temple, can I help indulging vanity?"

After quoting a portion of Sir David Dalrymple's letter, he proceeds:—

"Mr. Johnson was in vast good humour, and we had much conversation. I mentioned Fresnoy to him, but he advised me not to follow a plan, and he declared that he himself never followed one above two days. He advised me to read just as inclination prompted me, which alone, he said, would do me any good; for I had better go into company than read a set task. Let us study ever so much, we must still be ignorant of a good deal. Therefore the question is, what parts of science do we want to know? He said, too, that idleness was a distemper which I ought to combat against, and that I should prescribe to myself five hours a day, and in these hours gratify whatever literary desires may spring up. He is to give me his advice as to what books I should take with me from England. I told him that the *Rambler* shall accompany me round Europe, and so be a Rambler indeed. He gave me a smile of complacency."

The *tête-à-tête* with Dr. Johnson on the 14th of July, so described to Mr. Temple, also forms the subject of a letter to Sir David Dalrymple. That letter proceeds thus:—[22]

"On Wednesday evening, Mr. Johnson and I had another *tête-à-tête* at the 'Mitre.' Would you believe that we sat from half an hour after eight till between two and three! He took me cordially by the hand and said, 'My dear Boswell! I love you very much.' Can I help being somewhat vain? * * * He advises me to combat idleness as a distemper, to read five hours every day, but to let inclination direct me what to read. He is a great enemy to a stated plan of study. He advises me when abroad to go to places where there is most to be seen and learnt. He is not very fond of the notion of spending a whole winter in a Dutch town. He thinks I may do much more by private study than by attending lectures. He would have me to perambulate (a word in his own style) Spain. He says a man might see a good deal by visiting their inland towns and universities. He also advises me to visit the northern kingdoms, where more that is new is to be seen than in France and Italy, but he is not against my seeing these warmer regions."

These allusions to foreign travel refer to a proposal by Lord Auchinleck that his son should study civil law at Utrecht, and in which Boswell was disposed to acquiesce, believing that in thus gratifying his father's wishes he might be permitted before returning home to visit the principal countries of the Continent.

On Wednesday, the 21st July, Johnson supped at Boswell's chambers, when were also present Mr. George Dempster, M.P., and the host's paternal uncle, Dr. John Boswell, from Edinburgh. The occasion was one of the most memorable in the course of Boswell's intercourse with his illustrious associate. Dr. Boswell entertained loose notions of religion, and Mr. Dempster was a disciple of David Hume. Dempster made a violent attack on Christianity, repeating the arguments of Rousseau, and quoting approvingly the sentiments of Hume and Gibbon. Dr. Boswell preserved a general silence, but was disposed to smile approvingly at Dempster's sallies. In the society of his new acquaintance, Dr. Johnson was appalled to find a bold upholder of infidel sentiments, and his indignation was proportionate. He assailed Dempster with much severity, exposing the sophistry of his school. Boswell took notes of the conversation, doubtless intending to utilize what he had written. Next morning he hastened to Dr. Johnson's chambers to express disapproval of Dempster's sentiments. Dr. Johnson answered, "I have not met with any man for a long time who has given me such general displeasure. He is totally unfixed in his principles, and wants to puzzle other people." This utterance is presented by Boswell in Dr. Johnson's memoirs with the prefatory remark, "Of a gentleman who was mentioned he said," &c. Boswell became very intimate with Mr. Dempster, and so erased from his journal all memorials of the evening's conversation. Not very creditably he affirms, in Johnson's Life, that the evening was wholly occupied "in the discussion of social and political questions." But the truth, which Boswell sought to suppress, reaches us in his own words from two different channels. To Mr. Temple, on the 23rd of July, he wrote thus:—

> "On Wednesday evening, Mr. Johnson, Dempster, and my uncle Dr. Boswell, supped with me at my chambers. I had prodigious satisfaction to find Dempster's sophistry (which he has learned from Hume and Rousseau) vanquished by the solid sense and vigorous reasoning of Johnson. It was a very fertile evening, and *my journal is stored with its fruits*. Dempster was as happy as a vanquished argumentator could he; and the honest Doctor was cheerful and conversible and highly entertained."

On the same day Boswell communicated with Sir David Dalrymple in these words:—

> "Mr. Johnson did me the honour to sup with me at my chambers some nights ago. *Entre nous*, he said that Dempster, who was also with me, gave him more general displeasure than any man he has met with of a long time. He saw a pupil of

Hume and of Rousseau totally unsettled as to principles, and endeavouring to puzzle and shake other people with childish sophistry. I had infinite satisfaction in hearing solid truth confuting vain subtilty. * * * I thank God that I have got acquainted with Mr. Johnson. He has done me infinite service. He has assisted me to obtain peace of mind; he has assisted me to become a rational Christian; I hope I shall ever remain so."[23]

In referring to his having become a rational Christian, Boswell desired to satisfy his Scottish Mæcenas that he had personally abandoned the superstitions of Romish worship. Mr. Dempster's religious views, together with his personal history and his acquaintance with Boswell, may be finally disposed of. Grandson of George Dempster, merchant and banker at Dundee, he succeeded to several important estates, which his ancestor had acquired by granting extensive loans on mortgages to the former proprietors. Born in 1735, he studied at the University of Edinburgh, and in that city formed the intimacy of Dr. William Robertson, Alexander Carlyle, John Home, and other eminent clergymen. Under their auspices he sat as a lay member in the General Assembly; and in that court he opposed his friends by seconding the injunction of the House passed in 1757, forbidding the clergy to countenance theatricals.[24] Becoming acquainted with David Hume, he renounced Presbyterianism, and embraced infidelity. He abandoned the Scottish Bar to which he had been called, and became candidate for the parliamentary representation of the Fife and Forfar burghs. By a narrow majority he secured his seat, but he was convicted of bribery and the election was annulled. To accomplish his end he had sold two fine estates, and expended nearly £15,000. On presenting himself to the constituents the second time he was returned under less exceptionable circumstances. He retained his seat from 1762 till 1790. He would join no political party, probably owing to an uncertainty of judgment, which was partly an inheritance; two of his ancestors being deposed and afterwards restored to the ministry for certain changes in their civil and ecclesiastical opinions. According to Boswell he early cherished republican sentiments; latterly he resisted the revolutionary ferment created by the French Directory. By the general public he was esteemed a patriot, and was provincially known as "Honest George." The poet Burns held that he should have been ennobled. He supported some liberal measures, and certain important services are associated with his name. He denounced the conflict with the American colonies, opposed the sovereignty exercised by the East India Company, sought to remove all restraints from the national commerce, and advocated the abolition of sinecures. On retiring from Parliament, he devoted himself to the promotion of agriculture and manufactures in North Britain. He established an agricultural society on his estate.[25] He improved the condition of the Scottish fisheries, and discovered a method of preserving salmon for the London market. He was much respected on his estate, was benevolent to the poor, and exercised a generous hospitality. He did not attend church on the plea of feeble health, but he associated with the clergy of his neighbourhood, and to his household spoke reverently of religion. In some twenty of his letters, written at intervals during a period of twenty-five years preceding his decease, the writer has on a close examination been unable to detect any remark savouring of scepticism. Yet it is nearly certain that he cherished to the close of a long life the blighting infidelity of David Hume. To the Right Hon. John Wilson Croker was communicated by Sir Walter Scott the following metrical epitaph, which it was alleged Mr. Dempster composed upon himself:—

"Pray for the soul of deceased George Dempster,
In his youth a great fool, in his old age a gamester;
What you're to know, on this tomb you shall see,
Life's thread he let go when just ninety-three.
So sound was his bottom, his acquaintance all wonder'd
How old Nick had got him till he lived out the hundred.
To his money concerns he paid little attention,
First selling his land, then pawning his pension;[26]
But his precious time he much better did manage,
To the end of his life from his earliest nonage,
He divided his hours into two equal parts,
And spent one half in sleeping, the other at *cartes*."[27]

Mr. Dempster died on his estate of Dunnichen, Forfarshire, on the 13th February, 1818, at the age of eighty-four.

In May, 1763, two months before the period reached in the preceding narrative, Boswell asked Sir David Dalrymple to interpose with his father, who was threatening to disinherit him on account of his unsettled habits. He concludes a letter to Sir David in these words,—"Tell him to have patience with me for a year or two, and I may be what he pleases." In June he informs Sir David that his father's proposal that he should proceed to Utrecht, there to study civil law under the celebrated M. Trotz had met with his acceptance, and that his father was "much pleased to find in him so prudent a disposition."[28]

He adds,—

"My great object is to attain a proper conduct in life. How sad will it be if I turn no better than I am! I have much vivacity, which leads me to dissipation and folly. This I think I can restrain. But I will be moderate, and not aim at a stiff sageness and buckram correctness. I must, however, own to you that I have at bottom a melancholy cast, which dissipation relieves by making me thoughtless, and therefore an easier though a more contemptible animal. I dread a return of this malady. I am always apprehensive of it."

About the Utrecht scheme he writes to Mr. Temple on the 15th July, "I have had a long letter from my father, full of affection and good counsel. Honest man, he is now very happy: it is amazing to think how much he has had at heart my pursuing the road of civil life; he is anxious for fear I should fall off from my prudent system, and return to my dissipated, unsettled way of thinking; and in order to make him easy, he insists on having my solemn promise that I will persist in the scheme on which he is so earnestly bent: he knows my fidelity, and he concludes that my promise will fix me. Indeed he is much in the right; the only question is, how much I am to promise. I think I may promise this much,—that I shall from this time study propriety of conduct, and to be a man of knowledge and prudence, as far as I can; that I shall make as much improvement as possible while I am abroad, and when I return shall put on the gown as a member of the Faculty of Advocates, and be upon the footing of a gentleman of business, with a view to my getting into Parliament."

For the use of Mr. Temple's chambers Boswell paid his proportion of rent, but his occupancy was burdened with the condition that his friend's brother, a youth of seventeen, might as occasion suited share the accommodation. This young gentleman, Mr. Robert Temple, held a commission in the line, but was not very ardent in his military duties. Boswell's early intercourse with him was abundantly characteristic. To his brother he reported of him on the 15th July, that "his genius and application consisted in washing his face and brushing his hat, which he will execute in a few hours;" adding, "I find it somewhat inconvenient to have anybody in chambers with me.... I have allowed him to be too free with me; and I own it hurts me when I find my folly bringing me into the situation of being upon an equality with if not below the young man." On the 23rd of July he in these doggerel verses celebrated the youth on his returning from a visit to Salisbury:—

"Bob Temple has at Sarum been,
And all the pretty girls has seen;
But he came back in the machine

Because he was the barber!

"From Mother Bowles he got good wine;
He licked his lips and called it fine;
But now the dog at Cliff's must dine,

And is not that the barber?"

In a few days afterwards, Master Robert having begun to borrow one guinea after another, is described as "selfish," of a "heedless disposition," and having "no great powers either of understanding or imagination." Boswell sums up; "I am glad he goes down to Cambridge."

In his letter to Sir David Dalrymple of the 23rd July, Boswell enters into some details respecting the Utrecht scheme, and expresses a determination thoroughly to acquaint himself with the law of nations. He has resolved to transcribe the whole of Erskine's Institutes,[29] that the details might be impressed in his memory.

The progress of the Utrecht arrangement is reported in the following letter to Mr. Temple, dated 20th July:—

> "I have this night received a large packet from my father, with my letter of credit, and several letters of recommendation to different people in Holland. The letters have been sent open for me to seal, so I have been amused to see the different modes of treating that favourite subject myself. Sir David Dalrymple has written to Count Nassau; his letter is in French and is exceedingly genteel. He recommends Mr. Boswell as *un jeune homme de famille et de mérite*, and hopes he will find in the Count *le guide et le protecteur de sa jeunesse*. My father writes to Mynheer Abrahamus Gronovius, an old *literatus* at Leyden. It is an excellent letter, and recalls their old ideas with more liveliness than you would imagine. I have several other letters, so that I can be at no loss where I am going, especially as I have got some relations of the first fashion at the Hague. My father has allowed me £60 a quarter—£240 a year; that is not a great allowance, but with economy I may live very well upon it, for Holland is a cheap country. However, I am determined not to be straitened, nor to encourage the least narrowness of disposition as to saving money, but will draw upon my father for any sums I find necessary. My affairs being thus far settled, I must set out soon. I can have no excuse for indulging myself in a much longer stay in London; and yet I must own to you, my dear friend, that I feel a good deal of uneasiness at the thoughts of quitting the place where my affection is truly

centred, for there I enjoy most happiness; however, I am determined to go next week. I hope I shall not be feeble-minded, but pluck up manly resolution, and consider that I am leaving London in order to see the world, store my mind with more ideas, establish a proper character, and then return to the metropolis much happier, and more qualified for a solid relish of its advantages."

After the lapse of three days Boswell wrote to Mr. Temple as follows:—

"Inner Temple,

28th July, 1763.

MY DEAR TEMPLE,

  I have now fixed to-morrow se'nnight, Friday, the 5th of August, for the day of my departure; and on Saturday, the 6th, I shall be upon the Channel. Alas, my friend! let me disclose my weakness to you. My departure fills me with a kind of gloom that quite overshadows my mind. I could almost weep to think of leaving dear London and the calm retirement of the Inner Temple. I am now launching into the wide world, and am to be long at a distance from my dear Temple, whose kind and amiable counsel never failed to soothe my dejected mind. You may see I am somewhat melancholy; pray comfort me. This is very effeminate and very young, but I cannot help it. My time is fixed, and I will go; I have taken my resolution, and you shall see that I can keep to it. I enclose you a friendly dissertation, which you may read at your leisure; it will show how much stronger my mind was last night only. I am just going to meet Mr. Johnson at the 'Turk's Head.'"

The meeting with Johnson in the "Turk's Head" coffee-house is duly chronicled in the "Life." Boswell expressed himself as resolved on proceeding to Utrecht, and asked for advice.

"Come," said Johnson, "let us make a day of it; let us go down to Greenwich and dine, and talk of it fully, so that I shall say,—

'On Thames's bank in silent thought we stood,
Where Greenwich smiles upon the silver flood.'"[30]

The friends proceeded to Greenwich on Saturday, the 30th. They inspected the hospital, walked in the park, and returning to London by the river, closed the day's excursion by supping together at the "Turk's Head." During the evening Boswell entertained his Mentor by expatiating on the history of his House, and the extent and importance of the family estate. By Johnson no allusion was made to the ostensible purpose of the meeting; it was enough that on a day of the week when Boswell was likely to meet with bad counsellors, he and his purse were protected from their embrace. The friends met on Sunday. On Tuesday they were both morning and evening together. On Wednesday evening they supped at the "Turk's Head," when Johnson renewed his promise to start with his friend for Harwich early on Friday morning.

As Boswell was for a considerable period to be left to his own control, Sir David Dalrymple sent him a letter of advice, along with some commissions to be executed in course of his tour. To Sir David's letter Boswell on the 2nd August made the following answer:—

> "My scepticism was not owing to thinking wrong, but to not thinking at all. It is a matter of great moment to keep a sense of religion constantly impressed upon our minds. If that divine guest does not occupy part of the space, vain intruders will; and when once they have got in it is difficult to get them out again. I shall remember your commission about the Greek Lyrics. I shall hear what the librarian says, and I shall make diligent search myself. As to the MSS. of Anacreon, Mr. Johnson says he doubts much if there be such a thing at Leyden."

Of no settled convictions, Boswell was, under his protestations of orthodoxy, considerably tinged with Dempster's scepticism. Sir David Dalrymple, who had formerly sought to rescue him from the Scylla of credulity, was now attempting his deliverance from the Charybdis of doubt. Boswell on the 3rd August communicated with Mr. Temple:—

> "To-morrow morning, at five o'clock, I set out upon my travels. I am much hurried with putting all my things in order. I have left some parcels in one of the drawers, which I beg you will keep for me till I return. I have been a great deal with Mr. Johnson of late, and (would you believe it?) his friendship for me is so great that he insists on seeing me sail, and has actually taken a place in the coach to accompany me to Harwich."

In the "Life of Johnson" the narrative is continued:—

> "On Friday, August 5, we set out early in the morning in the Harwich stage-coach. A fat elderly gentlewoman and a young Dutchman seemed the most inclined among us to conversation. At the inn where we dined, the gentlewoman said that she had done her best to educate her children; and particularly that she had never suffered them to be a moment idle. *Johnson*: 'I wish madam, you would educate me too; for I have been an idle fellow all my life.' 'I am sure, sir,' said she, 'you have not been idle.' *Johnson*: 'Nay, madam, it is very true;

and that gentleman there,' pointing to me, 'has been idle. He was idle at Edinburgh. His father sent him to Glasgow, where he continued to be idle. He then came to London, where he has been very idle; and now he is going to Utrecht, where he will be as idle as ever.' I asked him privately how he could expose me so. *Johnson*: 'Pooh! pooh!' said he; 'they know nothing about you, and will think of it no more.' ... Next day we got to Harwich to dinner; and my passage in the packet-boat to Helvoetsluys being secured, and my baggage put on board, we dined at an inn by ourselves.... We went and looked at the church, and having gone into it, and walked up to the altar, Johnson, whose piety was constant and fervent, sent me to my knees, saying, 'Now that you are going to leave your native country, recommend yourself to the protection of your Creator and Redeemer.' ... My revered friend walked down with me to the beach, where we embraced and parted with tenderness, and engaged to correspond by letters. I said, 'I hope, sir, you will not forget me in my absence.' *Johnson*: 'Nay, sir, it is more likely that you should forget me than that I should forget you.' As the vessel put out to sea I kept my eyes upon him for a considerable time, while he remained rolling his majestic frame in his usual manner; and at last I perceived him walk back into the town, and he disappeared."

On the 8th December Dr. Johnson addressed to Boswell his first letter. He entreated him to study civil law as his father had advised, and the ancient languages, as he had personally resolved upon. He then proceeds to depict his friend's weaknesses in these forcible terms:—

"You know a gentleman, who when first he set his foot in the gay world, as he prepared himself to whirl in the vortex of pleasure, imagined a total indifference and universal negligence to be the most agreeable concomitants of youth, and the strongest indication of an easy temper and a quick apprehension. Vacant to every object, and sensible of every impulse, he thought that an appearance of diligence would deduct something from the reputation of genius, and hoped that he should appear to attain, amidst all the ease of carelessness, and all the tumult of diversion, that knowledge and those accomplishments which mortals of the common fabric obtain only by mute abstraction and solitary drudgery. He tried this scheme of life awhile, was made weary of it by his sense and his virtue; he then wished to return to his studies, and finding long habits of idleness and pleasure harder to be cured than he expected, still wishing to retain his claim to some extraordinary prerogatives, resolved the common consequences of irregularity into an unalterable decree of destiny, and concluded that nature had originally formed him incapable of rational enjoyment. Let all such fancies, illusive and destructive, be banished henceforward from your thoughts for ever. Resolve and keep your resolution; choose, and pursue your choice. If you spend this day in study, you will find yourself still more able to study to-morrow; not that you are to expect that you shall at once obtain a complete victory."

Johnson had commended his friend for keeping a journal.[31] He concludes his letter by expressing a hope that he is "enriching his journal with many observations upon the country" in which he was residing.

At Utrecht Boswell obtained the friendship of M. Trotz, the learned civilian, whose prelections on civil law he attended for some months. He also became intimate with the Rev. William Brown, pastor of the English congregation at Utrecht, subsequently Professor of Church History at St. Andrews. Anecdotes related by M. Trotz and Mr. Brown are preserved in Boswell's Commonplace-book.

Lord Auchinleck had designed that his son should prosecute his studies at Utrecht for two years. The proposal was not a hopeful one, and it was not realized. Before his first term was completed, Boswell longed for the pleasures of travel: as the term closed he hastened into the country. He visited Leyden and other noted localities in the Netherlands, and passed into Germany. He reached Berlin in July, where he delivered a letter of introduction to Mr., afterwards Sir Andrew Mitchell, British Ambassador at the Prussian Court. By this accomplished gentleman he was well received and hospitably entertained. From Berlin he wrote a letter to his father, expatiating on the advantages of travel, and entreating that such a remittance might be sent him as would carry him into Switzerland, and from thence into Italy. Pending his father's answer, he visited the duchies of Hanover and Brunswick. Returning to Berlin on the 27th of August he found a letter from his father, strongly disapproving his proposal for a lengthened tour, and allowing him only the indulgence of visiting France before resuming his legal studies at Utrecht. Mortified by his father's decision, and the severely peremptory character of his letter, he thought of waiting on Mr. Mitchell to entreat his aid and intervention. The ambassador was from home; he had gone with his family to Spa, where he was still to remain some weeks. Procuring his address, Boswell sent him a lengthened communication, which owing to its peculiar manner we present without abridgment:—

"You may believe, sir, that I was a good deal surprised to hear, upon my return to Berlin, that *onze Gezant*[32] was gone. There was indeed a surmise at Brunswick that you intended to return to England this season. I was asked if it was true, and very innocently affirmed that there was nothing in it. I find however, that when a man leaves a Minister at a foreign Court but for a fortnight, he is not sure of finding him upon his return. Your departure is a good deal unlucky for me, not only as it deprives me of conversation which gave me uncommon pleasure, and invariably accustomed me to rational thinking and honourable sentiment, but because I now particularly stand in need of your prudent and kind counsel with respect to my travels. I have had another letter from my father, in which he continues of opinion that travelling is of very little use, and may do a great deal of harm. I shall not repeat what I have formerly said of my father's particular character; I say *particular*, for rarely will you find a man of so excellent a frame of body, and so noble a mind as to have passed through life with uniform propriety of conduct.[33] For my own part, I own that I am not such a favourite of nature. Think not that I intend to plead machinery, and escape from the censure due to the faults which I have committed. I only would have you consider that judgment is a natural gift as well as imagination, and force of mind is in a great measure independent of our endeavours: think of me as I am, and pronounce accordingly.

"I esteem and love my father, and I am determined to do what is in my power to make him easy and happy; but you will allow that I may endeavour to make him happy and at the same time not be too hard upon myself. I must use you so much with the freedom of a friend as to tell you that, with the vivacity which you allowed me, I have a melancholy disposition. To escape from the gloom of dark speculation, I have made excursions into the fields of amusement, perhaps of folly. I have found that amusement and folly are beneath me, and that without some laudable pursuit my life must be insipid and wearisome. I therefore took the resolution of leaving London, and settled myself for the winter at Utrecht, where I recovered my inclination for study and rational thinking. I then laid my account with travelling for a couple of years, but I found my father's views to be entirely different. You saw the letter which I wrote him from this, and I flatter myself that you approved of it. I cannot expect his answer for some weeks; in the meantime he tells me that he would not oppose my passing another winter at Utrecht, so that he does not grudge the time which I ask. As for the money, I should think for one year a little extraordinary expense is not thrown away, when it is also to be considered that what I spend now I shall not have some years hence. My father seems much against my going to Italy, but gives me leave to go from there and pass some months in Paris. I own that the words of the apostle Paul, "I must see Rome," are strongly borne in upon my mind; it would give me infinite pleasure; it would give me talk for a lifetime, and I should go home to Auchinleck with serene contentment. I am no libertine, and have a moral certainty of suffering no harm in Italy; I can also assure you that I shall be as moderate as possible in my expenses. I do not intend to travel as *Mi Lord Anglois*, but merely as a scholar and a man of elegant curiosity, and I am told that in that character I may live in Italy very reasonably. I obviate your objection of my being obliged to live like others, by assuring you that I have none of that second-rate ambition which actuates most young men of fortune upon their travels. After passing four months on classic ground, I would come through France, and go home, as I said to my father, *uti conviva satur*.

"Now, sir, tell me fairly if I am unreasonable. Upon my honour I cannot think that I am. I give you my word that my father's inclinations shall be as inviolable laws to his son; but don't you think that I may just remonstrate before I consider an act as passed? Don't you think that, rather than go home contrary to what I much desire, and cannot help thinking very proper,—don't you think it worth while to humour me so far as to allow me my year and a reasonable sum, after which I return clear and contented, without any pretence for my stormy disposition to murmur at? I would beg, sir, that you may write to my father your opinion as to this matter, and put it in the light that you think it deserves. In the meantime I can see little advantage to be had at Berlin. I shall, however, remain here a fortnight, after which I intend passing by Mannheim, and one or two more of the German Courts, to Geneva; I am then at the point from which I may either steer to Italy or to France. I shall see Voltaire. I shall also see Switzerland and Rousseau; these two men are to me greater objects than most statues or pictures. I take this opportunity to assure the loved and respected friend of my father that I am serenely happy at having obtained his acquaintance. I would hope that I shall not be found unworthy of his regard, and I wish very honestly for an opportunity of showing my real esteem for such a character as I could draw to any one else but to himself."[34]

In a postscript Boswell begged an early reply. His letter, somewhat Johnsonian in style, actually reflected some of Dr. Johnson's sentiments respecting himself, in the letter received at Utrecht. It was sufficiently candid to induce friendship, and not more ambitious than the ardour of youth might have excused or justified. But Mr. Mitchell had no desire to arbitrate between father and son in a matter with which he was personally unconcerned. He contented himself with administering to the young traveller a lecture on filial obedience, and declined all further negotiation. Lord Auchinleck meanwhile relented without further pressure, assented to the Italian project, and sent the necessary funds. To the Ambassador Boswell addressed a letter from Geneva on the 26th December; it commenced in a style sufficiently exultant:—

"I thank you for your letter from Spa, although it gave me no great encouragement in my scheme of going to Italy. You tell me gravely to follow the plan which my father prescribed, whatever it may be, and in doing so I shall certainly act most wisely. I forgive you this, for I say just the same to young people when I advise. To enter into detail of the little circumstances which compose the felicity of another, is what a man of any genius can hardly submit to. We therefore give a good, wholesome, general counsel; and he who consults us thinks a little, and then endeavours to take his own way as well as he can. I have, however, the happiness to inform you that my father has consented that I shall go to Italy. Upon my soul, I am grateful to the most worthy of men: it will be hard if we are not well together, for I love him with the strongest affection. If I find that I cannot succeed in my own plans in such a way as to convince my father that I am in the right, I shall do my utmost to fulfil the plan beyond which he cannot think to look. You may suppose what my ideas are, for they are of your old acquaintances. One thing I am sure of, and by the undisguised honour of a man of probity I swear, shall chiefly influence me—a regard to the happiness of him to whom I owe so much, Believe me I have a soul."

Had Boswell concluded his letter at this point he might have merited some praise for snubbing the ambassador who had lectured him on filial duty. But he goes on to entreat Mr. Mitchell's influence on behalf of the father and brother of his friend Mr. Temple. The father he describes as formerly an officer in the Customs, who had forfeited his appointment by becoming insolvent. The son, Master Robert, is now a lieutenant on half-pay. Through Mr. Mitchell he desires a Government post for the one, and full pay for the other. He assures the ambassador that excepting his Sovereign he is "the only man in Britain" he would ask a favour of. "If you can aid me," he adds, "you will most truly oblige a worthy fellow, for such I am." To this second communication the ambassador vouchsafed no answer.

Through a part of Germany Boswell was accompanied by the Earl Marischal, who ordinarily resided at Berlin, and who had, during a recent visit to Scotland, formed the acquaintance of Lord Auchinleck. With introductions from his lordship he visited Voltaire at Ferney, and Rousseau in the wilds of Neufchatel. It is to be regretted that he did not record his conversations with these celebrated persons. Crossing the Alps, he visited the principal towns of Italy. He spent some time in Italy with Lord Mountstuart, eldest son of the Earl of Bute. To this nobleman he dedicated his thesis when he was called to the Bar.

The inhabitants of Corsica were at this time engaged against the Genoese in their memorable struggle for liberty, and Pascal Paoli, their patriotic leader, had become celebrated over Europe. To Boswell he had been warmly commended by Rousseau, who had corresponded with the Corsicans respecting the formation of their laws. Boswell hinted to Rousseau that he might proceed to Corsica, and when in April, 1765, he reached Rome, he addressed a letter to the philosopher, begging an introduction to Paoli. Not receiving a reply, he wrote to Rousseau a second time, informing him that should he withhold the introduction sought for "he should certainly go without it, and probably be hanged as a spy."[35] On his arrival at Florence, in August, he received a letter from "the wild philosopher," recommending him first to Mr. Buttafoco, Captain of the Royal Italian Regiment at Viscovado, and in his absence to General Paoli. At Leghorn he procured from Count Rivarola, the Sardinian Consul, a special letter to Paoli and other leading persons at Corsica.

Arriving in the island, Boswell was courteously received by Signor Antonetti, to whom he presented a letter from Count Rivarola. After entertaining him at his house, Antonetti facilitated his progress to the town of Sollacarò, the headquarters of Paoli. On his route Boswell heard that in the castle of Corte were detained three murderers, a woman and two men; he gratified his curiosity by conversing with them. At his request the executioner was also presented to him.

Reaching Sollacarò, Boswell was brought into the presence of Paoli, to whom he handed his credentials. Paoli received him with reserve, but afterwards became friendly. To the general he described himself in these terms:—"With a mind naturally inclined to melancholy, and a keen desire of inquiry, I have intensely applied myself to metaphysical researches, and reasoned beyond my depth on such subjects as it is not given to man to know. I have rendered my mind a comera (*sic*) obscura; in the very heat of youth I felt the *non est tanti*, the *omnia vanitas* of one who has exhausted all the sweets of his being, and is weary with dull repetition. I told him that I had almost become for ever incapable of taking a part in active life."[36]

Paoli introduced Boswell to his nobility, who severally honoured him with visits. He was one day mounted on Paoli's horse, with its rich garniture of crimson velvet and gold lace. In journeying he was attended by the general's guards, an honour from which he "enjoyed a sort of luxury of noble sentiment." From Paoli's palace at Corte, the capital of Corsica, he addressed a letter to Dr. Johnson, which he describes as "full of generous enthusiasm." Having related what he had done and seen, he summed up; "I dare to call this a spirited tour; I dare to challenge your approbation."[37]

From Corsica Boswell communicated to Rousseau, now in France, the details of his visit to Paoli, and on his reaching Paris received the philosopher's commands to bring with him into England, whither he had preceded him, the notorious companion of his household, Thérése La Vasseur. Boswell accepted the mission, and accompanied Rousseau's mistress from Paris to London. In reference to his intended progress, Mr. Hume, at whose instance Rousseau proceeded to England, thus communicated with his ingenious correspondent, the Countess de Bouflers:—

"12th of January, 1766.

"A letter has come open to me from Guy, the bookseller, by which I learn that Mademoiselle[38] sets out first in company with a friend of mine, a young gentleman very good-humoured, very agreeable, and very mad. He visited Rousseau in his mountains, who gave him a recommendation to Paoli, the King of Corsica; where this gentleman, whose name is Boswell, went last summer in search of adventures. He has such a rage for literature, that I dread some event fatal to our friend's honour. For remember the story of Terentia, who was first married to Cicero, then to Sallust, and at last, in her old age, married a young nobleman, who imagined that she must possess some secret which would convey to him eloquence and genius."

At Paris, in the house of Mr. Waters, an English banker, Boswell found a letter from Dr. Johnson, dated the 14th January. It proceeded thus:—

"Be assured for the present, that nothing has lessened either the esteem or love with which I dismissed you at Harwich. Both have been increased by all that I have been told of you by yourself or others, and when you return, you will return to an unaltered and, I hope, unalterable friend.

"All that you have to fear from me is the vexation of disappointing me. No man loves to frustrate expectations which have been formed in his favour; and the pleasure which I promise myself from your journals and remarks is so great, that perhaps no degree of attention or discernment will be sufficient to afford it.

"Come home, however, and take your chance. I long to see you and to hear you, and hope that we shall not be so long separated again. Come home, and expect such welcome as is due to him whom a wise and noble curiosity has led where perhaps, no native of this country ever was before.

******

"As your father's liberality has indulged you with so long a ramble, I doubt not but that you will think his sickness, or even his desire to see you, a sufficient reason for hastening your return. The longer we live, and the more we think, the higher value we learn to put on the friendship and tenderness of parents and friends. Parents we can have but once; and he promises himself too much who enters life with the expectation of finding many friends. Upon some motive I hope that you will be here soon, and am willing to think that it will be an inducement to your return that it is sincerely desired by, dear sir, your affectionate humble servant,

"SAM JOHNSON."

Boswell reached London in the beginning of February, and at once visited Dr. Johnson at his house in Johnson's Court. Received with much cordiality, he proceeded to entertain the lexicographer with Voltaire's opinions of some of the English poets. In the evening the friends supped together at the Mitre Tavern, when Boswell learnt, for the first time, that Johnson had become practically an abstainer. On Saturday, the 15th February, Boswell and Johnson again met at the "Mitre," the former being accompanied by his friend Mr. Temple. Boswell spoke of Rousseau, and said he had met with Mr. Wilkes in Italy, and had enjoyed his society. Johnson denounced both the philosopher and the politician in his severest manner.

In the course of their conversation General Paoli had remarked to Boswell that he might inform the members of his court that the Corsicans were worthy of greater support than they had hitherto received. Boswell construed the remark into a request, and, before he left the island, commissioned a Corsican dress in which he might, to members of the English Cabinet, plead the cause of Paoli. In this costume he waited on several members of Government, and some noted politicians. From Mr. Walpole he experienced a courteous reception. Mr. Pitt wrote him a short letter, which, in the hope of producing a correspondence between him and the minister, he acknowledged as follows:—

"*St. James' Street, Feb. 19, 1766.*

"Sir,—I have the honour to receive your most obliging letter, and can with difficulty restrain myself from paying you compliments on the very genteel manner in which you are pleased to treat me. But I come from a people among whom even the lowest arts of insinuation are unknown. However you may, by political circumstances, be in one view a simple individual, yet, sir, Mr. Pitt will always be the prime minister of the brave, the secretary of freedom and of spirit; and I hope that I may with propriety talk to him of the views of the illustrious Paoli. Be that as it may, I shall very much value the honour of being admitted to your acquaintance.

"I am, &c.,

JAMES BOSWELL."[39]

Informed of his mother's death, Boswell left London for Auchinleck. His father was pleased to find him somewhat less volatile, and quite reconciled to the legal profession. On the 26th July he was admitted advocate. His "Thesis on Civil Law," published at his admission, he transmitted to Dr. Johnson, who criticised it with severity; he, however, heartily commended his resolution to obey his father, and seriously to occupy himself with business. His proposal to write a history of Corsica Dr. Johnson objected to. "You have," he wrote, "no materials which others have not, or may have. You have, somehow or other, warmed your imagination. I wish there were some cure, like the lover's leap, for all heads of which some single idea has obtained an unreasonable and irregular possession. Mind your own affairs, and leave the Corsicans to theirs."

Aware of Boswell's tendency to form resolutions, which he afterwards departed from, Dr. Johnson entreated him to abandon his practice of vow-making. To a letter from the lexicographer on this subject Boswell made the following answer:—

"Auchinleck, 6th November, 1766.

"Might I venture to differ from you with regard to the utility of vows? I am sensible that it may be very dangerous to make vows rashly, and without a due consideration. But I cannot help thinking that they may often be of great advantage to one of a variable judgment and irregular inclinations. I always remember a passage in one of your letters to our Italian friend, Baretti; where, talking of the monastic life, you say you do not wonder that serious men should put themselves under the protection of a religious order, when they have found how unable they are to take care of themselves. For my own part, without affecting to be a Socrates, I am sure I have a more than ordinary struggle to maintain with the Evil Principle; and all the methods I can devise are little enough to keep me tolerably steady in the paths of rectitude."

In February, 1767, Boswell conveyed his congratulations to Mr. Temple on his being admitted to priest's orders, and instituted Rector of Mamhead. The following remarks with which his congratulations were accompanied would have reflected credit on Dr. Johnson:—

> "I am sincerely happy that you are at length the Reverend Mr. Temple. I view the profession of a clergyman in an amiable and respectable light. Don't be moved by declamations against ecclesiastical history, as if that could blacken the sacred order. I confess that it is not in ecclesiastical history that we find the most agreeable account of divines: their politics, their ambition, and their cruelty are there displayed; but remember, Temple, you are there reading the vices of only political divines,—of such individuals as in so numerous a body have

been very unworthy members of the Church, and should have rather been employed in the rudest secular concerns. But if you would judge fairly of the priests of Jesus, you must consider how many of the distressed they have comforted, how many of the wicked they have reclaimed, how many of the good they have improved; consider the lives of thousands of worthy pious divines who have been a blessing to their parishes. This is just, Temple. You say the truths of morality are written in the hearts of all men, and they find it their interest to practise them. My dear friend, will you believe a specious moral essayist against your own experience? Don't you in the very same letter complain of the wickedness of those around you? Don't you talk of the tares in society? My friend, it is your office to labour cheerfully in the vineyard, and, if possible, to leave not a tare in Mamhead.

* * * *
*

"In a word, my dear Temple, be a good clergyman, and you will be happy both here and hereafter."

Boswell proceeds to advise his friend to marry a suitable wife, and expresses a regret that he himself cannot wed so long as his father lives. Having administered these virtuous counsels, he intimates that he has involved himself in an illicit amour—or, as he expresses it, that he is attached to "a dear infidel." The person so described was a married woman, who had separated from her husband. Boswell had met her in the autumn of 1765 at Moffat Spa, where he had been sojourning with his friend Mr. Johnston, of Grange, a Dumfriesshire landowner. He had brought her to Edinburgh, and she was now maintained at his expense. In mitigation of his conduct in associating with her, he thus expatiates to Mr. Temple:—

"Don't think her unfaithful; I could not love her if she was. There is baseness in all deceit which my soul is virtuous enough to abhor, and therefore I look with horror on adultery. But my amiable mistress is no longer bound to him who was her husband: he has used her shockingly ill; he has deserted her; he lives with another. Is she not then free? She is, it is clear, and no arguments can disguise it. She is now mine; and were she to be unfaithful to me, she ought to be pierced with a Corsican poniard; but I believe she loves me sincerely. She has done everything to please me: she is perfectly generous, and would not hear of any present."

The first part of Boswell's letter embracing these incongruous details is dated "1st February," and occupies seven folio pages. With temporary discretion the writer hesitated to send off so strange a communication; at length, on the 28th of the month, he resumed his narrative, which after another interval was concluded on the 4th March, and thereupon despatched. Respecting his unhappy amour he writes:—

> "I have talked a great deal of my sweet little mistress; I am, however, uneasy about her. Furnishing a house and maintaining her with a maid will cost me a great deal of money, and it is too like marriage, or too much a settled plan of licentiousness; but what can I do? I have already taken the house, and the lady has agreed to go in at Whitsuntide; I cannot in honour draw back.... Now am I tormented because my charmer has formerly loved others. Besides, she is ill-bred, quite a rompish girl. She debases my dignity; she has no refinement, but she is very handsome and very lively. What is it to me that she has formerly loved? so have I. I am positive that since I first courted her at Moffat she has been constant to me; she is kind, she is generous. What shall I do? I wish I could get off; and yet how awkward would it be!... What is to be thought of this life, my friend? Hear the story of my last three days. After tormenting myself with reflecting on my charmer's former loves, and ruminating on parting with her, I went to her. I could not conceal my being distressed. I told her I was very unhappy, but I would not tell her why. She took this very seriously, and was so much affected that she went next morning and gave up her house. I went in the afternoon and secured the house, and then drank tea with her. She was much agitated; she said she was determined to go and board herself in the north of England, and that I used her very ill. I expostulated with her; I was sometimes inclined to let her go, and sometimes my heart was like to burst within me. I held her dear hand; her eyes were full of passion; I told her what made me miserable; she was pleased to find it was nothing worse. She had imagined I was suspicious of her fidelity, and she thought that very ungenerous in reconsidering her behaviour. She said I should not mind her faults before I knew her, since her conduct was now more circumspect. She owned that she loved me more than she had ever done her husband. All was well again."

Boswell went out, and the same evening got drunk, and committed gross follies. On the 30th March he wrote to Mr. Temple from Auchinleck. He informed him that as his Circe had gone to Moffat, he has "had time to think coolly," and to call up "that reason which he had so often contradicted." He proceeds:—

"Johnston, an old friend of mine, a writer in Edinburgh, but too much of an indolent philosopher to have great business, being rather a worthy country gentleman, with a paternal estate of £100 a year, was much distressed with my unhappy passion. He was at Moffat when it first began, and he marked the advance of the fever. It was he who assured me, upon his honour, that my fair one had a very bad character, and gave me some instances which made my lovesick heart recoil. He had some influence with me, but my brother David had more. To him I discovered my weakness, my slavery, and begged his advice. He gave it me like a man. I gloried in him. I roused all my spirit, and at last I was myself again. I immediately wrote her a letter, of which I enclose the scroll for your perusal. She and I have always corresponded in such a manner that no mischief could come of it, for we supposed a Miss— —, to whom all my amorous vows were paid.... I have not yet got her answer: what will it be, think you? I shall judge of her character from it. I shall see if she is abandoned or virtuous; I mean both in a degree; I shall at any rate be free. What a snare have I escaped! Do you remember Ulysses and Circe?—

'Sub domina meretrice vixisset turpis et excors.'

"My life is one of the most romantic that I believe either you or I really know of, and yet I am a very sensible, good sort of man. What is the meaning of this, Temple? You may depend upon it that very soon my follies will be at an end, and I shall turn out an admirable member of society. Now that I have given my mind the turn, I am totally emancipated from my charmer, as much as from the gardener's daughter who now puts on my fire and performs menial offices like any other wench, and yet just this time twelvemonth I was so madly in love as to think of marrying her. Should not this be an everlasting lesson to me?... How strangely do we colour over our vices! I startle when you talk of keeping another man's wife, yet that was literally my scheme, though imagination represented it just as being fond of a pretty, lovely, black little lady, who to oblige me stayed in Edinburgh, and I very genteelly paid her expenses."

From several letters to Mr. Temple at subsequent dates, it appears that Boswell's discreditable amour was protracted for some time longer. In the same letter he invited his friend's counsel respecting certain matrimonial projects on which he had embarked.

Amidst his dissipations and follies Boswell was not altogether idle. To Mr. Temple he reported, in March, that he had at the Bar earned sixty-five guineas during the winter, and that his employment was steadily on the increase. He stated that Mr. Hume augured favourably of his work on

Corsica; that Rousseau had quarrelled with him as he had done with Hume; that Dr. Gregory had sought his acquaintance, and that he had received a long letter from General Paoli, and one of three pages from Lord Chatham.

To Lord Chatham Boswell replied in characteristic fashion:—

"*Auchinleck, April 8th, 1767.*

"I have communicated to General Paoli the contents of your lordship's letter, and I am persuaded he will think as I do.... Your lordship applauds my 'generous warmth for so striking a character as the able chief.' Indeed, my lord, I have the happiness of being able to contemplate with supreme delight those distinguished spirits by which God is sometimes pleased to honour humanity, and as I have no personal favour to ask of your lordship, I will tell you, with the confidence of one who does not fear to be thought a flatterer, that your character, my lord, has filled many of my best hours with that noble admiration which a disinterested soul can enjoy in the bower of philosophy."

After informing his correspondent that he is about to publish an account of Corsica, he proceeds:—

> "As for myself, to please a worthy and respected father, one of our Scots judges, I studied law, and am now fairly entered to the bar. I begin to like it; I can labour hard, I feel myself coming forward, and I hope to be useful to my country. Could your lordship find time to honour me now and then with a letter?
>
> "I have been told how favourably your lordship has spoken of me. To correspond with a Paoli and with a Chatham is enough to keep a young man ever ardent in the pursuit of virtuous fame."

The cool egotism which prompted Boswell, an undistinguished youth, to beg an occasional letter from an illustrious and veteran statesman is without a parallel in biography. At Edinburgh, notwithstanding his obvious eccentricity, he enjoyed a kind of literary *status*. As a patron of histrionic art he led a considerable section of the Edinburgh youth; and we have already related, that at the request of Ross, the player, he composed the prologue spoken at the opening of the Edinburgh theatre in December, 1767. By an act of indiscretion he nearly crushed the institution he had helped to rear. He brought on the Edinburgh stage a comedy entitled "The Coquettes," to oblige Lady Houston, by whom it was composed. On the third performance it was condemned as a bad translation of one of Corneille's worst plays. Lady Houston was sister of Lord Cathcart, one of Boswell's friends, and creditably enough he was content to bear the censure of producing the piece rather than expose the foolish gentlewoman who had placed it in his hands.

In his letter to Mr. Temple of the 30th March, 1767, he reports concerning his forthcoming venture—"I am now seriously engaged in my account of Corsica; it elevates my soul, and makes me *spernere humum*. I shall have it finished by June." Through Mr. Hume he endeavoured to secure Mr. Andrew Millar as publisher; but negotiations being unsatisfactory, he sold his MS. for 100 guineas to Messrs. Edward and Charles Dilly, booksellers in the Poultry. In an ordinary octavo the work appeared in the spring of 1768, with the title, "An Account of Corsica: the Journal of a Tour to that Island, and Memoirs of Pascal Paoli, by James Boswell, Esq." It was dedicated, in flattering terms, to Paoli; but the peculiarities of the writer were more apparent in his preface. He there indicates his peculiar system of orthography. "Of late," he writes, "it has become the fashion to render our language more neat and trim by leaving out k after c, and u in the last syllable of words which used to end in our. The illustrious Mr. Samuel Johnson, who has alone executed in England what was the task of whole academies in other countries, has been careful in his dictionary to preserve the k as a mark of Saxon original. He has for most part, too, been careful to preserve the u, but he has also omitted it in several words. I have retained the k, and have taken upon me to follow a general rule with regard to words ending in our. Wherever a word originally Latin has been transmitted to us through the medium of the French I have written it with the characteristical u. Our attention to this may appear trivial, but I own I am one of those who are curious in the formation of language in its various modes; and therefore, with that, the affinity of English with other tongues may not be forgotten. If this work should at any future period be reprinted, I hope that care will be taken of my orthography."

Pursuant to his system, Boswell indulged the satisfaction of writing *authour* for author, and *tremenduous* for a word known only as tremendous. He closed his preface by intimating his literary aspirations:—

> "I should," he writes, "be proud to be known as an authour, and I have an ardent ambition for literary fame; for of all possessions I should imagine literary fame to be the most valuable. A man who has been able to furnish a book which has been approved by the world has established himself as a respectable character in distant society, without any danger of having that character lessened by the observation of his weaknesses. To preserve an uniform dignity among those who see us every day is hardly possible, and to aim at it must put us under the fetters of a perpetual restraint. The authour of an approved book may allow his natural disposition an easy play, and yet indulge the pride of superior genius when he considers that by those who know him only as an authour he never

ceases to be respected. Such an authour, when in his hours of gloom and discontent, may have the consolation to think that his writings are at that very time giving pleasure to numbers, and such an authour may cherish the hope of being remembered after death, which has been a great object to the noblest minds in all ages. Whether I may merit any portion of literary fame the public will judge. Whatever my ambition may be, I trust that my confidence is not too great, nor my hopes too sanguine."

Though subjected to some ridicule, owing to the extreme egotism of the writer, the Corsican Journey was well received. A second edition was called for within a few months. Boswell proceeded to London to enjoy an anticipated ovation. When he arrived Dr. Johnson was on a visit at Oxford, but Boswell by letter solicited his commendation. Contrary to his hopes he received this laconic answer—"I wish you would empty your head of Corsica, which I think has filled it rather too long." From Dr. Johnson such a reproof was intolerable. Boswell at once despatched the following reply:—

"How can you bid me empty my head of Corsica? My noble-minded friend, do you not feel for an oppressed nation bravely struggling to be free? Consider fairly what is the case. The Corsicans never received any kindness from the Genoese. They never agreed to be subject to them. They owe them nothing, and when reduced to an abject state of slavery by force, shall they not rise in the great cause of liberty, and break the galling yoke? And shall not every liberal soul be warm for them? Empty my head of Corsica! Empty it of honour, empty it of humanity, empty it of friendship, empty it of piety. No! while I live, Corsica and the cause of the brave islanders shall ever employ much of my attention, shall ever interest me in the sincerest manner."

Though Dr. Johnson imparted no praise, Boswell, on account of his book, met with considerable attention. To Mr. Temple he wrote on the 14th May,—

"I am really the great man now. I have had David Hume in the forenoon, and Mr. Johnson in the afternoon of the same day visiting me. Sir John Pringle, Dr. Franklin, and some more company, dined with me to-day; and Mr. Johnson and General Oglethorpe one day, Mr. Garrick alone another, and David Hume and some more *literati*, dine with me next week. I give admirable dinners and good claret; and the moment I go abroad again, which will be in a day or two, I set up my chariot.

> This is enjoying the fruit of my labours, and appearing like the friend of Paoli. By-the-bye, the Earl of Pembroke and Captain Meadows are just setting out for Corsica, and I have the honour of introducing them by letter to the General. David Hume came on purpose the other day to tell me that the Duke of Bedford was very fond of my book, and had recommended it to the Duchess."

In the beginning of 1769 Boswell issued under the publishing auspices of Messrs. Dilly, a duodecimo volume entitled "British Essays in favour of the brave Corsicans"—a work which was followed by the third edition of his work on Corsica. In a preface to this edition, dated at Auchinleck, 29th October, 1768, he thus disposes of his critics:—"To those who have imagined themselves very witty in sneering at me for being a Christian, I would recommend the serious study of theology; and I hope they will attain to the same comfort that I have in the belief of a revelation by which a Saviour is proclaimed to the world, and 'life and immortality are clearly brought to light.'" He closes by congratulating himself on having obtained literary reputation.

> "May I be permitted to say," he writes, "that the success of this book has exceeded my warmest hopes. When I first ventured to send it into the world I fairly owned an ardent desire for literary fame. I have obtained my desire; and whatever clouds may overcast my days, I can now walk here among the rocks and woods of my ancestors with an agreeable consciousness that I have done something worthy."

Complacently as he had expressed himself, Boswell was ill at ease, for though his book sold, and was generally approved, Dr. Johnson remained silent. After enduring the affront for eighteen months, he at length, in September, 1769, addressed a letter to the lexicographer, charging him with unkindness. In these terms Dr. Johnson rebutted the accusation:—

> "Why do you charge me with unkindness? I have omitted nothing that could do you good or give you pleasure, unless it be that I have forborne to tell you my opinion of your 'Account of Corsica.' I believe my opinion, if you think well of my judgment, might have given you pleasure; but when it is considered how much vanity is excited by praise, I am not sure that it would have done you good. Your history is like other histories, but your journal is in a very high degree curious and delightful. There is between the history and the journal that difference which there will always be found between notions borrowed from without and notions generated within. Your

history was copied from books; your journal rose out of your own experience and observation. You express images which operated strongly upon yourself, and you have impressed them with great force upon your readers. I know not whether I could name any narrative by which curiosity is better excited or better gratified."

These words from Dr. Johnson made Boswell happy. The Doctor's opinion as to the interest of the work mainly depending on the narrative of the writer's own experiences was shared generally. Respecting Boswell and his performance, Mr. Walpole, in a letter to the poet Gray, dated 18th February, 1768, thus expresses himself:—"Pray read the new account of Corsica; what relates to Paoli will amuse you much. There is a deal about the island and its dimensions that one does not care a straw for. The author, Boswell, is a strange being, and, like Cambridge,[40] has a rage for knowing anybody that was ever talked of. He forced himself upon me in spite of my teeth and my doors, and I see has given a foolish account of all he could pick up from me about King Theodore. He then took an antipathy to me on Rousseau's account, abused me in the newspapers, and expected Rousseau to do so too; but as he came to see me no more, I forgave all the rest. I see he is now a little sick of Rousseau himself, but I hope it will not cure him of his anger to me; however, his book will amuse you."

This is caustic enough. Gray's reply is equally in praise of Boswell's Journal and condemnatory of its author:—[41]

"Pembroke College, February 25, 1768.

"Mr. Boswell's book I was going to recommend to you when I received your letter. It has pleased and moved me strangely—all (I mean) that relates to Paoli.... The pamphlet proves what I have always maintained, that any fool may write a most valuable book by chance, if he will only tell us what he heard and said with veracity. Of Mr. Boswell's truth I have not the least suspicion, because I am sure he could invent nothing of the kind. The title of this part of his work is a dialogue between a Green Goose and a Hero."[42]

Inflated with his success as an author, and his supposed popularity as the friend of the Corsicans and of Paoli, Boswell, on his return to Edinburgh in the summer of 1768, began to eschew his legal duties and spend his evenings at the gambling-table. To this practice he had been formerly addicted, but he had temporarily renounced it, on the counsel of Mr. Sheridan. In August, 1768, he reported to Mr. Temple that "he found the fever still lurking in his veins," and so indulged his propensity. During the previous autumn he had experienced his father's resentment for his encouragement of theatricals and constant talk about Paoli. In reference to his father's displeasure he thus communicated with Mr. Temple in September, 1767:—

"How unaccountable is it that my father and I should be so ill together! He is a man of sense and a man of worth; but from some unhappy turn in his disposition he is much dissatisfied with a son whom you know. I write to him with warmth, with an honest pride, wishing that he should think of me as I am; but my letters shock him, and every expression in them is interpreted unfavourably. To give you an instance, I send you a letter I had from him a few days ago. How galling is it to the friend of Paoli to be treated so! I have answered him in my own style. I will be myself.... Temple, would you not like such a son? would you not feel a glow of parental joy? I know you would; and yet my worthy father writes to me in the manner you see, with that Scots strength of sarcasm which is peculiar to a North Briton. But he is offended with that fire which you and I cherish as the essence of our souls; and how can I make him happy? Am I bound to do so at the expense, not of this or the other agreeable wish, but at the expense of myself? The time was when such a letter from my father as the one I enclose would have depressed; but I am now firm, and as my revered friend Mr. Samuel Johnson used to say, I feel the privileges of an independent human being. However, it is hard that I cannot have the pious satisfaction of being well with my father."

To lose the paternal favour was perilous; so Boswell's next literary performance was of a professional character. When he commenced practice as an advocate, society in Edinburgh and in the country generally was much agitated in connection with the Douglas case. The question at issue was whether Mr. Archibald Douglas was the real heir to the estates of Douglas, the succession otherwise devolving on the Duke of Hamilton. The Lady Jane Douglas was twice married. By her first union, which subsisted for many years she had no children; she married secondly Mr. Stewart, afterwards Sir John Stewart, Bart., of Grandtully, an aged gentleman in feeble health, and by this marriage, as was alleged, gave birth to twin sons in her fifty-first year. Lady Jane long resided in France; her alleged *accouchement* took place in the house of a Madame le Brun, in Paris, and it was asserted that the children which she claimed as her sons were purchased from a Parisian rope-dancer. The younger of the two boys died in childhood, and on the death of the Duke of Douglas his Grace's estates were claimed by Archibald, the elder son. The validity of his claim was disputed, and the evidence adduced on both sides occupies several quarto volumes. In the Court of Session the claimant's birth was pronounced supposititious, on the casting vote of the Lord President Dundas. On appeal that decision was reversed by the House of Lords, Lord Camden, the Chancellor, alleging that "a more ample and positive proof of the child's being the son of a mother never appeared in a court of justice."

While the Douglas case was exciting its utmost interest, Boswell became a keen supporter of the claimant, Mr. Archibald Douglas; and in November, 1767, produced a pamphlet entitled "The Essence of the Douglas Cause." This *brochure* was issued in reply to a small publication entitled "Considerations on the Douglas Cause," but failed to excite any general attention. The author, however, cherished the belief that he had been of essential service to Mr. Douglas, and accordingly requested that his name might be added to the list of counsel retained on his behalf.

Boswell, we have seen, had begun to think of matrimony. In that direction his thoughts were sufficiently persistent, though in respect to the object of affection singularly variable. On the 30th March, 1767, he thus addressed Mr. Temple:—

> "What say you to my marrying? I intend, next autumn, to visit Miss Bosville in Yorkshire; but I fear, my lot being cast in Scotland, that beauty would not be content. She is, however, grave; I shall see. There is a young lady in the neighbourhood here who has an estate of her own between two and three hundred a year, just eighteen, a genteel person, an agreeable face, of a good family, sensible, good-tempered, cheerful, pious. You know my grand object is the ancient family of Auchinleck—a venerable and noble principle. How would it do to conclude an alliance with the neighbouring princess, and add her lands to our dominions? I should at once have a very pretty little estate, a good house, and a sweet place. My father is very fond of her: it would make him perfectly happy: he gives me hints in this way:—'I wish you had her,'—'No bad scheme this; I think it a very good one.' But I will not be in a hurry; there is plenty of time."

Writing to Mr. Temple on the 12th June, Boswell omits all reference to Miss Bosville, but extols "the young lady in his neighbourhood" as a kind of goddess.

> "The lady in my neighbourhood," he writes, "is the finest woman I have ever seen. I went and visited her, and she was so good as to prevail with her mother to come to Auchinleck, where they stayed four days, and in our romantic groves I adored her like a divinity. I have already given you her character. My father is very desirous I should marry her; all my

relations, all my neighbours, approve of it. She looked quite at home in the house of Auchinleck. Her picture would be an ornament to the gallery. Her children would be all Boswells and Temples, and as fine women as these are excellent men. And now my friend, my best adviser, comes to hear me talk of her and to fix my wavering mind."

In his next letter to Mr. Temple, Boswell reveals that his "angelic princess" is "Miss Blair, of Adamtown," adding that on the preceding Tuesday he had got inebriated in drinking her health, and in that condition had committed miserable follies. He proceeds:—

"You must resolve to visit my goddess. You are a stranger, and may do a romantic thing. You shall have consultation guineas, as an ambassador has his appointments. You see how I use you. In short, between us two, all rules and all maxims are suspended. Pray prepare yourself for this adventure; we shall settle it, I hope; I cannot go with you, though. You are to see our country for a jaunt upon my recommendation."

Boswell was practical for once. In assuring his reverend friend that he would have his "consultation guineas" he meant that his travelling costs would be defrayed should he consent to visit Ayrshire, and recommend him to Miss Blair. The proposal was acceded to. Mr. Temple agreed to proceed on his mission at once on being furnished with the needful instructions. Before the end of July he was in Scotland, provided with an itinerary, from which we extract the following:—

"*Wednesday.*—Thomas[43] will bring you to Adamtown a little after eleven. Send up your name; if possible, put up your horses there, they can have cut grass; if not, Thomas will take them to Mountain, a place a mile off, and come back and wait at dinner. Give Miss Blair my letter. Salute her and her mother; ask to walk. See the place fully; think what improvements should be made. Talk of my mare, the purse, the chocolate. Tell them you are my very old and intimate friend. Praise me for my good qualities, you know them; but talk also how odd, how inconstant, how impetuous, how much accustomed to women of intrigue. Ask gravely, 'Pray don't you imagine there is something of madness in that family?' Talk of my various travels, German princes, Voltaire and Rousseau. Talk of my father, my strong desire to have my own house. Observe her well. See how amiable! Judge if she would be happy with your friend. Think of me as the great man at Adamtown—quite classical, too! Study the mother. Remember well what passes. Stay tea. At six order horses and go to New Mills, two miles from Loudoun; but if they press you stay all night, do it. Be a man of as much ease as possible. Consider what a romantic expedition you are on; take notes; perhaps you now fix me for life."

Instructions more extraordinary were never before delivered by lovesick swain to the friend of his suit. That friend was to inform the lady of his affections that he was "much accustomed to women of intrigue;" that he was "odd," "inconstant," and "impetuous;" and he was even to hint that there was madness in his family. That Boswell should have brought his friend 500 miles so to describe him to the lady of his affections is not the least remarkable feature of his strange career. Mr. Temple, it is hoped, was more discreet than his client.

On his return to Mamhead Mr. Temple married a gentlewoman who brought him a fortune of £1,300. Boswell wrote to Miss Blair, thanking her for her attention to his friend, but the lady was silent. Her suitor became perplexed; he feared that a certain nabob had "struck in," or that Temple "had told her his faults too honestly." At length, after he had endured the miseries of "a feverish disorder, the lady relented, and sent him a most agreeable letter." She made an excuse that a letter of his had been delayed at the Ayr post office; but he had written several. On the 28th August he again communicates with Mr. Temple. He assumes the designation of a sovereign prince, and holds the clergyman as his ambassador.

> "Are you not happy," he writes, "to find that all is well between the Prince of Auchinleck and his fair neighbouring princess? In short, sir, I am one of the most fortunate men in the world. As Miss Blair is my great object at present, and you are a principal minister in forwarding the alliance, I enclose you the latest papers on the subject. You will find the letter I wrote her when ill, where you will see a Scots word *roving*, from the French *rêver*, as if to dream awake. I put it down as a good English word, not having looked in Johnson. You will next find the lady's answer, then a long letter from me, which required an extraordinary degree of good sense and temper to answer it with an agreeable propriety; then her answer, which exceeds my highest expectations. Read these papers in their order, and let me have your excellency's opinion. Am I not now as well as I can be? What condescension! what a desire to please! She studies my disposition, and resolves to be cautious, &c. Adorable woman! Don't you think I had better not write again till I see her? I shall go west in a fortnight, but I can

hardly restrain myself from writing to her in transport. I will go to Adamtown and stay a week. I will have no disguise; we shall see each other fairly. We are both independent; we have no temptation to marry but to make each other happy. Let us be sure if that would be the consequence."

On the 5th of November Boswell writes to Mr. Temple from Adamtown:—

"MY DEAR TEMPLE,—The pleasure of your countenance in reading the date of this letter is before me at this moment.... In short, I am sitting in the room with my princess, who is at this moment a finer woman than ever she appeared to me before. But, my valuable friend, be not too certain of your Boswell's felicity, for indeed he has little of it at present.... For ten days I was in a fever, but at last I broke the enchantment. However, I could not be too sullen in my pride; I wrote to her from Auchinleck, and wished her joy, &c.; she answered me, with the same ease as ever, that I had no occasion. I then wrote her a strange sultanish letter, very cold and very formal, and did not go to see her for near three weeks....

"But the princess and I have not yet made up our quarrel; she talks lightly of it. I am resolved to have a serious conversation with her to-morrow morning. If she can still remain indifferent as to what has given me much pain, she is not the woman I thought her, and from to-morrow morning shall I be severed from her as a lover. I shall just bring myself, I hope, to a good easy tranquillity. If she feels as I wish her to do, I shall adore her while my blood is warm."

After an interval of three days Boswell again communicated with Mr. Temple:—

"*Auchinleck, Sunday, 8th November, 1767.*

"I wrote you from Adamtown, and told you how it was with the princess and me. Next morning I told her that I had complained to you that she would not make up our last quarrel, but she did not appear in the least inclined to own herself in the wrong. I confess that, between pride and love, I was unable to speak to her but in a very awkward manner. I came home on Friday; yesterday I was extremely uneasy. That I might give her a fair opportunity, I sent her a letter, of which I enclose you a copy. Could the proud Boswell say more than you will see there? In the evening I got her answer; it was written with an art and indifference astonishing from so young a lady:—'I have not yet found out that I was to blame. If you have been uneasy on my account, I am indeed sorry for it; I should be sorry to give any person uneasiness, far more one whose cousin and friend I shall always be.'...

"In short, Temple, she is cunning, and sees my weakness. But I now see her; and though I cannot but suffer severely, I from this moment resolve to think no more of her. I send you the copy of a note which goes to her to-morrow morning. Wish me joy, my good friend, of having discovered the snake before too late. I should have been ruined had I made such a woman my wife. Luckily for me, a neighbour who came to Auchinleck last night told me that he had heard three people at Ayr agree in abusing her as a jilt. What a risk have I run! However, as there is still a possibility that all this may be mistake and malice, I shall behave to her in a very respectful manner, and shall never say a word against her but to you. After this I shall be upon my guard against ever indulging the least fondness for a Scotch lass. I am a soul of a more southern frame. I may, perhaps, be fortunate enough to find an Englishwoman who will be sensible of my merit, and will study to please my singular humour."

Subsequent letters from Boswell to Mr. Temple contain these passages:—"Upon my soul, the madness of which I have a strong degree in my composition is at present so heightened by love that I am absolutely deprived of judgment.... One great fault of mine is talking at random; I will guard against it." Referring to the object of his hopes at Adamtown, he writes:—"I will consecrate myself to her for ever. I must have her to learn the harpsichord and French; she shall be one of the first women in the island." "Temple, I ventured to seize her hand. She is really the finest woman to me I ever saw."

To Mr. Temple, on the 24th December, he wrote thus:—

> "In my last I told you that after I had resolved to give up with the Princess for ever, I resolved first to see her. I was so lucky as to have a very agreeable interview, and was convinced by her that she was not to blame. This happened on a Thursday; that evening her cousin and most intimate friend, the Duchess of Gordon, came to town. Next day I was at the concert with them, and afterwards supped at Lord Kames's. The Princess appeared distant and reserved. I could hardly believe that it was the same woman with whom I had been quite gay the day before; I was then uneasy. Next evening I was at the play with them: it was 'Othello.' I sat close behind the Princess, and at the most affecting scenes I pressed my hand upon her waist; she was in tears, and rather leaned to me. The jealous Moor described my very soul."

Boswell subjoins a dialogue between "the Princess" and himself. "You are very fond of Auchinleck," said Boswell in his pleading. "I confess I am," responded the lady; "I wish I liked you as well as I do Auchinleck." There had been repeated meetings and lengthy conversations, but Boswell could not extract a promise, and knew not what to think. He begs that Mr. Temple will consult with his wife, and thereupon advise him. Towards the close of his letter he writes, "Amidst all this love I have been wild as ever.... To-morrow I shall be happy with my devotions.... Could you assist me to keep up my real dignity among the illiterate race of Scots lawyers?"

To Mr. Temple he writes from Edinburgh on the 8th February, 1768:—

> "All is over between Miss Blair and me. I have delayed writing till I could give you some final account. About a fortnight after she went to the country a report went that she was going to be married to Sir Alexander Gilmour, Member of Parliament for Mid-Lothian, a young man about thirty, who has £1,600 a year of estate, was formerly an officer in the Guards, and is now one of the clerks of the Board of Green Cloth, a thousand a year—in short, a noble match, though a man of expense, and obliged to lead a London life. After the fair agreement between her and me, which I gave you in my last, I had a title to know the truth. I wrote to her seriously, and told her if she did not write me an answer I should believe the report to be true. After three days I concluded from her silence that she was at least engaged. I endeavoured to laugh off my passion, and I got Sir Alexander Gilmour to frank a letter to her, which I wrote in a pleasant strain, and amused myself with the whim; still, however, I was not absolutely certain, as her conduct has been so prudent all along."

To ask a gentleman to frank a letter for him addressed to a young lady of whom they were rival lovers was an act of eccentricity befitting Boswell only. In the letter above quoted he proceeds to inform Mr. Temple that the heiress having come to town, he began to apprehend that her affections were engaged by a Mr. Fullerton, whom he describes as his "old rival, the nabob." So he procured the nabob's acquaintance, and they called on the heiress together. She received them courteously, but with greater than wonted reserve. Boswell was determined to know the worst. He entertained Mr. Fullerton to supper at the house of a relative, and the same evening took him to a tavern and warmed him "with old claret." As anticipated, Mr. Fullerton became very communicative, admitting that he had been assiduous in attending Miss Blair, but had received no suitable encouragement. He and Boswell remained together long after midnight, and before separating agreed that each on the morrow should visit the heiress, and make proposals to her. Boswell made sure to reach first, as he went to breakfast; he proposed, and was refused. The nabob called on Miss Blair an hour or two afterwards, and was overpowered with her coldness.

"Now that all is over," Boswell sums up, "I see many faults in her which I did not see before.... I am, however, resolved to look out for a good wife either here or in England.... The heiress is a good Scots lass, but I must have an Englishwoman. You cannot say how fine a woman I may marry. Perhaps a Howard, or some other of the noblest in the kingdom."

Finally, to assure his correspondent that he was not distracted by rejection or disappointed hope, he embodied in his communication the following somewhat splenetic verses at the expense of the "princess:"—

"Although I be an honest laird,

In person rather strong and brawny,

For me the heiress never cared,

For she would have the knight Sir Sawney.[44]

"And when with ardent vows I swore,

Loud as Sir Jonathan Trelawney,

The heiress showed me to the door,

And said she'd have the knight Sir Sawney.

"She told me, with a scornful look,

I was as ugly as a tawny;

For she a better fish could hook,

The rich and gallant knight Sir Sawney."

In his next letter to Mr. Temple, dated London, 24th March, Boswell expresses his joy that he is rid of Miss Blair, and informs him that he and "a charming Dutchwoman" have renewed correspondence. Under the name of Zelide she is frequently mentioned in his previous letters; he had formed her acquaintance at Utrecht. Zelide is commended as fair, lively, sensible, and accomplished; and is so deeply attached to the writer that he feels he cannot be unhappy with her. By having translated into French his work on Corsica she has shown a just appreciation of his literary tastes.

Contrary to his usual habit, Boswell on this occasion consulted both his father and his friend. Zelide, he said, was "willing to meet him without any engagement;" but his counsellors were unwilling that any meeting should be held. Writing to Mr. Temple on the 16th April he admits that Zelide had faults, but time, he thinks, may have altered her for the better, as it had in some measure altered himself. However, he was willing, in deference to his advisers, to renounce Zelide. In a postscript he asks Mr. Temple's opinion of Miss Dick,[45] "with whom he dined agreeably." He describes her as "fine, healthy, young, and amiable," though lacking "a good fortune." He acknowledges that he had many wanton passions, "and had lately been wild as ever." He is much disappointed that his correspondent, to whom he had previously offered a visit, had no spare bed: he will visit him after all, and "they will sit up all night together."

On the 26th April he informs Mr. Temple that Zelide is not yet given up. He had received a letter from her, "full of good sense and tenderness," and he had asked his father to allow him to visit her at Utrecht. "How do we know," he proceeds, "but she is an inestimable prize? Surely it is worth while to go to Holland to see a fair conclusion, one way or other, of what has hovered in my mind for years. I have written to her and told her all my perplexity; I have put in the plainest light what conduct I actually require of her, and what my father will require. I have bid her be my wife at present, and comfort me with a letter, in which she shall show at once her wisdom, her spirit, and her regard for me. You shall see it. I tell you, man, she knows me and values me as you do." Boswell adds that he has been suffering from a distemper induced by social indulgence, and vows that he "shall never again behave in a manner so unworthy the friend of Paoli."

Disappointment still ruled. In a letter, dated 14th May, Boswell informs Mr. Temple that he had received a letter from Zelide. Most gently had he referred to her "levity and infidel notions," and she had proved a "termagant and scorched him." He had assured his father that Mademoiselle would not suit him as a wife; she, however, might be "a good correspondent."

Unaccepted as a lover, Zelide declined becoming a correspondent; she was soon forgotten. Mr. Temple was opposed to Miss Dick, and Boswell, though he disapproved his friend's opinion, began to look elsewhere. After two months,[46] he writes to Mamhead, that he had found another mistress— a certain Mary Anne, an Irish beauty. He congratulates himself on having escaped "the insensible Miss B. and the furious Zelide," and "rejoices in the finest creature that ever was formed, *la belle Irlandaise*." "Imagine to yourself, Temple," he adds, "a young lady just sixteen, formed like a Grecian nymph, with the sweetest countenance, full of sensibility, accomplished, with a Dublin education, always half the year in the north of Ireland, her father a councillor-at-law, with the estate of £1,000 a year, and above £10,000 in ready money; her mother a sensible, well-bred woman; she the darling of her parents, and no other child but her sister." He adds, "Upon my honour I never was so much in love; I never was before in a situation to which there was not some objection, but here every flower is united, and not a thorn to be found.... What a fortunate fellow am I! What a variety of adventures in all countries! I was allowed to walk a great deal with Miss——; I repeated my fervent passion to her again and again; she was pleased, and I could swear that her little heart beat. I carved the first letter of her name on a tree; I cut off a lock of her hair, *male pertinax*. She promised not to forget me, nor to marry a lord before March.... This is the most agreeable passion I ever felt; sixteen, innocence, and gaiety make me quite a Sicilian swain. Before I left London I made a vow in St. Paul's church that I would not allow myself ... for six months. I am hitherto firm to my vow, and already feel myself a superior being.... In short, Maria has me without any rival."

Amidst these vows and assurances of amendment, Boswell acknowledges that he had during the last two months "employed a great deal of time in gaming," and had thereby wasted his means. Within three months he has forgotten Mary Anne, is again a visitor at Adamtown, and on his knees before Miss Blair. That lady is provokingly curt, and Boswell is assured by her mother that he had made such a joke of his love for her in every company that she was piqued.[47] After "this relapse of fever" has continued a few weeks he bids a second adieu to Adamtown, and determines to renew his addresses to Mary Anne. "Then," he writes, "came a kind letter from my amiable aunt Boyd in Ireland, and all the charms of sweet Mary Anne revived. Since that time I have been quite constant to her, and as indifferent towards Kate as if I never had thought of her.... After her behaviour, do I, the candid, generous Boswell, owe her anything? Am I anyhow bound by passionate inclinations to which she did not even answer? Write to me, my dear friend. She will be here soon. I am quite easy with her. What should I do? By all that's enchanting I go to Ireland in March!"

To the letter just quoted Boswell adds two postscripts. In the first he intimates that he is "a good deal in debt." In the second, he remarks, "My present misfortune is occasioned by drinking. Since my return to Scotland I have fallen a great deal too much into that habit, which still prevails in Scotland. Perhaps the coldness of the Scots requires it, but my young blood is turned to madness by it. This will be a warning to me, and from henceforth I shall be a perfect man; at least, I hope so." Confessions which close the letter strongly proved that the writer's aspirations after perfection were altogether illusory.

In May, 1769, Boswell fulfilled his intention of visiting Ireland. Through the influence of Mr. Sibthorpe, a landowner in the county or Down, husband of one of his cousins, he was introduced into elegant and lettered society. At Dublin he dined with Lord Charlemont, and met such literary celebrities as Dr. Leland, Mr. Flood, Dr. Macbride, and George Falconer, the friend of Swift and Chesterfield. More conspicuous hospitalities which attended him at Dublin he deemed worthy of a place in a reputed organ of fashionable intelligence. At his request the *Public Advertiser* informed its readers on the

7th of July that "James Boswell, Esq., having now visited Ireland, he dined with his Grace the Duke of Leinster at his seat at Carton: he went also by special invitation to meet the Lord Lieutenant at his country seat at Leixlip, to which he was conducted, in one of his Excellency's coaches, by Lieut.-Colonel Walshe. He dined there and stayed all night, and next morning came in the coach with his Excellency to the Phœnix Park, and was present at a review of Sir Joseph Yorke's dragoons. He also dined with the Right Honourable the Lord Mayor. He is now set out on his return to Scotland." In Ireland he remained six weeks, chiefly occupied in prosecuting his suit. But the "charming Mary Anne" would only laugh at his protestations. In deepest mortification he complained to his cousin Margaret Montgomerie, who had accompanied him to Ireland. She offered her sympathy, and Boswell in gratitude tendered his hand. It was accepted cordially. Miss Montgomerie was not rich, but she possessed largely what her lover entirely lacked—discretion and common sense. Her pedigree justified her union with the heir of Auchinleck. Paternally she was related to the noble house of Eglinton, and her father, Mr. David Montgomerie, of Lainshaw, claimed the dormant peerage of Lyle. To Lord Auchinleck the proposed union gave entire satisfaction.

The solemnization of the marriage was deferred till autumn. Meanwhile Boswell resolved to pay another visit to the metropolis. Misfortune had attended Paoli. With the sum of £700, which he raised by subscription, Boswell, in August, 1768, shipped for Corsica a quantity of cannon from the Carron Ironworks.[48] Whether the artillery reached its destination, and to what extent it proved useful, has not been related. Unable to overcome Paoli, the Genoese transferred Corsica to the French, who accepting the gift, despatched an army under the Marshal de Vaux to take possession. The inhabitants fought bravely, but were overwhelmed by numbers. Paoli embarked on the 16th June, 1769, in an English vessel bound for Leghorn. Crossing the Continent he repaired to London, where he was hailed with the honours due to his patriotism. Boswell hastened from Scotland to offer his respects. Paoli received him warmly.

On the 6th September a national jubilee at Stratford-on-Avon celebrated the memory of Shakspere. Writing on this subject to the *Scots Magazine* of the same month, Boswell, while generally commending the proceedings, expressed regret that the demonstration commenced with an oratorio. "I could have wished," he wrote, "that prayers had been read, and a short sermon preached; it would have consecrated our jubilee to begin it with devotion—with gratefully adoring the Supreme Father of all spirits, from whom cometh every good and perfect gift." In strange contrast with these devotional sentiments was Boswell's own procedure at the jubilee. He took the part of a buffoon, in supposed tribute to patriotism. Rejoicing in his achievement, he published an account of his appearance in the *London Magazine* for September, accompanied with his portrait. His narrative proceeds thus:—

> "One of the most remarkable masks upon this occasion was James Boswell, Esq., in the dress of an armed Corsican chief. He entered the amphitheatre about twelve o'clock. He wore a short dark-coloured coat of coarse cloth, scarlet waistcoat and breeches, and black spatter-dashes; his cap or bonnet was of black cloth; on the front of it was embroidered in gold letters, "*Viva la Liberta*," and on one side of it was a handsome blue feather and cockade, so that it had an elegant as well as a warlike appearance. On the breast of his coat was sewed a Moor's head, the crest of Corsica, surrounded with branches of laurel. He had also a cartridge pouch into which was stuck a stiletto, and on his left side a pistol was hung upon the belt of his cartridge pouch. He had a fusee slung across his shoulder, wore no powder in his hair, but had it plaited at full length with a knot of blue ribbons at the end of it. He had, by way of staff, a very curious vine all of one piece, with a bird finely carved upon it emblematical of the sweet bard of Avon. He wore no mask, saying that it was not proper for a gallant Corsican. So soon as he came into the room he drew universal attention. The novelty of the Corsican dress, its becoming appearance, and the character of that brave nation concurred to distinguish the armed Corsican chief. He was first accosted by Mrs. Garrick, with whom he had a good deal of conversation. Mr. Boswell danced both a minuet and a country dance with a very pretty Irish lady, Mrs. Sheldon, wife to Captain Sheldon, of the 38th Regiment of Foot, who was dressed in a genteel domino, and before she danced threw off her mask."

In honour of Corsica, Boswell read to the assemblage at Stratford a poem which he published the same month in the *Scots Magazine*. These are the concluding lines:—

"Let me plead for liberty distressed,

And warm for her each sympathetic breast;
Amidst the splendid honours which you bear,
To save a sister island be your care;
With generous ardour make us also free,
And give to Corsica a noble jubilee."

On his return from Stratford, Dr. Johnson, in a letter dated 9th September, congratulated him on his approaching marriage. He wrote thus:—

> "I am glad that you are going to be married, and as I wish you well in things of less importance, wish you well with proportionate ardour in this crisis of your life. What I can contribute to your happiness I should be very unwilling to withhold, for I have always loved and valued you, and shall love you and value you still more as you become more regular and useful, effects which a happy marriage will hardly fail to produce."

Boswell was married to Miss Margaret Montgomerie, at Lainshaw, in Ayrshire, on the 25th November, 1769. On the same day his father entered on matrimony a second time, by espousing his cousin Elizabeth, daughter of Robert Boswell of Balmuto, and sister of Claude James Boswell, advocate, afterwards Lord Balmuto. This event, which Boswell did not anticipate, considerably modified his nuptial rejoicings. Boswell was afterwards reconciled; his father's wife proved kindly and generous, and she did not, by "multiplying," add to the family burdens.

In congratulating Boswell on his new condition Mr. Temple could not refer rejoicingly to his own matrimonial experiences. Mrs. Temple had not proved agreeable to her husband or pleasing to her neighbours. The occupancy of separate apartments did not rescue Mr. Temple from domestic disquietude, and he became desirous of abandoning his living of £80 a year for the humble station of a colonial chaplain.[49] In the hope of obtaining such an appointment by the influence of friends in the north, he proposed a visit to Boswell in the summer of 1770. Boswell adduced certain family prospects as a reason why the visit should be postponed.

About the end of August Mrs. Boswell gave birth to a son, who, much to the grief of both parents, survived only a few hours. Boswell sought comfort from his friend Mr. Temple, and expressed a hope that the visit he had announced he would fulfil soon. In a letter to Mr. Temple, dated 6th September, he wrote,—

> "Send your portmanteau on Monday, directed for me at my house in Chessel's Buildings, Canongate, and ride you over whenever you please. Give me all the time you can. My wife will be in her drawing-room next week, if it pleases God to continue to favour her. My dear friend, how happy will it make

me to have you under my roof, and enjoy with you some invaluable hours of elegant friendship and classical sociality!"

Mr. Temple remained at Chessel's Buildings several days. Though a persistent water-drinker, his visit was much enjoyed by his host. To a letter afterwards received from him Boswell replied thus:—

"*Edinburgh, 6th October, 1770.*

"I rejoice that you got so well to Gainslaw. I was afraid you might find the journey very fatiguing; but you water-drinkers are Herculean fellows. I believe it would be better for me were I to adopt your system; but this is only *en passant*. It is a bill which would meet with a good deal of opposition in my lower house. How agreeable is it to me to find that my old and most intimate friend was so happy in my house! We must really contrive it so as to pass a good part of our time together. I never will rest till you have a living in the north, I hope in Northumberland or Cumberland.

"You cannot say too much to me of my wife. How dare you quote to me *sua si bona norint*? I am fully sensible of my happiness in being married to so excellent a woman, so sensible a mistress of a family, so agreeable a companion, so affectionate and peculiarly proper helpmate for me. I own I am not so much on my guard against fits of passion or gloom as I ought to be; but that is really owing to her great goodness. There is something childish in it, I confess. I ought not to indulge in such fits; it is like a child that lets itself fall purposely, to have the pleasure of being tenderly raised up again by those who are fond of it. I shall endeavour to be better. Upon the whole I do believe I shall make her happy. God bless and preserve her!"

For eighteen months subsequent to his marriage Boswell applied himself with unwonted steadiness to literary study, and the systematic practice of his profession. If he corresponded regularly with Mr. Temple during this period few of his letters have been preserved, and he has recorded in his Life of Johnson that he and the lexicographer resumed, in June, 1771, a correspondence which had for a year and a half been intermitted. To a letter from Boswell, soliciting a renewal of epistolary intercourse, Dr. Johnson wrote as follows:—

"*London, June 20th, 1771.*

"I never was so much pleased as now with your account of yourself; and sincerely hope that, between public business, improving studies, and domestic pleasures, neither melancholy nor caprice will find any place for entrance. Whatever philosophy may determine of material nature, it is certainly true of intellectual nature that it abhors a vacuum. Our minds cannot be empty, and evil will break in upon them if they are not preoccupied by good. My dear sir, mind your studies, mind your business, make your lady happy, and be a good Christian. After this,—

'Tristitiam et metus,

Trades protervis in mare Creticum

Portare ventis.'

"If we perform our duty we shall be safe and steady, '*sive per*,' &c., whether we climb the Highlands or are tost among the Hebrides; and I hope the time will come when we may try our powers both with cliffs and water."

Dr. Johnson's letter contains the first published reference to the proposed journey to the Hebrides. In March, 1772, Boswell revisited London. He was retained as counsel in a case appealed to the House of Lords by one Hastie, a schoolmaster, who had been deprived of office for the cruel treatment of his pupils. That he might on this occasion properly acquit himself, he sought and obtained the aid of Dr. Johnson. During his visit he met Johnson frequently, and, with the intention of becoming his biographer, carefully recorded his conversations. He returned to Edinburgh in May.

Revisiting London in the spring of 1773, Boswell was for the first time invited to dinner at Dr. Johnson's private residence. He was, on Dr. Johnson's motion, admitted a member of the Literary Club. He had become known to Sir Joshua Reynolds, Dr. Goldsmith, and Mr. Garrick; he occasionally dined with General Oglethorpe, and continued on friendly terms with Paoli. He was a favourite with Mr. Thrale, and frequently enjoyed his hospitality. He returned to Edinburgh in May, and soon afterwards Mrs. Boswell presented him with a daughter. He named the child Veronica, in honour of his great-grandmother, the Countess of Kincardine, a descendant of the Dutch family of Somnelsdyck.

Dr. Johnson had talked of the proposed Hebridean journey more definitely. That his purpose might not waver, Boswell entreated some leading Scotsmen to send him letters of invitation and encouragement. Among those who responded by offers of hospitality were the chiefs Macdonald and Macleod, Principal Robertson, and Dr. Beattie. Johnson was much gratified, and fully determined to proceed to Scotland before the close of the summer. He left London early in August, in a post-chaise, along with Mr. Justice afterwards Sir Robert Chambers. The latter tarried at Newcastle, and Johnson was accompanied from thence to Edinburgh by Mr. Scott, afterwards Lord Stowell. From Newcastle he wrote to Boswell, on Wednesday, the 11th August, that he hoped to reach Edinburgh on the following Saturday. On the evening of that day he arrived at Boyd's Inn, Canongate, better known as the "White Horse." A note announcing his arrival brought Boswell at once. They embraced cordially, and Boswell led him up High Street to his house in James's Court.

To that house Boswell had removed lately from Chessel's Buildings. James's Court was entered from the Lawn Market by a low gateway. The court was quadrilateral, and opposite the entrance were two common stairs. Boswell occupied the dwelling reached by the western staircase, at the height of three storeys, his door being that at the top of the landing. The house was formerly occupied by David Hume, who here composed a portion of his history, and entertained Boswell when a youth. Dr. Hugh Blair had also occupied the dwelling.

Boswell having notified the arrival, his distinguished guest was, while he remained in Edinburgh, fêted at every meal. Among those invited by Boswell to meet him were such titled persons as the Duchess of Douglas, Lord Chief Baron Orde, Lord Hailes, Sir William Forbes, Bart., of Pitsligo, Sir Adolphus Oughton, and Sir Alexander Dick, Bart., of Prestonfield. Of those known in literature similarly privileged were Dr. William Robertson, Dr. Blair, Professor Adam Fergusson, Dr. Gregory, Dr. Alexander Webster, and Dr. Blacklock. It was an epoch in Boswell's life, and he was proportionately elated. In his "Tour," published fifteen years afterwards, he in reference to this period of his history presents of himself the following portraiture:—

"Think," he writes, "of a gentleman of ancient blood, the pride of which was his predominant passion. He was then in his thirty-third year, and had been about four years happily married. His inclination was to be a soldier, but his father, a respectable judge, had pressed him into the profession of the law. He had travelled a good deal and seen many varieties of human life; he had thought more than anybody had supposed, and had a pretty good stock of general learning and knowledge; he had all Dr. Johnson's principles, with some degree of relaxation; he had rather too little than too much prudence, and his imagination being lively, he often said things of which the effect was very different from the intention. He resembled sometimes—

'The best good man with the worst-natured muse.'"

He cannot deny himself the vanity of finishing with the encomium of Dr. Johnson, whose friendly partiality to the friend of his tour represents him as one "whose acuteness would help my inquiry, and whose gaiety of conversation and civility of manners are sufficient to counteract the inconveniences of travel in countries less hospitable than we have passed."

It was arranged that Boswell should accompany the lexicographer throughout the northern journey; and he made offer to attend to all business concerns, including those of finance. The travellers left Edinburgh on Wednesday, the 18th August. They crossed the Forth at Kinghorn, and proceeded to St. Andrews by post-chaise. By the professors of that ancient university they were cordially received and entertained with profuse hospitality. Among the ruins of the once magnificent cathedral Dr. Johnson inveighed against the ill-directed zeal of Presbyterian reformers. The travellers having rested two days at St. Andrews, proceeded northward by Dundee and Arbroath. When they reached Montrose, Boswell communicated with Lord Monboddo, who sent them a cordial invitation to his country seat. They dined with his lordship, and from thence posted to Aberdeen. There Dr. Johnson gratified his tastes by engaging in literary gladiatorship with several of the professors.

On Sunday, the 30th August, the travellers inspected a remarkable rock basin, known as the Buller of Buchan, and dined at Slains Castle with the Countess of Errol. Next day they proceeded to Banff, and on that following to Elgin, when they visited the ruins of the cathedral. On Friday, the 29th, they reached Nairn, and from thence inspected Cawdor Castle. By the Rev. Arlay Macaulay, minister of Cawdor, they were kindly entertained; he was known to them as author of a history of St. Kilda, and he has further claim to remembrance as member of a family which produced the celebrated Lord Macaulay. To his guests he presented a useful itinerary.

On Saturday, the 30th August, the travellers inspected Fort George, and dined with the governor, Sir Eyre Coote. Next day, at Inverness, they attended the Episcopal Chapel, when Boswell mentions as an odd coincidence, as to what might be said of his connecting himself with Dr. Johnson, that Mr. Tait, the clergyman, remarked in his discourse "that some connected themselves with men of distinguished talents, and since they could not equal them, tried to deck themselves with their merit by being their companions." The coincidence, puzzling to Boswell, admitted of simple solution, for Mr. Collector Keith, of the Excise, a native of Ayrshire, had met the travellers at Fort George, and to the clergyman notified their approach. Mr. Tait's allusion, apart from its truthfulness, was in the worst taste, and not to be justified. Boswell and Dr. Johnson dined with Mr. Keith.

At Inverness the travellers hired horses and procured guides. They remained one night at Fort Augustus, entertained by the governor, and thence pursued their journey to the opposite shores of Skye. Inconvenienced by rough roads, Dr. Johnson became irritable. As they approached Glenelg, Boswell, without apprising his companion, rode forward to secure at the inn the necessary accommodations. Johnson called him back with an angry shout, and on his return reproved him lustily. Boswell felt hurt, but did not venture to recriminate. His reflections on this occasion are thus recorded in his journal:—

"I wished to get on to see how we were to be lodged, and how we were to get a boat; all of which I thought I could best settle myself, without his having any trouble. To apply his great mind to minute particulars is wrong; it is like taking an immense balance (such as is kept on quays for weighing cargoes of ships) to weigh a guinea. I knew I had neat little scales which would do better, and that his attention to everything which falls in his way, and his uncommon desire to be always in the right, would make him weigh, if he knew of the particulars; it was right, therefore, for me to weigh them, and let him have them only in effect. I, however, continued to ride by him, finding he wished I should do so."

The travellers found the inn at Glenelg nearly destitute of provisions, but Macleod's factor sent them rum and sugar, and at night they rested on beds of hay. Next morning they sailed for Skye, and landing at Armidale, were met by Sir Alexander Macdonald and his lady, formerly Miss Bosville, of Yorkshire, with whom they remained several days. They received much generous hospitality from Mr. Mackinnon, a farmer who had entertained Pennant, and were pleased to find that he possessed a considerable library. Invited to Rasay by the insular Chief, they had at his house a distinguished reception. After spending some days at Rasay they returned to Skye, and were conducted to the residence of Mr. Macdonald, of Kingsburgh. His wife had earned a reputation which secured her a visit from every traveller penetrating into the Hebrides. She was the celebrated Flora Macdonald, who under circumstances of peril enabled Prince Charles Edward to elude the vigilance of his pursuers. At Kingsburgh Dr. Johnson slept in the bed on which the Prince rested twenty-seven years before. To her guests Mrs. Macdonald related the circumstances of the Prince's escape.

The travellers were conducted to Dunvegan Castle, where they were entertained by the Laird of Macleod and his accomplished mother, Lady Macleod. At Dunvegan, Boswell attempting wit at Dr. Johnson's expense, paid dearly for his rashness. Johnson retaliated, sarcastically presenting his assailant under a variety of degrading images, so as to render him the sport of the company.[50]

For two weeks the travellers were attended by Mr. Donald McQueen, a clergyman in Skye, whose respectable scholarship gratified Dr. Johnson, while his personal influence availed in opening channels of hospitality. With Mr. McQueen they parted on Saturday, the 25th September. On the evening of that day, Dr. Johnson having retired at an early hour, Boswell sat up drinking till five o'clock, when, much intoxicated, he was helped to bed. In the afternoon Johnson entered his apartment, and denounced him as "a drunken dog." The words were uttered playfully, and the inebriate, who had begun to dread a more terrible reproof, was pleased to find his companion in good humour. He rose, and opened the Church of England Prayer-book, and in the Epistle for the day read these words,—"And be not drunk with wine, wherein is excess." "Some," he wrote, "would have taken this as a divine interposition."

On Sunday, the 3rd October, the travellers left Skye for the island of Col. When they had got to sea a tempest arose; Dr. Johnson went into the hold and lay down, overcome with sickness. Conscious of danger, Boswell became meditative.

> "Piety," he writes, "afforded me comfort; yet I was disturbed by the objections that have been made against a particular Providence, and by the arguments of those who maintain that it is in vain to hope that the petitions of an individual, or even of congregations, can have any influence with the Deity; objections which have been often made, and which Dr. Hawkesworth has lately revived in his preface to the 'Voyages to the South Seas;' but Dr. Ogden's excellent doctrines on the efficacy of intercession prevailed."

At Col the travellers enjoyed the hospitality of Donald Maclean, the young *laird* who some time previously was a companion of their journey. Owing to unfavourable winds they remained at Col till Wednesday, the 13th October, when they sailed for Tobermory, in Mull. From thence they proceeded to Ulva and Inchkenneth, enjoying on both islands the hospitality of the owners, Mr. M'Quane and Sir Allan Maclean. Sir Allan accompanied them in their voyage round Mull to the island of Iona. They reached the island at nightfall, and procured beds in a barn among hay. Boswell records that he was much impressed with the solemnity of the scene; while Sir Allan and Dr. Johnson were at breakfast he quietly left his companions and returned to the cathedral. In these words he records his reflections:—

> "While contemplating the venerable ruins I reflected with much satisfaction that the solemn scenes of piety never lose their sanctity and influence, though the cares and follies of life may prevent us from visiting them, or may even make us fancy that their effects are only as yesterday when it is past, and never again to be perceived. I hoped that ever after having been in this holy place I should maintain an exemplary conduct. One has a strong propensity to fix upon some point of time from whence a better course of life may begin."

Accompanied by Sir Allan Maclean the travellers returned to Mull. After enjoying a series of hospitalities they sailed for Oban, on the mainland. Next day they posted to Inverary. Boswell reported their arrival to the Duke of Argyll, who cordially invited them to dinner. To Dr. Johnson the Duke and Duchess were extremely courteous, but Boswell's presence was by the Duchess studiously ignored. As widow of the late Duke of Hamilton she directed her displeasure at Boswell's zeal on behalf of Mr. Archibald Douglas in claiming the Douglas estates, which she believed to belong lawfully to her former husband. Boswell took her Grace's displeasure as a compliment to his talents, and has in his "Journey" playfully remarked that, his "punishment being indicted by so dignified a beauty,[51] he had the consolation which a man would feel who is strangled by a silken cord."

Arriving on the shores of Lochlomond, the travellers visited Sir James Colquhoun, Bart., at Rossdhu, and Mr. Commissary Smollett, cousin of Dr. Tobias Smollett. They posted for Glasgow, inspecting *en route* the ancient castle of Dumbarton. At Glasgow they visited the university, and two of the professors dined with them at their inn. Proceeding to Ayrshire, they dined with the Earl of Loudoun, and visited the aged Countess of Eglinton.

During the journey Boswell received a letter from his father, permitting him to bring his friend to Auchinleck. They arrived there on Sunday, the 2nd November, and remained a week. Lord Auchinleck and Dr. Johnson contended keenly on various points, but the social current moved more smoothly than Boswell had anticipated. Lord Auchinleck regarded Dr. Johnson's politics with aversion, and had denounced him as a "Jacobite." Illustrative of his dislike, an anecdote has been preserved by Sir Walter Scott. When Boswell left Edinburgh with Johnson on their northern tour, Lord Auchinleck remarked to a friend, "There's nae hope for Jamie, man; Jamie's gane clean gyte. What do you think, man? He's aff wi' the landlouping scoundrel of a Corsican. And whase tail do ye think he has pinned himself to now, man? a *dominie*, man,—an auld dominie, that keepit a schule and ca'd it an academy." Boswell has denied the truth of a report which had gained credit, that on his representing the lexicographer to his father as a *constellation of genius*, he replied, "*Ursa Major.*" Lord Auchinleck, he admits, did use the expression, but it was spoken aside to a brother judge as Dr. Johnson was standing in the Court of Session.[52]

After an absence of eighty-three days the travellers returned to Edinburgh. They were complimented and entertained by Lord Elibank, Lady Colville, Lord Hailes, Principal Robertson, and others. Mrs. Boswell, though she did not oppose her husband taking part in the Hebridean journey, was not reconciled to it. On his return she remarked to him, "I have seen a bear led by a man, but I never before saw a man led by a bear." Boswell accepted the remark facetiously, and, in the belief he would enjoy it, repeated it to Dr.

Johnson. As might have been expected, the lexicographer felt most keenly the allusion to his rough manners, and he was placed in circumstances in which retort was impossible. Removal was his only refuge, and he hastened his departure. He left Edinburgh in the stage-coach on the 22nd November—just twelve days after his return to the city. But he did not forget Mrs. Boswell's censure. For several years he alluded to her disliking him in many letters to her husband. Writing to Boswell on the 29th January, 1774, he sends his compliments to Mrs. Boswell, adding, "Tell her I do not love her the less for wishing me away." On the 5th March he wrote, "Mrs. Boswell is a sweet lady—only she was so glad to see me go that I have almost a mind to come again, that she may again have the same pleasure." In the same strain he writes to Boswell on the 27th August, 1775,—

> "Of Mrs. Boswell, though she knows in her heart that she does not love me, I am always glad to hear any good, and hope that she and the dear little ladies will have neither sickness nor any other affliction. But she knows that she does not care what becomes of me, and for that she may be sure that I think her very much to blame."

Dr. Johnson prepared his "Journey to the Hebrides" most leisurely; it was not published till January, 1775. Boswell received a parcel of copies, one for himself, others for persons who had shown particular attention to the writer. In distributing the volumes he invited special attention to an encomium upon himself in the earlier portion of the work. Obtaining charge of several cases appealed from the Court of Session to the House of Lords, he hastened to London to enjoy the honours which he conceived Dr. Johnson's eulogy must have secured him.

On the evening of Saturday, the 18th March, Boswell by the Edinburgh diligence reached Grantham. Travelling being suspended till Monday, he in the interval wrote a long letter to Mr. Temple. An extract follows.

"I am now," he proceeded, "so far on my way to London in the fly. It is Saturday night, and we repose here all Sunday. I have an acquaintance in Grantham, the Rev. Mr. Palmer, who was chaplain to the late Speaker; he is a worthy, learned, social man. I sent him a card that I would breakfast with him to-morrow, if not inconvenient to him. His answer is just come, which you shall hear: As breakfasting will be attended with some inconveniences in the present state of his family, he will be very glad of the favour of his company to a family dinner to-morrow at two o'clock. What can be the meaning of this? *How can breakfasting be inconvenient to a family that dines?* Can he wish to lie long in the morning that Queen Mab may be with him, 'tickling the parson as he lies asleep'? or can his wife and daughter not dress early enough? Pray guess in your next, with a sacerdotal sagacity, what this can be.

I shall try to learn and let you know. It is now early in the morning. I am writing in a great English parlour, to have my letter ready for the post at nine. It is comfortable to have such an acquaintance as Palmer—so situated. I have thought of making a good acquaintance in each town on the road. No man has been more successful in making acquaintance easily than I have been. I even bring people quickly on to a degree of cordiality. I am a quick fire, but I know not if I last sufficiently, though surely, my dear Temple, there is always a warm place for you. With many people I have compared myself to a taper, which can light up a great and lasting fire, though itself is soon extinguished....

"Mr. Johnson, when enumerating our club, observed of some of us that they talked from books,—Langton in particular. Garrick, he said, would talk from books, if he talked seriously. 'I,' said he, 'do not talk from books; you do not talk from books.' This was a compliment to my originality, but I am afraid I have not read books enough to be able to talk from them. You are very kind in saying that I may overtake you in learning. Believe me, though, that I have a kind of impotency of study; however, *nil desperandum est*....

"For my own part, I have continued schemes of publication, but cannot fix. I am still very unhappy with my father. We are so totally different that a good understanding is scarcely possible. He looks on my going to London just now as an *expedition*, as idle and extravagant, when in reality it is highly improving to me, considering the company which I enjoy; and I think it is also for my interest, as in time I may get something. Lord Pembroke was very obliging to me when he was in Scotland, and has corresponded with me since. I have hopes from him. How happy should I be to get an independency by my own influence while my father is alive!

"I am in charming health and spirits. There is a handsome maid in this inn, who interrupts me by coming sometimes into the room—I have no confession to make, my priest, so be not curious.

******

"Dr. Young says,—

  'A fever argues better than a Clarke.'

It is as fair reasoning for me to say that this handsome maid (Matty is her name) argues better than—whom you please."

Boswell reached London on the 21st March, and at once waited on Dr. Johnson, who received him cordially. On the 4th April he despatched a long letter to Mr. Temple, of which a portion is subjoined:—

"My dear Temple,

"My last was indeed a characteristical letter: I was quite in my old humour. My mind, formerly a wild, has been for some years pretty well enclosed with moral fences; but I fear the fences are stone hedges (to use a strange expression of Mr. Johnson in his 'Journey') of a loose construction, for a storm of passion would blow them down. When at Grantham there was a pretty brisk gale, which shook them; but now Reason, that steady builder and overseer, has set them firm, or they have proved to be better than I thought them, for my enclosures are in as good order as ever. I thank you, however, for your friendly props; your kind counsels pleased me much.

******

"Your soft admonitions would at any time calm the tempests of my soul. I told you that my arguments for concubinage were only for theory; the patriarchs might have a plurality, because they were not taught that it was wrong; but I, who have always been taught that it is wrong, cannot have the same enjoyment without an impression of its being so, and consequently without my moral sense suffering. But is not this prejudice? Be it so....

"I had last night an unexpected call to be at the bar of the House of Commons this day for Captain Erskine, brother to Miss Floyer's husband, as counsel for him in the Clackmannan election, where he is petitioner. I had neither wig nor gown with me. I posted to Claxton's early this morning, and he has kindly lent me both. I know not but in equity he should have a share of the guineas which they bring....

"To-day I dine at Sir John Pringle's; to-morrow at Dilly's, with Mr. Johnson and Langton, &c.; Thursday at Tom Davies's, with Mr. Johnson and some others; Friday at the Turk's Head, Gerrard Street, with our club, Sir Joshua Reynolds, &c., who now dine once a month, and sup every Friday. My forenoons are spent in visiting, and you know the distances of London make that business enough. Mr. Johnson has allowed me to write out a supplement to his Journey, but I wish I may be able to settle to it. This House of Commons work will be good ballast for me. I am little in what is called the gaiety of London; I went to Mrs. Abingdon's benefit to please Sir Joshua Reynolds. I have been at no other public place except exhibitions of pictures with Lord Mountstuart;[53] he is warmly my friend, and has engaged to do for me. His brother's lady,[54] a sweet, handsome, lively little woman, is my wife's intimate friend. I pass many of my morning hours with her. Paoli and I (for his simple designation is the highest) are to be at Wilton some time between the 10th and 26th of this month; I shall go from thence to your parsonage and overpower you with vivacity, and return to Bath."

Boswell proceeded to Mamhead, and there, though his host was an abstainer, got very drunk. Mr. Temple entreated him, when he became sober, to abandon his intemperate habits. As they talked together under an aged yew, Boswell vowed that he should henceforth avoid excess and cherish moderation. In a letter to Mr. Temple, dated the 10th May, he remarked that Dr. Johnson was now discouraging his proposal to add a supplement to his "Journey." This proceeding he attributes to Dr. Johnson's unwillingness that any one should share his laurels. "But don't you think," he adds, "I may write out my remarks on Scotland, and send them to be revised by you? and then they may be published freely. Give me your opinion of this."

Good Friday, which fell upon the 14th of April, Boswell spent with Dr. Johnson. They were present at three religious services, and in the evening they sat "a long while together in a serene, undisturbed frame of mind." On Easter Sunday Boswell "attended the solemn service at St. Paul's." Writing next day to Mr. Temple, he informs him that he had "received the holy sacrament, and was exalted in piety." In the same letter he reports that he is enjoying "the metropolis to the full," and that he has had "too much dissipation." He asks his friend not to fear "his Asiatic multiplicity," except when he happens to "take too much claret."

Boswell remained in London about two months, and though chiefly engaged in driving out, contrived to pocket forty guineas of professional fees. From Grantham, *en route* for Scotland, he wrote to Mr. Temple that, much to his disgust, "Henry Dundas,[55] a coarse, unlettered, unfanciful dog," was to be made Lord Advocate "at thirty-three," and that he had personally resolved to join the English Bar on obtaining his father's consent. He proceeds,—

> "I passed a delightful day yesterday. After breakfasting with Paoli and worshipping at St. Paul's, I dined *tête-à-tête* with my charming Mrs. Stuart, of whom you have read in my Journal. She refused to be of a party at Richmond, that she and I might enjoy a farewell interview. We dined in all the elegance of two courses and a dessert, with dumb waiters, except when the second course and the dessert were served. We talked with unreserved freedom, as we had nothing to fear; we were *philosophical*, upon honour—not deep, but feeling we were pious; we drank tea, and bid each other adieu as purely as romance paints. She is my wife's dearest friend, so you see how beautiful our intimacy is."

Boswell adds that "the handsome chambermaid had gone from the inn," and that he had promised Dr. Johnson to accept a chest of books of the moralist's own selection, and to "read more and drink less." He sums up,

"Tell Mrs. Temple that I am a favourite with her, because she knows me better, and that she may be assured that the more she knows me the more allowance will she make for my faults." A postscript is added. "There is," he writes, "a Miss Silverton in the fly with me, an amiable creature, who has been in France. I can unite little fondnesses with perfect conjugal love. Remember to put my letters in a book neatly,—see which of us does it first."

From Edinburgh, on the 3rd June, Boswell wrote to Mr. Temple as follows:—

> "On my arrival here I had the pleasure to find my wife and two little daughters as well as I could wish; but indeed, my worthy friend, it required some philosophy to bear the change from England to Scotland. The unpleasing tone, the rude familiarity, the barren conversation, of those whom I found here, in comparison with what I had left, really hurt my feelings.... The General Assembly is sitting, and I practise at its bar. There is *de facto* something low and coarse in such employment, though on paper it is a Court of *Supreme Judicature*; but guineas must be had."

"Low and coarse" as Boswell regarded the practice of his profession in the General Assembly of the Church of Scotland, he acknowledges that he did not perform his part without some misgiving. "Do you know," he proceeds, "it requires more than ordinary spirit to do what I am to do this very morning; I am to go to the General Assembly and arraign a judgment pronounced last year by Dr. Robertson, John Home, and a good many more of them, and they are to appear on the other side. To speak well, when I despise both the cause and the judges, is difficult; but I believe I shall do so wonderfully. I look forward with aversion to the little dull labours of the Court of Session."

Besides being disgusted with the Scottish Lord Advocate, Scottish manners, and Scottish courts, ecclesiastical and civil, Boswell was particularly dissatisfied with his father. He had sent him, he writes, "a conciliatory letter, but he fears he is callous." In dread of the paternal allowance being discontinued, he writes,—

> "If Lord Mountstuart would but give me an independency from the King while my father lives, I should be a fine fellow." He adds, "My promise under the venerable yew has kept me sober."

Boswell's habits were not more pleasing to his father than were his professional diligence and domestic economy. In the belief that his son was an incorrigible idler, Lord Auchinleck seriously meditated a withdrawal of his pension. But for his two children, disinheritance might have followed. To Mr. Temple on the 19th of June he wrote thus:—

> "My father is most unhappily dissatisfied with me. My wife and I dined with him on Saturday; he did not salute her, though he had not seen her for three months; nor did he so much as ask her how she did, though she is advanced in pregnancy. I understand he fancies that if I had married another woman, I might not only have had a better portion with her, but might have been kept from what he thinks idle and extravagant conduct. He harps on my going over Scotland with a brute[56] (think how shockingly erroneous!), and wandering, or some such phrase, to London. In vain do I defend myself; even the circumstance that my last jaunt to London did not cost me £20—as I got forty-two guineas in London—does not affect him. How hard it is that I am totally excluded from parental comfort! I have a mind to go to Auchinleck next autumn, and try what living in a mixed stupidity of attention to common objects, and restraint from expressing any of my own feelings, can do with him. I always dread his making some bad settlement."

Lord Auchinleck had solid grounds for indignation. He allowed his son £300 per annum, besides having provided him with a very expensive education. In the Scottish courts Boswell had abundant employment when he evinced the slightest inclination to attend to it. He had run himself aground; he owed a thousand pounds, which he could not pay, and his creditors were clamorous. Fretting under the unexpected burden which he was expected to sustain, Lord Auchinleck felt disposed to blame his daughter-in-law for encouraging his son's extravagance, and it is not certain that Boswell took the blame solely upon himself. The worthy judge was at length got over, and Boswell recovered his elasticity. To Mr. Temple on the 12th August he writes as follows:—

> "Tell me, my dear Temple, if a man who receives so many marks of more than ordinary consideration can be satisfied to drudge in an obscure corner, where the manners of the people are disagreeable to him? You see how soon I revive again. Could I but persuade my father to give me £400 a year, and let me go to the English Bar, I think I should be much better. That, however, seems to be impossible. As he is bound for £1,000 which I owe, he has resolved to lessen his allowance to me of £300 to £200. I must not dispute with him, but he is really a strange man. He is gone to Auchinleck. I intend to pass

a little while with him there soon, and sound him; or there see just what attention can produce."

In allusion to the request that his letters might be preserved, Boswell was assured by Mr. Temple that he too contemplated a publication. Boswell pronounces it "a charming thought."[57] He refers exultingly to the attention he had lately received from Paoli. "For the last fortnight that I was in London," he writes, "I lay at his house, and had the command of his coach.... I felt more dignity when I had several servants at my devotion, a large apartment, and the convenience and state of a coach; I recollected that this dignity in London was honourably acquired by my travels abroad, and my pen after I came home, so I could enjoy it with my own approbation; and in the extent and multiplicity of the metropolis other people had not even the materials for finding fault, as my situation was not particularly known."

Referring to his resolution to read more constantly, Boswell informs Mr. Temple, on the 19th June, that he has not yet "begun to read," but that "his resolution is lively." Lord Kames had asked him to become his biographer, a piece of intelligence which does not again crop up. In a conversation about Dr. Johnson he had disputed with Mr. Hume. The quarrel is thus described:—

> "Mr. Hume said he would give me half a crown for every page of his dictionary in which he would not find an absurdity, if I would give him half a crown for every page in which he did find one; he talked so insolently, really, that I calmly determined to be at him; so I repeated, by way of telling that Dr. Johnson could be touched, the admirable passage in your letter, how the Ministry had set him to write in a way that they 'could not ask even their infidel pensioner Hume to write.' Upon honour, I did not give the least hint from whom I had the letter. When Hume asked if it was from an American, I said 'No; it was from an English gentleman.' 'Would a gentleman write so?' said he. In short, Davy was finely punished for his treatment of my revered friend; and he deserved it richly, both for his petulance to so great a character, and for his talking so before me."

In a letter dated 12th August he informed his reverend correspondent that he had been suffering from his "atrabilious temperament." In his melancholy he had been strongly impressed by the phrase in Scripture, "Seek ye the Lord while He may be found." From sleep at night he had awakened "dreading annihilation or being thrown into some horrible state of being." He proceeds:—

"My promise under the solemn yew I have observed wonderfully, having never infringed it till the other day a very jovial company of us dined at a tavern, and I unwarily exceeded my bottle of old hock; and having once broke over the pale I run wild. But I did not get drunk; I was, however, intoxicated, and very ill next day. I ask your forgiveness, and I shall be more strictly cautious for the future. The drunken manners of this country are very bad."

The distinction between being *intoxicated* and *drunk* is not very obvious, and the allusion by way of defence to the intemperate habits of the country is *Boswellian*. Amidst his general gloom Boswell experienced comfort in the assurance by Mr. Temple that he was preparing for the press a portion of their correspondence. A specimen was transmitted, and Boswell tendered his advice. He insisted that anonymous authorship would not suit, and suggested that his own name as "James Boswell, Esq.," should be displayed upon the title-page. Mr. Temple subsequently published selections from his own letters under the title of "Selection of Historical and Political Memoirs."

About the middle of August Boswell begged Dr. Johnson for a prescription against melancholy. The moralist replied:—

"For the black fumes which rise in your mind I can prescribe nothing but that you disperse them by honest business or innocent pleasure, and by reading, sometimes easy and sometimes serious. Change of place is useful, and I hope your residence at Auchinleck will have many good effects.... Never, my dear sir," added Dr. Johnson, "do you take it in your head to think that I do not love you; you may settle yourself in full confidence both of my love and esteem. I love you as a kind man, I value you as a worthy man, and hope in time to reverence you as a man of exemplary piety. I hold you, as Hamlet has it, 'in my heart of hearts,' and therefore it is little to say that I am, sir, your affectionate, humble servant,

"SAM. JOHNSON."

To check his "atrabilious" complaint Boswell did not have recourse to reading. He informed Mr. Temple that since his return from England his reading had been confined to some small treatises on midwifery. On the 2nd September he communicated with Mr. Temple from Auchinleck. He had been there a week, and had experienced an unsupportable distress. Next day being Sunday, he proposed to worship in the parish church, and on Monday to join at Edinburgh his "valuable spouse and dear little children." To his dissension with his father he refers in characteristic fashion:—

"My father, whom I really both respect and affectionate (if that is a word, for it is a different feeling from that which is expressed by *love*, which I can say of you from my soul), is so different from me. We *divaricate* so much, as Dr. Johnson said, that I am often hurt when I dare say he means no harm; and he has a method of treating me which makes me feel myself like a *timid boy*, which to *Boswell* (comprehending all that my character does in my own imagination and in that of a wonderful number of mankind) is intolerable. His wife, too, whom in my conscience I cannot condemn for any capital bad quality, is so narrow-minded, and, I don't know how, so set upon keeping him under her own management, and so suspicious and so sourishly tempered that it requires the utmost exertion of practical philosophy to keep myself quiet. I, however, have done so all this week to admiration; nay, I have appeared good-humoured, but it has cost me drinking a considerable quantity of strong beer to dull my faculties....

"I have sauntered about with my father, and he has seen that I am pleased with his works. But what a discouraging reflection it is that he has in his possession a renunciation of my birthright which I madly granted him, and which he has not the generosity to restore now that I am doing beyond his utmost hopes, and that he may incommode and disgrace me by some strange settlement, while all this time not a shilling is secured to my wife and children in case of my death.... My father is visibly failing. Perhaps I may get him yet to do as I wish. In the meantime I have written plainly to my brother David, to see if he will settle on my wife and daughters, in case of his succeeding. I shall now know whether trade has destroyed his liberal spirit."

Amidst his many aberrations, and in spite of Dr. Johnson's discouragement, Boswell put into shape his travels in the Hebrides. He forwarded the MS. to Johnson, who remarked on it to Mrs. Thrale, "One would think the man had been hired to be a spy upon me." To Boswell he conveyed Mrs. Thrale's favourable judgment, but reserved his own. On this subject Boswell thus communicated with Mr. Temple:—

"Dr. Johnson has said nothing to me of my remarks during my journey with him which I wish to write. Shall I task myself to write so much of them a week, and send you for revisal? If I do not publish them now they will be good materials for my 'Life of Dr. Johnson.'"

On the 9th October Boswell was enabled to rejoice in an important event,—Mrs. Boswell presented him with a son. To Mr. Temple he wrote on the 6th November:—

> "My wife is recovered remarkably well. This son has been quite a cordial to her. He has been a little unlucky; the nurse had not milk enough, and as he is a big-boned fellow he cannot subsist without plentiful sustenance. We have got another nurse, a strong, healthy woman, with an abundant breast. His mother is quite unfit for nursing, she is of a temper so exceedingly anxious."

Boswell named his infant son Alexander, after his father. The compliment was well received, and in a few months afterwards Boswell was relieved of all apprehensions respecting his inheritance. By his father he was consulted as to the provisions of a deed of entail. He solicited counsel from Dr. Johnson[58] and Lord Hailes on a point respecting which he and his father disagreed. Lord Auchinleck proposed that in the series of heirs to be established under the entail, all males descending from his grandfather should be preferred to females, but he would not extend that privilege to males deriving their descent from a higher source. Boswell, on the other hand, desired that heirs male, however remote, should be preferred. As both Dr. Johnson and Lord Hailes supported the view of Lord Auchinleck, and Boswell at length acquiesced in his father's wishes, the entail, a document extending to thirty-seven folio pages, was executed at Edinburgh on the 7th August, 1776. The instrument proceeds thus:—[59]

> "I ALEXANDER BOSWEL of Auchinleck Esquire one of the Senators of the College of Justice considering that having long intended to make a full settlement of my estate, but which I have put off a long time, not having fallen upon a plan which gave me satisfaction, notwithstanding I have seen a multiplicity of settlements, I am now come to the resolution to execute what follows, which though it appears to me better calculated to answer the ends of a family settlement, and to be more free from objections than others I have seen, I am conscious is not exempt from faults, for I see them. But when one is providing for futurity it is impossible to obviate all inconveniences. I have, however, chose this form as appearing to me subject to the fewest. The Settlement I am to make is a Taillie or Deed of Entail intended to be perpetual, which notwithstanding the prejudices of the ignorant and dissipated part of mankind to the contrary I have always approved of, if

properly devised. My motive to it is not the preservation of my name and memory, for I know that after death our places here know us no more. But my motives are that the strength of the happy constitution with which this kingdom is blest, depends in a great measure upon there being kept up a proper number of Gentlemen's families of independent fortunes. It was this which at first introduced the right of primogeniture amongst us, a right well adapted to the good of the younger, as well as the eldest, as it prevents estates crumbling down by division into morsels. It enables the several successive heirs to educate their whole children properly, and thereby fit them for different employments, so that these families are useful nurseries. On the other hand a danger arises from an accumulation of different estates into the hands of overgrown rich men. Again the estate which I have, though not great, is sufficient for answering all the reasonable expenses of a gentleman's family and is situate in an agreeable country with the people of which I and my worthy predecessors have had the happiness to live in great friendship, which I hope shall always be the case with those that succeed me; and the place of residence has many uncommon beauties and conveniences, which several considerations would make any wise man careful to preserve such an estate. But as an heir may happen to get it who by weakness or extravagance would soon put an end to it, I cannot think any wise man will condemn me if while I allow the heirs of Taillie every power which a man of judgment would wish to exercise, I restrain them only from acting foolishly. If a person saw his next heir a weak foolish and extravagant person he would justly be censured if in place of giving his estate to his other children, or bestowing it upon some worthy friend who would make a proper use of it, he let it drop into the hands of a person who had nothing to recommend him but the legal character of an heir who directly on his succession would let it fly. I say he would justly be censured for this unless he laid that unhappy heir under proper restraints. And if this would be an advisable precaution to follow where the person is seen, it must be equally so whenever an heir happens to exist of that unhappy disposition at any period however remote, for no time can come when any reasonable man can think it would be beneficial to allow a person to act foolishly, do therefore hereby,—with the special advice and consent of James Boswell, Esquire, Advocate, younger of Auchinleck my eldest son, and under these

> impressions and in the hope and belief that I have fallen on a method of preventing children from being independent of their parents and of securing a proper provision for younger children, not only at first, which is all that is commonly done, but in all future times, the want of which appeared to me the most solid objection to Taillies—give, grant, and dispose heretably and Irredeemably to myself and the heirs male procreated and to be procreated of my body whom failing the lands of Auchinleck to Dr. John Boswell physician in Edinburgh my brother german and the heirs male lawfully procreated or to be procreated of his body, whom failing to Claude Boswell of Balmuto Esquire advocate, only son of the deceast John Boswell of Balmuto who was the only brother of the deceast Mr. James Boswell of Auchinleck advocate my father and the heirs male lawfully procreated or to be procreated of the body of the said Claude Boswell, whom failing to the heirs whatsoever lawfully procreated or to be procreated of my body, whom failing, to my own nearest heirs whatsoever descended of the body of Thomas Boswell of Auchinleck my predecessor, whom all failing to my own nearest heirs and assignes whatsoever—the eldest heir female and the descendants of her body always excluding heirs portioners and succeeding still without division, throughout the whole course of succession of heirs whatsoever as well as heirs of provision."

After excluding from the succession all fatuous persons, and regulating annuities for females and younger children, Lord Auchinleck proceeds to guard against the extinction of the family name.

> "It is hereby," he adds, "specially provided and declared That in case any of the heirs male of my body who shall succeed to my said lands and estate shall also succeed to a peerage or to any other estate entailed under such conditions as may restrain the heir from carrying my name and arms then and in every such case the person so succeeding to the said peerage or other such entailed estate when he is possessed of my said estate or succeeding to my estate when having right to such peerage or possessed of such other entailed estate shall forfeit all right and title to my said lands and estate and that not only for himself but also for his apparent heir and for all the apparent heirs of such an apparent heir in a direct line downwards whether in a nearer or remoter degree and my said estate shall devolve and belong to the next heir of Taillie

though descending of the body of the person excluded or of his apparent heir in the same manner as if the person excluded and all the apparent heirs in the said peerage were naturally dead."

On Friday, the 15th March, 1776, Boswell arrived in London. Four days thereafter he accompanied Dr. Johnson, first to Oxford and afterwards to Lichfield. At Oxford they had agreeable intercourse with Dr. Wetherell, Master of University College; Dr. Adams, Master of Pembroke College; Dr. Bentham, Professor of Divinity; Mr. Thomas Warton, and Dr. Horne, Bishop of Norwich. *En route* for Lichfield they paused at Birmingham, to visit Dr. Johnson's schoolfellow, Mr. Hector. Boswell improved the occasion by visiting, at Soho, Mr. Matthew Boulton, the celebrated mechanician, and partner of James Watt. Finding Mr. Boulton at the head of seven hundred mechanics, he describes him as "an iron chief," and a "father to his tribe." At Lichfield he was introduced to Mrs. Lucy Porter, Dr. Johnson's stepdaughter, "an old maid, of simple manners," living on a fortune of £10,000 bequeathed to her by her brother, a captain in the navy. On Friday, the 29th March, the travellers returned to London.

Good Friday, which fell on the 5th of April, Boswell spent with Dr. Johnson. They worshiped together morning and evening in St. Clement's Church. On Easter Sunday Boswell attended morning service in St. Paul's Cathedral, and in the evening accompanied Dr. Johnson to his pew in St. Clement's.

In the preceding January the brothers Daniel and Robert Perreau were hanged for forgery. They were convicted on the evidence of Margaret Caroline Rudd, who cohabited with one of them, and who, to save her own life, proved informer. This woman possessed uncommon powers of fascination, and it was believed that she had duped the brothers into the crime for which they suffered. Like other great criminals, Mrs. Rudd had acquired a temporary celebrity, and on this account Boswell determined to visit her. He carried out his intention, and confessed himself charmed by Mrs. Rudd's conversation and manners. Under the plea that he would interest Mrs. Boswell, he made a full record of Mrs. Rudd's conversation, transmitting the MS. to Mr. Temple, that he and his patron, Lord Lisburne, might "enjoy" its perusal. To his many whims and vagaries in the past Mr. Temple had submitted with more than befitting good nature, but the celebration of Mrs. Rudd was beyond his endurance. He denounced the interview, and the record of it; and Boswell, satisfied that he had been imprudent for once, took back his MS.

Writing to Mr. Temple on the 28th April he remarks that he "must eat commons in the Inner Temple this week and next, to make out another term, that he may still be approximating to the English Bar." He then proceeds:—

> "I don't know but you have spoken too highly of Gibbon's book; the Dean of Derry,[60] who is of our club, as well as Gibbon, talks of answering it. I think it is right that as fast as infidel wasps or venomous insects, whether creeping or flying, are hatched, they should be crushed. Murphy says he has read thirty pages of Smith's 'Wealth,' but says he shall read no more. Smith too is now of our club. *It has lost its select merit.* He has gone to Scotland at the request of David Hume, who is said to be dying. General Paoli had a pretty remark when I told him of this: "Ah! je suis fâché qu'il soit détrompé si tôt."

In a subsequent letter Boswell describes Gibbon as "an ugly, affected, disgusting fellow," adding, "he poisons our Literary Club to me." Gibbon was elected a member of the club in March, 1774. With an agreeable presence and elegant manners his conversational powers were of a high order. His religious sentiments being obnoxious to Dr. Johnson led to Boswell's personal dislike. Dr. Adam Smith was admitted to the club on the 24th December, 1775. He and Dr. Johnson had been at variance, but the quarrel was made up. Doubtless in connection with this controversy Boswell thought meet to censure the philosopher and his work. That a literary club which had added to its membership Edward Gibbon and Adam Smith should thereby have lost "its select merit," reads strangely, even as a *dictum* of James Boswell.

Boswell's personal habits remained much the same. He informed Mr. Temple that his "promise under the solemn yew" had not been "religiously kept." He had lately given "his word of honour" to General Paoli that "he would not taste fermented liquor for a year." He adds, "I have kept the promise now about three weeks; I was really growing a drunkard."

At the end of April Boswell proceeded to Bath, and there joined Dr. Johnson at the residence of the Thrales. He accompanied Dr. Johnson to Bristol, where they inspected the church of St. Mary, Redcliff, and discoursed on the genius and errors of Chatterton. Returning to London, Boswell realized a project on which he had set his heart—that of bringing together Dr. Johnson and Mr. Wilkes. On this subject he writes:—

> "My desire of being acquainted with celebrated men of every description had made me much about the same time obtain an introduction to Dr. Samuel Johnson and to John Wilkes, Esq. Two men more different could perhaps not be selected out of all mankind. They had even attacked one

another with some asperity in their writings; yet I lived in habits of friendship with both. I could fully relish the excellence of each, for I have ever delighted in that intellectual chemistry which can separate good qualities from evil in the same person."

Boswell contrived a meeting between Dr. Johnson and Mr. Wilkes by the exercise of considerable craft. Having been invited to meet Mr. Wilkes at the table of Mr. Edward Dilly, he bore a message from that gentleman to Dr. Johnson, requesting him to join the party. In conveying it he played on the Doctor's "spirit of contradiction." Having repeated Mr. Dilly's message without reference to the other guests, the following conversation ensued:—

Johnson: "Sir, I am obliged to Mr. Dilly; I will wait upon him."

Boswell: "Provided, sir, I suppose, that the company which he is to have is agreeable to you?"

Johnson: "What do you mean, sir? What do you take me for? Do you think I am so ignorant of the world as to imagine that I am to prescribe to a gentleman what company he is to have at his table?"

Boswell: "I beg your pardon, sir, for wishing to prevent you from meeting people whom you might not like. Perhaps he may have some of what he calls his patriotic friends with him."

Johnson: "Well, sir, and what then? What care I for his patriotic friends? Poh!"

Boswell: "I should not be surprised to find Jack Wilkes there."

Johnson: "And if Jack Wilkes should be there, what is that to me, sir? My dear friend, let us have no more of this. I am sorry to be angry with you, but it is treating me strangely to talk to me as if I could not meet any company whatever occasionally."[61]

Johnson and Wilkes met not unpleasantly, and Boswell had his triumph. In May he returned to Edinburgh. Before leaving London he repeated to Dr. Johnson his former promise that he would devote a portion of his time to reading. Johnson despatched to him at Edinburgh several boxes of books, thereby relieving his collection of supernumerary volumes, and by placing on the books a marketable value discharging a debt which he owed on the Hebridean journey. After an interval Boswell reported that owing to a renewed attack of melancholy the boxes remained unopened. Johnson in these words administered reproof:

> "To hear that you have not opened your boxes of books is very offensive. The examination and arrangement of so many

volumes might have afforded you an amusement very seasonable at present, and useful for the whole of life. I am, I confess, very angry that you manage yourself so ill."

Boswell opened the boxes, and found what he describes as "truly a numerous and miscellaneous stall library thrown together at random." It was not further disturbed.

Boswell's melancholy did not proceed from any constitutional disorder. He was involved in debt, and his creditors were importunate. His father was again appealed to, and the liabilities were discharged. Rejoicing in his deliverance he communicated the good news to Dr. Johnson. On the 16th November the Doctor thus conveyed his congratulations:—

> "I had great pleasure in hearing that you are at last on good terms with your father. Cultivate his kindness by all honest and manly means. Life is but short: no time can be afforded but for the indulgence of real sorrow, or contest upon questions seriously momentous. Let us not throw away any of our days upon useless resentment, or contend who shall hold out longest in stubborn malignity. It is best not to be angry, and best, in the next place, to be quickly reconciled. May you and your father pass the remainder of your time in reciprocal benevolence!"

In December Mrs. Boswell presented her husband with a second son, who was christened David. A delicate child, he survived only a few months.

Writing to Dr. Johnson on the 8th July, 1777, Boswell claims merit in having refrained from visiting London since the spring of 1776, and proposes that the Doctor should meet him at Carlisle, and from thence complete his tour of the English cathedrals. To this proposal Johnson did not accede, but the friends agreed to meet in September at Ashbourne, in the hospitable residence of Dr. Taylor. At this meeting Boswell intimated his desire to obtain a permanent residence in London as an English barrister. This scheme Dr. Johnson warmly disapproved, and entreated his companion to be satisfied with his prospective advantages as a Scottish landowner.

In his more important legal causes Boswell had recourse to Dr. Johnson's assistance. At Ashbourne he asked help in a case of importance. Joseph Knight, a negro, having been brought to Jamaica in the usual course of the slave trade, was purchased by a Scottish gentleman in the island, who afterwards returned to Scotland. Soon after his arrival Knight claimed his freedom, and brought an action to enforce it.[62] The case was now pending, and Boswell induced Dr. Johnson to dictate an argument on the negro's behalf. In recording it he is careful to add that he was personally an upholder of the slave trade. He writes:—

"I record Dr. Johnson's argument fairly upon this particular case; where, perhaps, he was in the right. But I beg leave to enter my most solemn protest against his general doctrine with respect to the slave trade. For I will resolutely say that his unfavourable notion of it was owing to prejudice and imperfect or false information. The wild and dangerous attempt which has for some time been persisted in to obtain an Act of our Legislature to abolish so very important and necessary a branch of commercial interest must have been crushed at once, had not the insignificance of the zealots, who vainly took the lead in it, made the vast body of planters, merchants, and others, whose immense properties are involved in that trade, reasonably enough suppose that there could be no danger. The encouragement which the attempt has received excites my wonder and indignation; and though some men of superior abilities have supported it, whether from a love of temporary popularity when prosperous, or a love of general mischief when desperate, my opinion is unshaken. To abolish a *status* which in all ages God has sanctioned and man has continued, would not only be robbery to an innumerable class of our fellow-subjects, but it would be extreme cruelty to the African savages, a portion of whom it saves from massacre, or intolerable bondage in their own country, and introduces into a much happier state of life, especially now when their passage to the West Indies, and their treatment there, is humanely regulated. To abolish that trade would be to—

"———Shut the gates of mercy on mankind."

The political success of Edmund Burke induced Boswell to indicate his readiness to co-operate with him in regard to the American colonies. To Mr. Burke he wrote as follows:—

"Edinburgh, March 3, 1778.

"DEAR SIR,—Upon my honour I began a letter to you some time ago, and did not finish it because I imagined you were then near your *apotheosis*, as poor Goldsmith said upon a former occasion, when he thought your party was coming into administration; and being one of your old Barons of Scotland, my pride could not brook the appearance of paying my court to a minister amongst the crowd of interested expectants on his accession. At present I take it for granted that I need be under no such apprehension, and therefore I resume the indulgence of my inclination. This may be perhaps a singular method of beginning a correspondence; and in one sense may not be very complimentative. But I can sincerely assure you, dear sir, that I feel and mean a genuine compliment to Mr. Burke himself. It is generally thought no meanness to solicit the notice and favour of a man in power; and surely it is much less a meanness to endeavour by honest means to have the honour and pleasure of being on an agreeable footing with a man of superior knowledge, abilities, and genius.

"I have to thank you for the obligations which you have already conferred upon me by the welcome which I have, upon repeated occasions, experienced under your roof. When I was last in London you gave me a general invitation, which I value more than a Treasury warrant:—an invitation to 'the feast of reason,' and, what I like still more, 'the flow of soul,' which you dispense with liberal and elegant abundance, is, in my estimation, a privilege of enjoying certain felicity; and we know that riches and honour are desirable only as means to felicity, and that they often fail of the end.

"Most heartily do I rejoice that our present ministers have at last yielded to conciliation. For amidst all the sanguinary zeal of my countrymen I have professed myself a friend to our fellow-subjects in America, so far as they claim an exemption from being taxed by the representatives of the King's British subjects. I do not perfectly agree with you; for I deny the Declaratory Act, and I am a warm Tory in its true constitutional sense. I wish I were a commissioner, or one of the secretaries of the commission for the grand treaty. I am to be in London this spring, and if his Majesty should ask me what I would choose, my answer will be, to assist in the compact between Britain and America. May I beg to hear from you, and in the meantime to have my compliments made acceptable to Mrs. Burke?—I am, dear sir, your most obedient, humble servant,

"JAMES BOSWELL."[63]

On the 18th March Boswell arrived in London, and at once renewed his intercourse with Dr. Johnson. They spent Good Friday together, Boswell accompanying the lexicographer to morning and evening service in St. Clement's Church. Next evening, while taking tea with him, Boswell severely experienced Dr. Johnson's resentment. The narrative we present in his own words:—

"We talked of a gentleman (Mr. Langton) who was running out his fortune in London, and I said, 'We must get him out of it. All his friends must quarrel with him, and that will soon drive him away.' *Johnson*: 'Nay, sir, we'll send you to him; if your company does not drive a man out of his house, nothing will.' This was a horrible shock, for which there was no visible cause. I afterwards asked him why he had said so harsh a thing. *Johnson*: 'Because, sir, you made me angry about the Americans.' *Boswell*: 'But why did you not take your revenge directly?' *Johnson* (*smiling*): 'Because, sir, I had nothing ready. A man cannot strike till he has his weapons.' This," adds Boswell, "was a candid and pleasant confession."[64]

Dr. Johnson made a second attack a fortnight afterwards, which Boswell endured with less patience. On the 2nd May they met at Sir Joshua Reynolds'. The wits of Queen Anne's reign were talked of, when Boswell exclaimed, "How delightful it must have been to have lived in the society of Pope, Swift, Arbuthnot, Gay, and Bolingbroke! We have no such society in our days." Sir Joshua answered, "I think, Mr. Boswell, you might be satisfied with your great friend's conversation." "Nay, sir, Mr. Boswell is right," said Johnson, "every man wishes for preferment, and if Boswell had lived in those days he would have obtained promotion." "How so, sir?" asked Sir Joshua. "Why, sir," said Johnson, "he would have had a high place in the Dunciad." Boswell felt so much hurt that, contrary to his custom, he omits the conversation.[65] He refers to the occurrence in these terms:—

"On Saturday, May 2, I dined with him at Sir Joshua Reynolds's, when there was a very large company, and a great deal of conversation; but owing to some circumstance, which I cannot now recollect, I have no record of any part of it, except that there were several people there by no means of the Johnsonian school, so that less attention was paid to him than usual, which put him out of humour, and upon some imaginary offence from me, he attacked me with such rudeness that I was vexed and angry, because it gave those persons an opportunity of enlarging upon his supposed ferocity, and ill-treatment of his best friends. I was so much hurt, and had my pride so much roused, that I kept away from him for a week, and perhaps might have kept away much longer, nay, gone to Scotland without seeing him again, had we not fortunately met and been reconciled."

The reconciliation is thus described:—

"On Friday, May 8, I dined with him at Mr. Langton's. I was reserved and silent, which I supposed he perceived, and might recollect the cause. After dinner, when Mr. Langton was called out of the room and we were by ourselves, he drew his chair near to mine and said, in a tone of conciliating courtesy, 'Well, how have you done?' *Boswell*: 'Sir, you have made me very uneasy by your behaviour to me at Sir Joshua Reynolds's. You know, my dear sir, no man has a greater respect and affection for you, or would sooner go to the end of the world to serve you. Now to treat me so——' He insisted that I had interrupted, which I assured him was not the case, and proceeded, 'But why treat me so before people who neither love you nor me?' 'Well, I'm sorry for it. I'll make it up to you twenty different ways, as you please.' *Boswell*: 'I said to-day to Sir Joshua, when he observed that you *tossed* me sometimes, I don't care how often or how high he tosses me when only friends are present, for then I fall upon soft ground; but I do not like falling on stones, which is the case when enemies are present. I think this is a pretty good image, sir.' *Johnson*: 'Sir, it is one of the happiest I have ever heard.'"

Boswell left London on the 19th of May. On his return to Edinburgh he was seized with an irrepressible longing for an early settlement in London, and forthwith communicated his sentiments to Dr. Johnson. He had the following answer:—

> "I wish you would a little correct or restrain your imagination, and imagine that happiness such as life admits may be had at other places as well as London. Without affecting stoicism, it may be said that it is our business to exempt ourselves as much as we can from the power of external things. There is but one solid basis of happiness, and that is, the reasonable hope of a happy futurity. This may be had everywhere. I do not blame your preference of London to other places, for it is really to be preferred if the choice is free; but few have the choice of their place or their manner of life, and mere pleasure ought not to be the prime motive of action."

In August Mrs. Boswell gave birth to her third son, who was christened James. Dr. Johnson sent suitable congratulations.

In March, 1779, Boswell again repaired to the metropolis. He spent Good Friday with Dr. Johnson, attending him at both diets of worship in St. Clement's Church. Johnson, he relates, preferred silent meditation during the interval of worship, and for his improvement handed him "Les Pensées de Paschal," a book which he perused with reverence. On Easter Sunday he worshipped in St. Paul's, and afterwards dined with Dr. Johnson.

A letter to Mr. Temple, which Boswell commenced at London on the 31st May, and finished at Newcastle on the 8th June, contains the following passages:—

> "Had you been in London last week, you would have seen your friend sadly changed for a little. So trifling a matter as letting the nails of my great toes grow into the flesh, particularly in one foot, produced so much pain and inflammation and lameness and apprehension, that I was

confined to bed, and my spirits sank to dreary dejection.... I am now much better, but still unable to walk; and having received a very wise letter from my dear, sensible, valuable wife, that although my father is in no immediate danger, his indisposition is such that I ought to be with him, I have resolved to set out to-morrow, being the very first day after completing another term at the Temple.... Is it not curious that at times we are in so happy a frame that not the least trace of former misery or vexation is left upon the mind? But is not the contrary, too, experienced?—Gracious Author of our being, do Thou bring us at length to steady felicity.—What a strange, complicated scene is this life! It always strikes me that we cannot seriously, closely, and clearly examine almost any part of it. We are at pains to bring up children, just to give them an opportunity of struggling through cares and fatigues; but let us hope for gleams of joy here, and a blaze hereafter.... I got into the fly at Buckden, and had a very good journey. An agreeable young widow nursed me, and supported my lame foot on her knee. Am I not fortunate in having something about me that interests most people at first sight in my favour?... You ask me about Lowth's 'Isaiah.' I never once heard it mentioned till I asked Dr. Johnson about it.... I do not think Lowth an engaging man; I sat a good while with him this last spring. He said Dr. Johnson had *great genius*. I give you this as a specimen of his talk, which seemed to me to be neither discriminating, pointed, nor animated; yet he certainly has much curious learning, and a good deal of critical sagacity.... I did not know Monboddo's new book, 'The Metaphysics of the Ancients,' had been advertised. I expect it will be found to be a very wonderful performance. I think I gathered from a conversation with him that he believes the 'metempsychosis.'"

On his arrival in Edinburgh, learning that the celebrated Mr. John Wesley was on a visit to the city, Boswell waited on him with a letter from Dr. Johnson. The writer expressed a wish that "worthy and religious men should be acquainted with each other." Mr. Wesley received Boswell with politeness, but did not encourage any closer intimacy.

For two months after his return to Scotland Boswell despatched no letters to Dr. Johnson. He in this fashion made trial of his friend's fidelity. At length receiving a letter from the Doctor inquiring for his welfare, he resolved "never again to put him to the test."[66]

The friendship which subsisted between Mrs. Boswell and Mrs. Stuart, wife of the second son of John, third Earl of Bute, has been referred to. Boswell was, we have seen, also a favourite with Mrs. Stuart. To her regard for him Boswell delighted to refer, however, inopportunely. In his *Boswelliana* he relates that Lord Mountstuart having remarked that he resembled Charles Fox, Colonel Stuart (Mrs. Stuart's husband) ejaculated, "You are much uglier." Boswell replied, looking his tormentor in the face, "Does your wife think so, Colonel James?" Colonel Stuart knew Boswell intimately, and, in common with his wife, enjoyed his humour and excused his egotism. Being in command of the Bedfordshire Militia, he invited Boswell to accompany him and the regiment to London and some other stations. Boswell readily complied. He delighted "to accompany a man of sterling good sense, information, discernment, and conviviality," and he hoped in his society "to have a second crop, in one year, of London and Johnson."

On Monday, 4th October, Boswell waited on Dr. Johnson, thereafter attending him daily during a fortnight's residence in London. On the 18th October he departed for Chester, in company with Colonel Stuart. He tarried a few hours at Lichfield, where he visited some of Dr. Johnson's relatives. His proceedings at Chester are related in the following letter to Mr. Temple, dated Edinburgh, 4th January, 1780:—

> "From London, after an excellent fortnight there, I accompanied Colonel Stuart to Chester, to which town his regiment was ordered from Leeds, and there I passed another fortnight in mortal felicity. I had from my earliest years a love for the military life, and there is in it an animation and relish of existence which I have never found amongst any other set of men, except players, with whom you know I once lived a great deal. At the mess of Colonel Stuart's regiment I was quite the great man, as we used to say; and I was at the same time all joyous and gay. Such was my home at Chester. But I had the good fortune to be known to the bishop, who is one of the most distinguished prelates for piety and eloquence, and one of the most pleasing men in social life that you can imagine. His palace was open to me, morning, noon, and night; and I was liberally entertained at his hospitable board. At Chester, too, I found Dean Smith, the translator of 'Longinus,' with whom you and I were so well acquainted when we were studying under Mr. John Stevenson. I was surprised to find him, for I somehow had imagined that he was an ancient English author, comparatively speaking. He is very old, but is quite cheerful and full of anecdotes. He lives very retired, with

a disagreeable wife, and they told me I was the only man who had been in the deanery for a long time. I found too at Chester Mr. Falconer, a gentleman of fortune and extraordinary learning and knowledge, who is preparing a new edition of Strabo, at the desire of the University of Oxford; he was exceedingly obliging to me."

At Chester Boswell found the young ladies to be especially charming. Forgetting that he and his correspondent were both married, he informed Mr. Temple that several of the ladies had "capital fortunes." He wrote to Dr. Johnson that he had complimented Miss Letitia Bainston, niece of one of the prebendaries, in these words:—"I have come to Chester, madam, I cannot tell how; and far less can I tell how I am able to get away from it." In his journey from Chester to Scotland Boswell lingered at Carlisle. He wrote to Dr. Johnson that he had received the sacrament in the cathedral, and that it was "divinely cheering to him that there was a cathedral so near Auchinleck." Dr. Johnson reminded his correspondent that Carlisle cathedral was at least one hundred and fifty miles from Auchinleck, adding, "If you are pleased, it is so far well."

In the spring of 1777 Boswell obtained a connection with the *London Magazine*. He then commenced in its pages a series of papers, which he styled "The Hypochondriack." These papers are generally short, and often disconnected; they abound in allusions to the writer's personal tastes and peculiar opinions, while classical quotations are interspersed without point and without purpose. But Boswell was pleased to see himself in print, and so he complacently reports to Mr. Temple, in January, 1780, that his "Hypochondriack gets on wonderfully well." In his paper for March, 1780, he thus alludes to his love of dissipation:—

> "I do fairly acknowledge," he writes, "that I love drinking; that I have a constitutional inclination to indulge in fermented liquors, and that were it not for the restraints of reason and religion, I am afraid I should be as constant a votary of Bacchus as any man."[67]

At the close of his letter of January he informs Mr. Temple that his father had been ill of fever, with his pulse at ninety-five; he then begs a loan of £200, to satisfy a demand which his father could not be informed of. The loan was not granted, and Boswell afterwards sought repayment of an advance made to his friend at a former period, and which remained undischarged.

In September Boswell experienced a family loss in the death of Dr. John Boswell, his father's brother. Of his deceased relative he writes to Mr. Temple that he was "a good scholar and affectionate relative," but "had no conduct." He adds, "He had a strange kind of religion, but I flatter myself he will be ere long, if he is not already in heaven." This passage might imply that in abandoning the Romish faith he had not abjured the doctrine of purgatory; yet that doctrine is inconsistent with the following aspiration contained in the same letter:—

> "I comfort myself with the Christian revelation of our being in a state of purification, and that we shall, in course of time, attain to felicity. It is delightful, Temple, to look forward to the period when you and I shall enjoy what we now imagine. In the meantime let us be patient, and do what we can."

Writing to Mr. Temple in November, Boswell thus refers to an unpleasantness which had for some months subsisted between him and his father:—

> "I could not help smiling at the expostulation which you suggest to me to try with my father. It would do admirably with some fathers, but it would make mine much worse, for he cannot bear that his son should talk with him as a man. I can only lament his unmelting coldness to my wife and children, for I fear it is hopeless to think of his ever being more affectionate towards them. Yet it must be acknowledged that his paying £1,000 of my debt some years ago was a large bounty. He allows me £300 a year; but I find that what I gain by my practice and that sum together will not support my family. I have now two sons and three daughters. I am in hopes that my father will augment my allowance to £400 a year. I was indeed very imprudent in expressing my extreme aversion to his second marriage; but since it took place I am conscious of having behaved to himself and his lady with such respectful attention, and imposed such restraint upon myself as is truly meritorious. The woman is very implacable, and I imagine it is hardly possible that she can ever be my friend. She, however, behaves much better to the children than their grandfather does. We are all to dine at my father's to-day; he is better now than he has been for several years."

In thus writing Boswell lacked candour. Had he chosen to observe his usual frankness he would not have heaped censure on his father's wife, but attributed the paternal resentment to its true cause—the payment of that sum of £200 which Mr. Temple had declined to lend. His correspondent's advice respecting the plan for a London settlement was, for the time not unacceptable. On this subject he writes:—

"Your counsel to me to set my mind at rest, and be content with promotion in Scotland, is, I believe, very wise. My brother David enforced it earnestly. If my father lives a few years longer, age will, I suppose, fix me here without any question; for to embark in a new sphere when one is much after forty is not advisable. Yet, my dear Temple, ambition to be in Parliament or in the metropolis is very allowable. Perhaps my exalted notions of public situation are fallacious, for I begin to think that true elevation is to be acquired from study and thinking, and that when one is used to the most eminent situations they become familiar and insipid, and perhaps vexatious."

The embarrassed condition of his affairs kept Boswell in Scotland during the whole of 1780. In March, 1781, he again presented himself in London. Good Friday was, as usual, spent with Dr. Johnson, the friends worshipping together in St. Clement's church. On Easter Sunday he performed his wonted devotions in St. Paul's Cathedral. Not long afterwards he afforded sad evidence of persistent recklessness. Dining with the Duke of Montrose, he became inebriated, and in this condition joined an evening party at the Honourable Miss Monckton's. He talked incoherently, and Dr. Johnson, who was present, endeavoured to shield him from observation.[68] Next, day being made conscious of his lamentable aberration, he despatched to his hostess the following verses as an apology for violating good manners:—

"Not that with th' excellent Montrose

I had the happiness to dine;

Not that I late from table rose,

From Graham's wit, from generous wine;

"It was not these alone which led

On sacred manners to encroach,

And made me feel what most I dread,

Johnson's just frown and self-reproach:

"But when I entered, not abashed,

From your bright eyes were shot such rays,

At once intoxication flashed,

And all my frame was in a blaze.

"But not a brilliant blaze, I own;

Of the dull smoke I'm yet ashamed,

I was a dreary ruin grown,

And not enlightened, though enflamed.

"Victim at once to wine and love,

I hope, Maria, you'll forgive;

While I invoke the powers above,

That henceforth I may wiser live."

Boswell remained in London till the beginning of June. *En route* for Scotland, he accompanied Dr. Johnson to Southill, Bedfordshire, on a visit to Mr. Charles Dilly, publisher, who had there established his country seat. The friends reached Southill on Saturday, the 2nd June. Next day they accompanied Mr. Dilly's family to the parish church. Boswell remained behind to receive the sacrament. During the evening he sought religious conversation with Dr. Johnson, commencing thus:—"My dear sir, I would fain be a good man; and I am very good now. I fear God and honour the king; I wish to do no ill, and to be benevolent to all mankind." Dr. Johnson said impressions were deceitful and dangerous, and explained the nature of the Christian atonement. Boswell requested him to repeat his remarks, and proceeded to record them.[69]

Neglecting the practice of his profession, Boswell became wholly dependent on his allowance from Lord Auchinleck, and again ran himself aground. He explained his condition to Dr. Johnson as a reason why he could not visit London in the spring of 1782, adding that could he possibly reach the metropolis, he might obtain a post which would restore his fortunes. Dr. Johnson replied as follows:—

> "To come hither with such expectations at the expense of borrowed money, which I find you know not where to borrow, can hardly be considered prudent. I am sorry to find, what your solicitations seem to imply, that you have already gone the length of your credit. This is to set the quiet of your whole life at hazard. If you anticipate your inheritance, you can at last inherit nothing; all that you receive must pay for the past. You must get a place, or pine in penury, with the empty name of a great estate. Poverty, my dear friend, is so great an evil, and pregnant with so much temptation, and so much misery, that I cannot but earnestly enjoin you to avoid it. Live on what you have; live if you can on less; do not borrow either for vanity or pleasure; the vanity will end in shame, and the pleasure in

regret; stay therefore at home till you have saved money for your journey hither."

In a letter written some months subsequently, Johnson resumed his discourse on the miseries of improvidence:—

> "Whatever might have been your pleasure or mine, I know not how I could have honestly advised you to come hither with borrowed money. Do not accustom yourself to consider debt only as an inconvenience; you will find it a calamity. Poverty takes away so many means of doing good, and produces so much inability to resist evil, both natural and moral, that it is by all virtuous means to be avoided. Consider a man whose fortune is very narrow; whatever be his rank by birth, or whatever his reputation by intellectual excellence, what can he do, or what evil can he prevent? That he cannot help the needy is evident; he has nothing to spare. But perhaps his advice or admonition may be useful. His poverty will destroy his influence; many more can find that he is poor than that he is wise; and few will reverence the understanding that is of so little advantage to its owner. I say nothing of the personal wretchedness of a debtor, which, however, has passed into a proverb."

After a long illness, patiently borne, Lord Auchinleck died at Edinburgh on the 31st August. He had settled on his eldest son the ancestral estate, with an unencumbered rental of £1,600 a year. On receipt of the tidings, Dr. Johnson wrote to Boswell as follows:—

> "Your father's death had every circumstance that could enable you to bear it; it was at a mature age, and it was expected; and as his general life had been pious, his thoughts had doubtless for many years past been turned upon eternity. That you did not find him sensible must doubtless grieve you; his disposition towards you was undoubtedly that of a kind, though not of a fond father. Kindness, at least actual, is in our power, but fondness is not; and if by negligence or imprudence you had extinguished his fondness, he could not at will rekindle it. Nothing then remained for you but mutual forgiveness of each other's faults, and mutual desire of each other's happiness. I shall long to know his final disposition of his fortune."

At Auchinleck the deceased judge was deeply revered. In the Kirk-Session Records of that parish, Mr. David Murdoch,[70] schoolmaster and session clerk, has accompanied the entry of his death with the following lines, entitled "Essay towards a character of Lord Auchinleck:"—

"For every sovereign virtue much renowned,
 Of judgment steady, and in wisdom sound,
 Through a long life in active bus'ness spent,
 For justice and for prudence eminent;
 Well qualified to occupy the line
 Allotted him by Providence divine;
 Employed with indefatigable pains
 In very num'rous and important scenes;
 And as his fame for justice was well known,
 His clemency no less conspicuous shone;
 Reliever of the needful and opprest,
 The gen'rous benefactor of distrest,
 Ready to hear and rectify a wrong,
 To re-establish harmony among
 Contending friends, or such as disagreed,
 And of his interposing aid had need;
 Successfully he laboured much and long
 As healer of the breaches us among;
 And still from jarring order brought about,
 Carefully searching unknown causes out.

A foe to vice, detesting liars much,

Of shrewd acuteness in discerning such;
Averse to flattery, hating all deceit,
Though in resentment mod'rate and discreet;
And ready still, with sympathizing grace,
To wipe the tear from every mourning face.

Whether we see him talking at the Bar,

Or on the Bench, a step exalted far,
Display the spirit of his country's laws,
Or ruminate the merits of a cause;
Or in retirement from such legal strife
View him a gentleman in private life,—
In all connections, and in him we find
The husband loving and the parent kind,
The easy master and the faithful friend,
The honest counsellor, as all will own,
And most indulgent landlord ever known.

In all departments on the earthly stage,
In every scene in which he did engage,
Such steadiness, such truth and candour shone,
As equalled is by few, surpassed by none;
In everything important less or more,
Supporting well the character he bore.
A person thus disposed and thus endowed
Must have been universally allowed
The tribute of our praises heretofore,
And claims our tears when now he is no more.
All ranks in him a mighty loss sustain,
Both rich and poor, the noble and the mean;
For why? his services did far extend
Through town and country to the kingdom's end;
The whole to him in obligations bound,
As to his honour ever will redound.

Revere his memory, and his death lament,

As well becomes, with uniform assent;
Your high concern by loud encomiums show,
Unite the shout of praise and tear of woe;
Your warm effusions only can reveal
(And faintly too) what every heart must feel.

This benefactor lost, the meaner man

May quiver, and so he will, that's all he can;
Let those descended of a station higher,
To imitate his virtuous life aspire;
Transcribe the bright example set by him,
Best way to evidence their true esteem.
May after generations who succeed,
From Register, his famed remembrance read.
Alive his character afar was known,
So may it long continue when he's gone;
And let the undissembled voice of fame
To distant ages celebrate his name—
A name of veneration and respect,
Of honour and esteem, Lord Auchinleck."

    On Friday, the 21st March, 1783, Boswell arrived in London. He found Dr. Johnson at Mrs. Thrale's in feeble health. As on former occasions, the friends worshipped together in St. Clement's Church on Good Friday, while Boswell again kept Easter in St. Paul's. When congratulating his friend on his position as a landowner, Dr. Johnson unsparingly exposed his egotism.

"Boswell," said he, "you often vaunt so much, as to provoke ridicule. You put me in mind of a man who was standing in the kitchen of an inn with his back to the fire, and thus accosted the person next him:—'Do you know, sir, who I am?' 'No, sir,' said the other, 'I have not that advantage.' 'Sir,' said he, 'I am the great Twamley, who invented the new floodgate iron.'"[71]

Boswell left London for Scotland on the 29th of May. From Dr. Johnson he received these parting counsels:—"Get as much force of mind as you can. Live within your income. Always have something saved at the end of the year. Let your imports be more than your exports, and you'll never go far wrong."

On the opening of Parliament in November, 1783, Mr. Fox introduced in the House of Commons his celebrated East India Bill. By this measure he proposed to vest the Government of India for five years, in a commission of seven, who were to be appointed by Parliament, and to be irremovable by the Crown. The Bill was accepted by the Commons, but was, on the 17th December, rejected in the Upper House, through the influence of the King. The rejection of this measure compelled the coalition ministry to resign, and Mr. Pitt became Prime Minister on the understanding that he would appeal to the country without loss of time. Having become a landowner, Boswell conceived himself a fit candidate for parliamentary honours, and in prospect of a dissolution resolved to offer his services to a constituency. He published a pamphlet entitled "A Letter to the People of Scotland on the Present State of the Nation" (43 pp. 12mo.). In this composition he denounces Mr. Fox's India Bill as "an attempt to deprive the sovereign of his lawful authority;" and urges "his fellow-countrymen in their several counties" to express their satisfaction that the Bill had been rejected by the Lords. He celebrates the memory of Sir John Lowther, ancestor of Lord Lowther,[72] who had lately promised him support. Then, passing to his favourite theme, he announces himself as "a firm loyalist, holding an estate transmitted to him by charters from a series of kings." He concludes by the offer of parliamentary service. His composition he transmitted to Dr. Johnson, begging his opinion. The lexicographer was in declining health, and was proportionally amiable. He complimented the writer on his knowledge of constitutional history, adding that his pamphlet would "raise his character, though it might not make him a Minister of State." Mr. Pitt sent a polite acknowledgment, commending "the author's zeal in the cause of the public."

His "Letter to the People of Scotland" Boswell followed up by the following address to the Ayrshire constituency:—

"To the Real Freeholders of the County of Ayr.

"GENTLEMEN,—If my friend Colonel Montgomerie shall not be a candidate at the next election, I intend to offer my services as your representative in Parliament. If Colonel Montgomerie stands, he shall have my warmest support; for I have never ceased to think that great injustice was done both to you and him when he was deprived of the seat given him by your voice; and I am very desirous to have ample reparation made for that injustice. Indeed, gentlemen, you have at the two last general elections been disappointed of your representation by the unconstitutional means of those votes, which, upon a notice that I glory in having made, were, at a meeting of this county, 29th October, 1782, declared to be *nominal* and *fictitious.*

"Colonel Montgomerie and I will probably at no time be on different sides. We are both connected with the respectable old interest of the county; and I trust we should both be exceedingly sorry to hurt it by a division, of which its enemies are eagerly watchful to take advantage.

"I pledge my word and honour that if there is not a greater number of the *real freeholders* for me than for any other candidate, I shall retire from the contest. I disdain to avail myself of what I condemn; and I am not callous enough to bear the indignant and reproachful looks of my worthy neighbours, who would consider that, by an artful use of the letter of that law which so loudly calls for reformation, I had triumphed over their wishes, and annihilated their most valuable privileges.

"My political principles I have avowed, in the most direct and public manner, to be those of a steady Royalist, who reveres monarchy, but is at the same time animated with genuine feelings of liberty; principles which, when well understood, are not in any degree inconsistent, but are happily united in the true British Constitution.

"The confidences with which I have been honoured by many of you in my profession as a lawyer, and other marks of attention which you have been pleased to show me, emboldens me to believe that you think well of my integrity and abilities. On the other hand, I declare that I should pay the utmost deference to your instructions as my constituents; and as I am now the representative of a family which has held an estate in the county, and maintained a respectable character for almost three centuries, I flatter myself that I shall not be reckoned too presumptuous when I aspire to the high distinction of being your representative in Parliament, and that you will not disapprove of my indulging an ambition that this family shall rather advance than fall off in my time.

"Though I should not be successful at the next, or at any future election, I am so fortunate as to have resources enough to prevent me from being discontented or fretful on that account; and I shall ever be, with cordial regard,

"Gentlemen,

"Your very faithful, and most obedient, humble servant,

"JAMES BOSWELL.

"*Auchinleck, March 17, 1784.*"

Boswell was at York on the 28th March, 1784, *en route* for London, when he was informed that Parliament was dissolved. Having in a brief note intimated to Dr. Johnson his political aspirations, he posted to Ayrshire, to contest the county. From Johnson he received a letter entreating him to be "scrupulous in the use of strong liquors," as "one night's drunkenness might defeat the labour of forty days well employed."

On reaching Auchinleck, Boswell learned what he might have ascertained sooner, that Colonel Montgomerie was re-soliciting the suffrages of the constituency. He was the successful candidate. Boswell again proceeded southward, and on the 5th May reached London. He dined out almost daily, frequently meeting Dr. Johnson, who though an invalid, rejoiced in the intercourse of his friends. By his physicians Johnson had been advised to proceed to Italy, and as the journey was delayed, Boswell apprehended that his friend was suffering from lack of funds. He applied to Lord Chancellor Thurlow, entreating an augmentation of Johnson's pension, or a special grant for the Italian journey. To the Treasury the Chancellor presented the application, but it was not entertained. Dr. Johnson expressed his grateful sense of Boswell's consideration and enterprise.

After a period of severe suffering, Dr. Johnson expired on the 13th December, 1784. He had prepared an autobiography, but destroyed it, with a portion of his correspondence, some weeks before his decease. He appointed no literary executor, nor left instructions respecting a memoir. Boswell contemplated a different result, but did not publicly complain. From respect to Johnson's wishes he had abstained from publishing his Hebridean tour. He now seriously employed himself in preparing it for the printer. As the first proof-sheet was being sent him from Mr. Baldwin's printing office, it happened to attract the attention of Mr. Edmund Malone, who proceeded to read the account of Dr. Johnson's character. He was struck with the fidelity of the representation, and begged Mr. Baldwin to introduce him to the writer.[73] Boswell rejoiced to cultivate the acquaintance of one who not only belonged to Dr. Johnson's circle, but was himself a celebrity, as editor of Goldsmith's works, and as a writer on Shakespeare's plays.[74] He visited Mr. Malone almost daily, submitting to his revision the MS. of his work. Accompanied by a flattering dedication to Mr. Malone, the work appeared in 1786 as a bulky octavo, bearing on the title-page the following copious inscription:—

"The Journal of a Tour to the Hebrides, with Samuel Johnson, LL.D., by James Boswell, Esq., containing some poetical pieces by Dr. Johnson, relative to the Tour, and never before published: a series of his conversation, Literary Anecdotes, and Opinions of Men and Books, with an authentick account of the Distresses and Escape of the Grandson of King James II. in the year 1746.

'O! while along the stream of time, thy name
Expanded flies, and gathers all its fame,
Say, shall my little book attendant sail,
Pursue the triumph, and partake the gale?'

"POPE."

Above the imprint was placed a small woodcut representing a falcon—the author's crest, with his family motto, *vraye foy*. The work was published by Mr. Charles Dilly, and the edition was rapidly distributed. The author was thus commended by Mr. Courtenay in his "Poetical Review:"[75]—

"With Reynolds' pencil, vivid, bold and true
So fervent Boswell gives him to our view:
In every trait we see his mind expand;
The master rises by the pupil's hand:
We love the writer, praise his happy vein,
Graced with the *naiveté* of the sage Montaigne;
Hence not alone are brighter parts display'd,
But e'en the specks of character portray'd:
We see the 'Rambler' with fastidious smile
Mark the lone tree, and note the heath-clad isle;
But when the heroic tale of 'Flora'[76] charms,
Deck'd in a kilt, he wields a chieftain's arms;
The tuneful piper sounds a martial strain,
And Samuel sings 'The King shall have his *ain*.'

****

"Can Boswell be forgot,

Scarce by North Britons now esteem'd a Scot?
Who to the sage devoted from his youth
Imbib'd from him the sacred love of truth;
The keen research, the exercise of mind,
And that best art, the art to know mankind."

Much as his performance was appreciated by friendly persons, it was impossible that Boswell's morbid egotism should escape ridicule. Thomas

Rowlandson, the noted caricaturist, issued twenty cartoons, presenting the unguarded tourist in absurd and grotesque scenes and attitudes, founded on descriptions in his book. They were placed in the shop windows and hawked about the streets, while the laughter-rousing Peter Pindar[77] addressed Boswell in a "Poetical and Congratulatory Epistle," mercilessly castigating him in sarcastic and crushing rhymes. Here is a specimen:—

"At length, ambitious Thane, thy rage

To give one spark to Fame's bespangled page
Is amply gratified. A thousand eyes
Survey thy book with rapture and surprize!
Loud of thy tour, a thousand tongues have spoken,
And wonder'd that thy bones were never broken.

*****

Nay, though thy Johnson ne'er had bless'd thine eyes,
Paoli's deeds had rais'd thee to the skies;
Yes! his broad wing had rais'd thee (no bad luck)
A tomtit twitt'ring on an eagle's back."

Equally pungent was the savage Pindar in a subsequent poem, entitled "Bozzy and Piozzi." He wrote:—

"For thee, James Boswell, may the hand of Fate
Arrest thy goose-quill and confine thy prate!
Thine egotism the world disgusted hears—
Then load with vanities no more our ears.
Like some lone puppy, yelping all night long,
That tires the very echoes with his tongue.
Yet, should it lie beyond the pow'rs of Fate
To stop thy pen, and still thy darling prate;
To live in solitude, oh! be thy luck
A chattering magpie on the Isle of Muck."

Than the shafts of ridicule, Boswell experienced even more substantial discomfort. Respecting Sir Alexander Macdonald, Bart., chief of the Macdonalds, he had written thus unguardedly:—

> "Instead of finding the head of the Macdonalds surrounded with his clan, and a festive entertainment, we had a small company, and cannot boast of our cheer. The particulars are minuted in my Journal, but I shall not trouble the publick with them. I shall mention but one characteristick circumstance. My shrewd and hearty friend Sir Thomas (Wentworth) Blacket, Lady Macdonald's uncle, who had preceded us on a visit to this

chief, upon being asked by him if the punch-bowl then upon the table was not a very handsome one, replied, 'Yes,—if it were full.' Sir Alexander Macdonald having been an Eton scholar, Dr. Johnson had formed an opinion of him which was much diminished when he beheld him in the Isle of Skye, where we heard heavy complaints of rents racked, and the people driven to emigration. Dr. Johnson said, 'It grieves me to see the chief of a great clan appear to such disadvantage. This gentleman has talents, nay, some learning; but he is totally unfit for this situation. Sir, the Highland chiefs should not be allowed to go farther south than Aberdeen. A strong-minded man, like his brother Sir James, may be improved by an English education, but in general they will be turned into insignificance.' I meditated an escape from this house the very next day; but Dr. Johnson resolved that we should weather it out till Monday."

In charging the chief of the Macdonalds with an unwarrantable parsimony, Boswell is justified in a letter written by Dr. Johnson to Mrs. Thrale.[78] But he evinced his wonted imprudence in making public what had better have been concealed, and in dragging into the controversy Sir Thomas Blacket, a near relative of Sir Alexander's wife.[79] Both baronets made loud complaint, and the chief of the Macdonalds spoke of vengeance by personal chastisement. To this threat Peter Pindar thus pungently alludes:—

"Let Lord Macdonald[80] threat thy breech to kick,
And o'er thy shrinking shoulders shake his stick
Treat with contempt the menace of this Lord,
'Tis Hist'ry's province, Bozzy, to record."

The displeasure which Boswell had excited was appeased by a compromise. He agreed in his next edition to exclude Blacket's anecdote, and to substitute allusion to Macdonald's shabbiness by quoting his Latin verses, welcoming the lexicographer to Skye.

In 1786 Boswell executed his Will, and it seems probable that "the apprehension of danger to his life"[81] to which in that document he refers was due to the menace of the Highland chief. If this conjecture is well founded, it is interesting to remark that Boswell especially provides that his own tenantry should in the matter of rent be treated with leniency.

In the preface to his third edition, issued in 1786, Boswell vigorously denounces his critics on both sides the Tweed. His Scottish compeers, he alleges, have displayed "a petty national spirit unworthy of his countrymen." The English critics are styled "shallow and envious cavillers." In opposition to their assertions that he has *lessened* Dr. Johnson's character, he maintains that he was assured by persons of taste that he had *greatly heightened* it. He appeals to the judgment of posterity.

Elated by his popularity as a tourist, he determined to reassert his political pretensions. An opportunity for displaying patriotic ardour seasonably occurred. A Bill was introduced into the House of Commons by Mr. Islay Campbell, the Lord Advocate, and Mr. Dundas, Dean of Faculty, for reconstructing the Court of Session. By this Bill it was proposed to reduce the judges from fifteen to ten, and with the funds secured by the reduction to augment the salaries of those who remained. In opposition to this measure Boswell issued a pamphlet, sensationally entitled "A Letter to the People of Scotland on the alarming attempt to infringe the Articles of Union, and introduce a most pernicious innovation, by diminishing the number of the Lords of Session." This composition, extending to 107 octavo pages, was published by Dilly, and sold for half a crown. There were few sales, but copies of the pamphlet were presented to the author's friends.[82]

In his characteristic manner Boswell sets forth that the number of judges was fixed unalterably by the Act of Union, "an Act which, entering into the constitution of Parliament itself, Parliament dare not alter." The number of fifteen was declared by George Buchanan to be small enough to avoid the character of a tyrannical junto.—"Is a court of ten," he proceeds, "the same with a court of fifteen? Is a two-legged animal the same with a four-legged animal? I know nobody who will gravely defend that proposition, except one grotesque philosopher, whom ludicrous fable represents as going about avowing his hunger, and wagging his tail, fain to become cannibal and eat his deceased brethren."[83] Lords of Session, he argues, do the work of English juries in civil cases, and exercise the functions of English Grand Juries. Mr. Dundas he denounces as "Harry the Ninth," and Mr. Islay Campbell is censured, though less abusively. Boswell next introduces himself, and proceeds to expatiate on his personal merits. He had in his previous letter "kindled the fire of loyalty and saved the constitution." He is "a true patriot," and begs that he may not be misunderstood by associating with Mr. Wilkes, "he being so pleasant," and an "old classical companion." He declares himself a scholar and a gentleman—"a scholar," as he is familiar with Latin authors; and a gentleman, "since his friends were persons of title and influence." His wife, whom "he loved as dearly as when she gave him her hand," is "a relation of Lord Eglinton, a true Montgomery." The M.P. for Plymouth, Captain Macbride, is "the cousin of his wife, and the friend of his heart." His intimate friend, Colonel Stuart, has "sterling good sense, information, discernment, honour, honesty, and spirit." Lord Lowther is apostrophised thus:—

"Let not the Scottish spirit be bowed. Let Lowther come forth and support us. We are his neighbours. *Paries proximus ardet*. We all know what HE can do. He upon whom the thousands of Whitehaven depend for *three* of the elements. *He* whose soul is all great; whose resentment is terrible, but whose liberality is boundless. I know that he is dignified by having hosts of enemies; but I have fixed his character in my mind upon no slight inquiry. I have traversed Cumberland and Westmoreland; I have sojourned at Carlisle and at Kendal; I know of the Lonsdale Club at Lancaster. Lowther! be kindly interested. Come over to Macedonia, and help us. With such personal qualities and such friends Boswell holds himself admirably qualified for a seat in the Legislature. He will present himself at next election as a candidate for Ayrshire. I have reason to hope," he proceeds, "that many of the real freeholders of Ayrshire will support me at the election for next Parliament, against which I have declared myself a candidate. I shall certainly stand upon the substantial interest of the gentlemen of landed property; and if upon a fair trial I should not succeed in that object of ambition, which I have most ardently at heart, I have resources enough to prevent me from being discontented and fretful."

The project of settling in London and forming a connection with the English Bar, which Boswell had long cherished, was now to be carried out. After keeping his terms, according to the usual practice, he was called to the English Bar, at Hilary term, 1786. His professional *début* prognosticated failure. Some of the junior barristers, to whom he was known as *Johnson's Bozzy*, prepared an imaginary case full of absurdity, which was submitted for his opinion. Unsuspecting a trap, he prepared an elaborate note of judgment. The laughter was prodigious, and the merriment penetrated into private circles. A ridiculous appearance in court, made soon afterwards, put a final check on his career as a practising barrister.[84] About three years after joining the English Bar he represented his condition to Mr. Temple in these terms:—

"*London, January 10th, 1789.*

"I am sadly discouraged by having no practice nor probable prospect of it; and to confess fairly to you, my friend, I am afraid that were I to be tried, I should be found so deficient in the forms, the quirks, and the quiddities, which early habit acquires, that I should expose myself. Yet the delusion of Westminster Hall, of brilliant reputation and splendid fortune as a barrister, still weighs upon my imagination. I must be seen in the courts, and must hope for some happy openings in causes of importance. The Chancellor, as you observe, has not done as I expected; but why did I expect it? I am going to put him to the test. Could I be satisfied with being Baron of Auchinleck, with a good income for a gentleman in Scotland, I might, no doubt, be independent. But what can be done to deaden the ambition which has ever raged in my veins like a fever? In the country I should sink into wretched gloom, or at best into listless dulness and sordid abstraction. Perhaps a time may come when I may by lapse of time be grown fit for it. As yet I, really from a philosophical spirit, allow myself to be driven along the tide of life with a good deal of caution not to be much hurt; and still flattering myself that an unexpected lucky chance may at last place me so that the prediction of a fortunate cap appearing on my head at my birth will be fulfilled."

Not long after writing this letter Boswell obtained his only professional appointment; he was, through the influence of Lord Lowther, appointed Recorder of Carlisle. The emoluments of the office were small, and as an attendance of several weeks was required annually, the acquisition was inconsiderable. But the wits did not permit the new Recorder to enter on his post without ridicule. The following *jeu d'esprit* obtained circulation:—

"Boswell once flamed with patriot zeal,

His bow was ever bent;

How he no public wrongs can feel

Till Lowther nods assent.

To seize the throne which faction tries,

And would the Prince command,

The Tory Boswell coolly cries,

My King's in Westmoreland."

At the close of the first edition of Boswell's Tour to the Hebrides, appeared the following advertisement:—

"Preparing for the Press, in one volume quarto,
The Life of Samuel Johnson, LL.D.
By James Boswell, Esq.

"Mr. Boswell has been collecting materials for this work for more than twenty years, during which he was honoured with the intimate friendship of Dr. Johnson; to whose memory he is ambitious to erect a literary monument, worthy of so great an authour, and so excellent a man. Dr. Johnson was well informed of his design, and obligingly communicated to him several curious particulars. With these will be interwoven the most authentick accounts that can be obtained from those who knew him best; many sketches of his conversation on a multiplicity of subjects, with various persons, some of them the most eminent of the age; a great number of letters from him at different periods, and several original pieces dictated by him to Mr. Boswell, distinguished by that peculiar energy which marked every emanation of his mind."

This advertisement, more befitting the announcement of a play than the memoir of a moralist, did not escape the witty criticism of the sarcastic Pindar. In a postscript to his "Poetical Epistle" he has thus written:—

"As Mr. Boswell's 'Journal' hath afforded such universal pleasure, by the relation of minute incidents and the great moralist's opinion of men and things during his northern tour, it will be adding greatly to the anecdotical treasury, as well as making Mr. B. happy, to communicate part of a dialogue that took place between Dr. Johnson and the author of this congratulatory epistle, a few months before the Doctor paid the great debt of nature. The Doctor was very cheerful that day, had on a black coat and waistcoat, a black plush pair of breeches, and black worsted stockings, a handsome grey wig, a shirt, a muslin neckcloth, a black pair of buttons in his shirt-sleeves, a pair of shoes ornamented with the very identical little buckles that accompanied the philosopher to the Hebrides; his nails were very neatly pared, and his beard fresh shaved with a razor fabricated by the ingenious Mr. Savigny.

"*P. P.*: 'Pray, Doctor, what is your opinion of Mr. Boswell's literary powers?'

"*Johnson*: 'Sir, my opinion is, that whenever Bozzy expires, he will create no vacuum in the region of literature—he seems strongly affected by the *cacoëches scribendi*; wishes to be thought a *rara avis*, and in truth so he is—your knowledge in ornithology, sir, will easily discover to what species of bird I allude.' Here the Doctor shook his head and laughed.

"*P. P.*: 'What think you, sir, of his account of Corsica?—of his character of Paoli?'

"*Johnson*: 'Sir, he hath made a mountain of a wart. But Paoli hath virtues. The account is a farrago of disgusting egotism and pompous inanity.'

"*P. P.*: 'I have heard it whispered, Doctor, that should you die before him, Mr. B. means to write your life.'

"*Johnson*: 'Sir, he cannot mean me so irreparable an injury,—which of us shall die first, is only known to the Great Disposer of events; but were I sure that James Boswell would write *my* life, I do not know whether I would not anticipate the measure by taking *his*.' (Here he made three or four strides across the room, and returned to his chair with violent emotion.)

"*P. P.*: 'I am afraid that he means to do you the favour.'

"*Johnson*: 'He dares not—he would make a scarecrow of me. I give him liberty to fire his blunderbuss in *his own* face, but not murder *me*, sir. I heed not his [Greek: autos epha]. Boswell write my life! why, the fellow possesses not abilities for writing the life of an ephemeron.'"

Naturally indolent and procrastinating, Boswell was, like persons of his temperament, aroused to enterprise by harsh and ungenerous criticism. Johnson's "Life" was commenced at once, and for some time prosecuted vigorously. Abandoned for many months, it was taken up in 1787, and worked upon at intervals in the year following.

The progress of the undertaking is in February 1788, thus reported to Mr. Temple:—

> "Mason's Life of Gray is excellent, because it is interspersed with letters which show us the man.... I am absolutely certain that my mode of biography, which gives not only a history of Johnson's visible progress through the world, and of his publications, but a view of his mind in his letters and conversations, is the most perfect that can be conceived, and will be more of a life than any work that has ever yet appeared. I have been wretchedly dissipated, so that I have not written a line for a fortnight; but to-day I resume my pen, and shall labour vigorously."

To Mr. Temple a further report is presented in January, 1789:—

> "I am now very near my rough draft of Johnson's Life. On Saturday I finished the Introduction and Dedication to Sir Joshua, both of which had appeared very difficult to be accomplished. I am confident they are well done. Whenever I have completed the rough draft, by which I mean the work without nice correction, Malone and I are to prepare one-half perfectly, and then it goes to press, whence I hope to have it early in February, so as to be out by the end of May."

After joining the English Bar, and establishing his headquarters in London, Boswell rented inexpensive chambers near the law courts; but in the winter of 1788-9 he removed to a house in Queen Anne Street West, Cavendish Square. He was joined by his two sons, and his daughter Veronica,—the sons attending an academy in Soho. His attendants were "a butler and Scotch housekeeper," whom he kept "on account of their fidelity and moderate wages."[85]

Mrs. Boswell made a trial of London, but soon returned to Auchinleck. She disapproved her husband's preference for the English Bar, and feared that the fogs of London would prove injurious to her health. She had been an asthmatic patient, and at the commencement of 1789 the complaint returned in an aggravated form. Writing to Mr. Temple on the 5th March, Boswell expresses himself deeply concerned about his "valuable and affectionate wife," but he feels that joining her in the country would destroy the completion of the Life of Johnson, and remove him from "the great whirl of the metropolis," from which he hoped "in time to have a capital prize." He had visited Ayrshire at the close of 1788, and there prosecuted an active canvass among his supposed friends, the parliamentary freeholders. The visit and its prospective results are thus detailed to Mr. Temple:—

"*London, 10th January, 1789.*

"As to my canvass in my own county, I started in opposition to a junction between Lord Eglintoun and Sir Adam Fergusson, who were violent opponents, and whose coalition is as odious there as the Great One is to the nation. A few friends and real independent gentlemen early declared for me; three other noble lords, the Earls of Cassilis, Glencairn, and Dumfries, have lately joined and set up a nephew of the Earl of Cassilis: a Mr. John Whitefoord, who as yet stands as I do, will, I understand, make a bargain with this alliance. Supposing he does, the two great parties will be so poised that I shall have it in my power to cast the balance. If they are so piqued that either will rather give the seat to me than be beaten by the other, I may have it. Thus I stand, and I shall be firm. Should Lord Lonsdale give me a seat he would do well, but I have no claim upon him for it. In the matter of the regency he adds that he had 'almost written one of his very warm popular pamphlets in favour of the Prince;' but as Lord Lonsdale was ill, and he had no opportunity of learning his sentiments, he had 'prudently refrained.' He accuses Pitt of 'behaving very ill,' in neglecting him, and denounces Dundas 'as a sad fellow in his private capacity.'"

Boswell returned to Ayrshire in April. Mrs. Boswell had written that she was "wasting away," and her physician was not hopeful of her improvement. Her husband thus describes her condition to Mr. Temple:[86]—

"I found," he writes, "my dear wife as ill, or rather worse than I apprehended. The consuming hectic fever had preyed upon her incessantly during the winter and spring, and she was miserably emaciated and weak. The physician and surgeon-apothecary, whom she allows occasionally, though rarely, to visit her, told me fairly, as to a man able to support with firmness what they announced, that they had no hopes of her recovery, though she might linger they could not say how long.... No man ever had a higher esteem or a warmer love for a wife than I have for her. You will recollect, my Temple, how our marriage was the result of an attachment truly romantic;

yet how painful is it to me to recollect a thousand instances of inconsistent conduct! I can justify," he adds, "my removing to the great sphere of England upon a principle of laudable ambition, but the frequent scenes of what I must call dissolute conduct are inexcusable; and often and often, when she was very ill in London, have I been indulging in festivity with Sir Joshua Reynolds, Courtenay, Malone, &c., and have come home late and disturbed her repose."

In these expressions of affection Boswell was sincere, but he would have better indicated regret for past inattention to his suffering helpmate if his conduct during her last illness had been more suited to her condition. During the five weeks he remained at Auchinleck, he was, according to his own acknowledgment, "repeatedly from home," and both "on these occasions, and when neighbours visited him, drank too much wine." Returning from a neighbour's house in a state of inebriety, he experienced an accident, the particulars of which he thus related to Mr. Temple:—

"On Saturday last, dining at a gentleman's house where I was visiting for the first time, and was eager to obtain political influence; I drank so freely that, riding home in the dark without a servant, I fell from my horse and bruised my shoulder severely. Next morning I had it examined by a surgeon, who found no fracture or dislocation, but blooded me largely to prevent inflammation."

The presence in Auchinleck House of one whose habits were so irregular, and who had narrowly escaped death in a fit of drunkenness, was not likely to soothe the dying gentlewoman. Some days after the occurrence of his accident, Boswell was invited by a friend of Lord Lonsdale to accompany his lordship in an early journey to London. Though still a sufferer and in bed on account of his fall, he resolved to obey the summons, and Mrs. Boswell "animated him to set out." With his arm in a sling he posted to Carlisle. Reaching Lowther Castle, he found Lord Lonsdale "in no hurry to proceed on the London journey." Meanwhile his shoulder became more uneasy, the pain extending to the breast and over the entire arm, so that he was unable to put on his clothes without help.[87]

Two weeks after he had reached London a letter from the Auchinleck physician informed him that Mrs. Boswell was rapidly sinking. He at once set out for Ayrshire, accompanied by his two sons, and, as he is particular in relating, the journey was performed in "sixty-four hours and a quarter." On his arrival he found that Mrs. Boswell had died four days before. In a letter to Mr. Temple, dated 3rd July, he wrote thus:—

> "I cried bitterly and upbraided myself for leaving her, for she would not have left me. This reflection, my dear friend, will, I fear, pursue me to my grave.... I could hardly bring myself to agree that the body should be removed, for it was still a consolation to me to go and kneel by it, and talk to my dear, dear Peggy.... Her funeral was remarkably well attended. There were nineteen carriages followed the hearse, and a large body of horsemen, and the tenants of all my lands. It is not customary in Scotland for a husband to attend a wife's funeral, but I resolved, if I possibly could, to do her the last honours myself; and I was able to go through it very decently. I privately read the funeral service over her coffin in presence of my sons, and was relieved by that ceremony a good deal. On the Sunday after Mr. Dun delivered, almost *verbatim*, a few sentences which I sent him as a character of her."

Boswell's religious views were still unsettled. During his wife's illness he wrote to Mr. Temple, "What aid can my wife have from religion, except a pious resignation to the great and good God? for indeed she is too shrewd to receive the common topics; she is keen and penetrating." What "the common topics" were, belief in which Boswell regarded with contempt, he has not informed us, and it might be hazardous to conjecture.

The dissolution of Parliament expected in the spring of 1789 did not occur, but the representation of Ayrshire became vacant in July, owing to the acceptance of a public office by the sitting member, Colonel Montgomerie. Obtaining intimation of the vacancy, Boswell, four weeks a widower, hastened from London to Ayrshire to renew his claims. There were two other candidates—Sir Adam Fergusson and Mr. John Whitefoord. The former was chosen. Boswell informed Mr. Temple that "he would make an admirable figure even if he should be unsuccessful." He stood alone!

Since his failure at the English Bar, Boswell had been most energetic in the pursuit of patronage. He rested his hopes on Mr. Dundas and Mr. Pitt, but more especially on Mr. Burke and Lord Lonsdale. Concerning the two former he thus communicated with Mr. Temple in the spring of 1789. After censuring Mr. Dundas for neglecting to promote his brother David, he proceeds:—

> "As to myself, Dundas, though he *pledged himself* (as the modern phrase is) to assist me in advancing in promotion, and though he last year assured me, upon his honour, that my letter concerning the Scottish judges made no difference; yet, except when I in a manner compelled him to dine with me last winter,

he has entirely avoided me, and I strongly suspect has given Pitt a prejudice against me. The excellent Langton says it is disgraceful; it is utter folly in Pitt not to reward and attach to his administration a man of my popular and pleasant talents, whose merit he has acknowledged in a letter under his own hand. He did not answer several letters which I wrote at intervals, requesting to wait upon him; I lately wrote to him that such behaviour to me was certainly not generous. 'I think it is not just, and (forgive the freedom) I doubt if it be wise. If I do not hear from you in ten days, I shall conclude that you are inclined to have no further communication with me; for I assure you, sir, I am extremely unwilling to give you, or indeed myself, unnecessary trouble.' About two months have elapsed, and *he has made no sign*. How can I still delude myself with dreams of rising in the great sphere of life."

Mr. Burke knew Boswell's good qualities, and had sought to befriend him. In 1782 he recommended him for employment to General Conway,[88] though without success. Boswell still hoped to obtain a post through his influence, and not infrequently reminded him that he was unprovided for. To Mr. Temple, in March, 1789, he describes Mr. Burke in these terms:—

"I cannot help thinking with you that Pitt is the ablest and most useful minister of any of those whom we know; yet I am not sure that after the *pericula* which should give caution, others (and amongst them Burke, whom I visited yesterday, and found as ably philosophical in political disquisition as ever) might not do as well; and if he has treated me unjustly in his stewardship for the public, and behaved with ungrateful insolence to my *patron*,[89] who first introduced him into public life, may I not warrantably arraign many articles, and great ones too, in his conduct which I can attack with forcible energy? At present I keep myself quiet, and wait till we see how things will turn out."

While thus distrusting or despising his other patrons, Boswell rested strongly on Lord Lonsdale. To Mr. Temple he communicated in March that his lordship showed him "more and more regard." He was his last star of hope; but the setting was at hand.

Checked in his legal, political, and parliamentary aspirations, Boswell began to devote some attention to family affairs. By his brother David he was advised to return to Scotland, and there attend to the education of his children. Concerning this proposal he remarks to Mr. Temple:—

> "Undoubtedly my having a house in Edinburgh would be best for them (the children); but, besides that my withdrawing thither would cut me off from all those chances which may in time raise me in life, I could not possibly endure Edinburgh now, unless I were to have a judge's place to bear me up; and even then I should deeply sigh for the metropolis."

He determined to remain in London. Plans for the disposal of his children were, after much wavering, at length resolved upon. Alexander, his eldest son, having "begun to oppose him,"[90] was removed from Soho Academy to Eton. He was afterwards to be sent to the University of Edinburgh, and latterly to Holland and Germany for the study of civil law. James, the second son, described to Mr. Temple as "an extraordinary boy, much of his father," was to be educated as a barrister. Meanwhile, being in his eleventh year, he was to be continued at the Soho school. Veronica, the eldest daughter, was kept in London under the charge of Mrs. Buchanan, a widow. Euphemia, the second daughter, was sent to a boarding-school in Edinburgh; and Elizabeth, the youngest, was placed in an educational institution at Ayr. By thus dispersing the members of his family, Boswell secured himself against any interference with his habits. For his children the arrangement was salutary, since they could not have profited by the exhibition of his weaknesses.

Amidst incessant place-hunting and a round of social indulgences, the "Life of Johnson" proceeded slowly. The public were meanwhile entertained by Mrs. Piozzi's Anecdotes.[91] This work and the "Life of Johnson," by Sir John Hawkins, seemed to satisfy general curiosity. The latter work, which appeared in 1787, deeply mortified Boswell; he was mentioned in it only once, and then as "Mr. James Boswell, a native of Scotland."[92] Indignation inspired him with energy. As specimens of his forthcoming work, he issued in quarto form two portions of its contents, with these titles:—"The Celebrated Letter from Samuel Johnson, LL.D., to Philip Dormer Stanhope, Earl of Chesterfield, now first published, with notes by James Boswell, Esq. London: Printed by Henry Baldwin for Charles Dilly, in the Poultry, 1790. [Price Half a Guinea.]" "A Conversation between His Most Sacred Majesty George III. and Samuel Johnson, LL.D., illustrated with Observations by James Boswell, Esq. London: Printed by Henry Baldwin for Charles Dilly, in the Poultry, 1790. [Price Half a Guinea.]"

The former of these *fasciculi* occupied four, and the latter eight quarto pages. Intimating to Mr. Temple that "a part of his *magnum opus* was ready for the press," he added that Hawkins should not be spared. His labours were interrupted by Mrs. Boswell's illness and his return to inebriate habits. On the 28th November he wrote to Mr. Temple:—

"Let me first address you from Cato:—

'Thou best of friends,

Pardon a weak distemper'd soul that swells,
In sudden gusts, and sinks again in calms.'

Your last letter supposes too truly my situation. With grief continually at my heart, I have been endeavouring to seek relief in dissipation and in wine, so that my life for some time past has been unworthy of myself, of you, and of all that is valuable in my character and connections. For a week past, as the common phrase is, 'I have taken up,' and by a more regular and quiet course find myself, I think, rather better."

As in the case of his "Tour to the Hebrides," Boswell submitted each successive chapter of the "Life of Johnson" to the revision of Mr. Malone. In his letter to Mr. Temple of the 28th November he remarks:—

> "The revision of my 'Life of Johnson' by so acute and knowing a critic as Mr. Malone is of most essential consequence, especially as he is *Johnsonianissimus*; and as he is to hasten to Ireland as soon as his Shakspere[93] is fairly published, I must avail myself of him *now*. His hospitality and my other invitations, and particularly my attendance at Lord Lonsdale's, have lost us many evenings; but I reckon that a third of the work is settled, so that I shall get to press very soon. You cannot imagine what labour, what perplexity, what vexation I have endured in arranging a prodigious multiplicity of materials, in supplying omissions, in searching for papers, buried in different masses, and all this besides the exertion of composing and polishing. Many a time have I thought of giving it up. However, though I shall be uneasily sensible of its many deficiencies, it will certainly be to the world a very valuable and peculiar volume of biography, full of literary and characteristical anecdotes (which word, by the way, Johnson always condemned, as used in the sense that the French, and we from them, use it, as signifying particulars), told with authenticity, and in a lively manner. Would that it were in the booksellers' shops! Methinks, if I had this *magnum opus* launched, the public has no further claim upon me; for I have promised no more, and I may die in peace, or retire into dull obscurity, *reddarque tenebris*."

Writing to Mr. Temple on the 8th February, 1790, Boswell thus reports progress:—

> "I am within a short walk of Mr. Malone, who revises my 'Life of Johnson' with me. We have not yet gone over quite a half of it, but it is at last fairly in the press. I intended to have printed it upon what is called an *English* letter, which would have made it look better; but upon calculation it would have made two quarto volumes, and two quarto volumes for one life would have appeared exorbitant, though in truth it is a view of much of the literature, and many of the literary men of Great Britain for more than half a century. I have therefore taken a smaller type, called *Pica*, and even upon that I am afraid its bulk will be very large. It is curious to observe how a printer calculates; he arranges a number of pages, and the words in them at different parts of the 'copy' (as the MS. is called), and so finds the number of words. Mine here are four hundred and one thousand six hundred. Does not this frighten you. By printing a page the number of words it holds is discovered; and by dividing the sum-total of words by that number we get the number of pages. Mine will be eight hundred. I think it will be, without exception, the most entertaining book you ever read. I cannot be done with printing before the end of August."

In excellent terms with himself, and rejoicing in his literary aptitude, he thus addresses Mr. Temple on the 13th February:—

> "I dine in a different company almost every day, at least scarcely ever twice running in the same company, so that I have fresh accessions of ideas. I drink with Lord Lonsdale one day; the next I am quiet in Malone's elegant study revising my Life of Johnson, of which I have high expectations, both as to fame and profit. I surely have the art of writing agreeably. The Lord Chancellor[94] told me he had read every word of my Hebridean Journal; he could not help it."

On the 4th December Boswell addressed Mr. Malone:[95]—

> "The *magnum opus* advances. I have revised p. 216. The additions which I have received are a Spanish quotation from Mr. Cambridge, an account of Johnson at Warley Camp from Mr. Langton, and Johnson's letters to Mr. Hastings—three in all,—one of them long and admirable; but what sets the diamonds in pure gold of Ophir is a letter from Mr. Hastings to me, illustrating them and their writer. I had this day the honour of a long visit from the late Governor-General of

India. There is to be no more impeachment. But you will see his character nobly vindicated, depend upon this."

Though still ambitious of professional advancement, Boswell began to dread the merriment of the Circuit mess, promoted too frequently at his personal cost. On the plea of saving £50, and "avoiding rough, unpleasant company," he informed Mr. Temple in February, 1789, that he would omit the spring Northern Circuit. In August he communicated to the same correspondent that he had proceeded to Lord Lonsdale's with the intention of joining the autumn Circuit at Carlisle; but that considering his "late severe loss," and "the rough scenes of the roaring, bantering society of lawyers," he preferred to remain at Lowther Castle. At the castle he was subjected to a practical jest, which as an annoying incident he thus describes to Mr. Temple:—

"A strange accident happened; the house at Lowther was so crowded that I and two other gentlemen were laid in one room. On Thursday morning my wig was missing; a strict search was made, all in vain. I was obliged to go all day in my night-cap, and absent myself from a party of ladies and gentlemen who went and dined with the Earl on the banks of the lake,—a piece of amusement which I was glad to shun, as well as a dance which they had at night. But I was in a ludicrous situation. I suspected a wanton trick which some people think witty; but I thought it very ill-timed to one in my situation. Next morning the Earl and a colonel, who I thought might have concealed my wig, declared to me, upon honour they did not know where it was; and the conjecture was that a clergyman who was in the room with me, and had packed up his portmanteau in a great hurry to set out in the morning early, might have put it up among his things. This is very improbable; but I could not long remain an object of laughter, so I went twenty-five miles to Carlisle on Tuesday, and luckily got a wig there fitted for me in a few hours."

On the 13th October Boswell informed Mr. Temple that on lately visiting Lowther Castle he received back his wig. "The way in which it was lost," he adds, "will remain as secret as the author of Junius."

Mr. Temple became urgent for repayment of a loan of £200, and in obtaining the necessary means Boswell severely taxed his resources. Referring to the debt, he assured his correspondent that he had, after deducting family costs, a free income of not more than £350, and that while he had been in straitened circumstances for twenty years, he dreaded that his embarrassments would continue. In a letter dated 28th November he returns to his pecuniary difficulties.

> "The state of my affairs is very disagreeable; but be not afraid of your £200, as you may depend upon its being repaid. My rent-roll is above £1,600; but deducting annuities, interest of debts, and expenses absolutely necessary at Auchinleck, I have but about £850 to spend. I reckon my five children at £500 a year. You see what remains for myself."... "I am this year to make one trial of the Lord Chancellor. In short, I cast about everywhere. I do not see the smallest opening in Westminster Hall; but I like the scene, though I have attended only one day this last term, being eager to get my 'Life of Johnson' finished. And the delusion that practice may come at any time (which is certainly true) still possesses me." He adds, "I have given up my house, and taken good chambers in the Inner Temple, to have the appearance of a lawyer. O Temple! Temple! is this realizing any of the towering hopes which have so often been the subject of our conversation and letters? Yet I live much with a great man, who, upon any day that his fancy shall be so inclined, may obtain for me an office which would make me independent."

Boswell could cherish no reasonable hope of professional advancement, save through the patronage of Lord Lonsdale. And the recent escapade at Lowther Castle might have shown him that sentiments of respect were unassociated with his lordship's friendship. What he could not perceive in August, 1789, was made sufficiently plain in the following June. The narrative must be presented in his own words. Writing from Carlisle to Mr. Temple on the 21st June, 1790, he proceeds:—

> "At no period during our long friendship have I been more unhappy than at present. The day on which I was obliged to set out from London I had no time allowed me after a most shocking conversation with Lord Lonsdale, and I hastened home in hopes of finding you, but you were gone out. It was to inform you that upon his seeing me by no means in good humour, he challenged it roughly, and said, 'I suppose you thought I was to bring you into Parliament. I never had any such intention.' In short, he expressed himself in the most degrading manner, in presence of a low man from Carlisle, and one of his menial servants. The miserable state of low spirits I had, as you too well know, laboured under for some time before made me almost sink under such unexpected insulting behaviour. He insisted rigorously on my having solicited the

office of Recorder of Carlisle; and that I could not, without using him ill resign it until the duties which were now required of it were fulfilled, and without a sufficient time being given for the election of a successor. Thus was I dragged away as wretched as a convict; and in my fretfulness I used such expressions as excited him almost to fury, so that he used such expressions towards me that I should have, according to the irrational laws of honour sanctioned by the world, been under the necessity of risking my life, had not an explanation taken place.... I am down at an inn, in wretched spirits, and ashamed and sunk on account of the disappointment of hopes which led me to endure such grievances. I deserve all that I suffer. I may be kept hanging on for weeks, till the election and Midsummer Sessions are over; and I am at the same time distracted what to do in my own county, as to the state of which I expect letters every day. I am quite in a fever. O my old and most intimate friend, what a shocking state am I now reduced to! I entreat of you, if you possibly can, to afford me some consolation, directed to me here, and pray do not divulge my mortification. I will endeavour to appear indifferent; and as I now resign my Recordership, I shall gradually get rid of all communication with this brutal fellow."

In Boswell's correspondence Lord Lonsdale's name only reappears once. Writing to Mr. Temple on the 21st July, he remarks, "I parted from the northern tyrant in a strange equivocal state, for he was half irritated, half reconciled; but I promise you I shall keep myself quite independent of him."

Parliament was dissolved in July, and Boswell proposed once more to offer his services to the Ayrshire constituency. He ultimately determined more wisely, remarking to Mr. Temple that "he did not go to Ayrshire, finding that he could only show how small a party he had."

Amidst these distractions, Boswell found leisure warmly to interest himself in two objects to which he had pledged his support. The first of these was to obtain subscribers for two volumes of sermons, published by his former tutor and early friend, Mr. John Dun, parish minister of Auchinleck.[96] In these volumes the reverend author attempted to ridicule the poet Burns. The following verses, a parody on the bard's "Address to the Deil," were regarded by Boswell without disfavour:—

"THE DEIL'S ANSWER TO HIS VERRA FREEND R. BURNS.

"So zealous Robin, stout an' fell,
True champion for the cause o' hell,
Thou beats the righteous down pell mell,

Sae frank and frothy,

That o' a seat where devils dwell,

There's nane mair worthy.

****

"Thou does as weel's could be expectit,
O' ane wha's wit lay long neglectet;
Some *godly folk* your rhyme, I trow,

Ca' worthless blether;

But be na feart, ye's get your due,

When we forgather.

****

"In hell when I read o'er your sang,
Where rhymes come thun'ring wi' a bang,
Quoth I, trouth I's see Rab or lang,

An' that's be seen.

Giff Nick should on me ride the stang

To Aberdeen."

Mr. Dun's work was still-born. In a letter to Mr. Temple, Boswell regrets that his friend would, by his performance, be "a sad loser."

While thus abetting the ridicule of the Ayrshire poet, Boswell's other enterprize was more creditable. He gave assistance in raising funds for a monument to Dr. Johnson in Westminster Abbey. To this undertaking he thus refers in a letter to Mr. Temple, dated the 28th November, 1789:—

> "Last Sunday I dined with him (Malone), with Sir Joshua Reynolds, Sir Joseph Banks, Mr. Metcalfe, Mr. Windham, Mr. Courtenay, and young Mr. Burke, being a select number of Dr. Johnson's friends, to settle as to effectual measures for having a monument erected to him in Westminster Abbey; it is to be a whole-length statue of him, by Bacon, which will cost £600. Sir Joshua and Sir William Scott, his executors, are to send circular letters to a number of people, of whom we make a list, as supposing they will contribute. Several of us subscribed five guineas each, Sir Joshua and Metcalfe ten guineas each, Courtenay and young Burke two guineas each. Will you not be one of us, were it but for one guinea? We expect that the Bench of Bishops will be liberal, as he was the greatest supporter of

the hierarchy. That venerable sound brings to my mind the ruffians of France, who are attempting to destroy all order, ecclesiastical and civil. The present state of that country is an intellectual earthquake, a whirlwind, a mad insurrection, without any immediate cause, and therefore we see to what a horrible anarchy it tends."

The subject of the monument is resumed in Boswell's letter to Mr. Temple, dated 8th February, 1790:—

"You will have seen that Johnson's friends have been exerting themselves for his monument, which is to cost six hundred guineas. We have now near to £400 of the money. Can we have no Cornish coin? I wish you could assist us in your neighbourhood. As your character of Gray was adopted by him it would appear well if you sent two guineas. We shall have a great dispute as to the epitaph. Flood, the orator, though a distinguished scholar, says it should be in English, as a compliment to Johnson's having perpetuated our language; he has compressed his opinion in these lines:—

"No need of Latin, or of Greek to grace

Our Johnson's memory and inscribe his grave;

His native tongue demands this mournful space,

To pay the immortality he gave."

Johnson's monument in Westminster Abbey was erected in 1796 at the cost of eleven hundred guineas; it was inscribed with a Latin epitaph composed by Dr. Parr. Mr. Temple's name does not appear among the subscribers.

With the entire prostration of his political and professional expectations, Boswell relapsed into melancholy. In a letter to Mr. Temple dated 21st July he expresses himself in this earnest manner:—

"Surely, my dear friend, there must be another world in which such beings as we are will have our misery compensated. But is not this a state of probation? and if it is, how awful is the consideration! I am struck with your question, 'Have you confidence in the Divine aid?' In truth I am sensible that I do not sufficiently '*try* my ways' as the Psalmist says, and am ever almost inclined to think with you *that* my great *oracle Johnson did allow too much credit to good principles, without good practice.*"

In this passage Dr. Johnson's sentiments on practical religion are strangely perverted. Had not the great moralist warned his companion against vanity and self-deceit, and the substitution of good intentions for the active practice of virtue? In the autumn of 1790, Boswell's intemperance was excessive. On the 4th December, he wrote to Mr. Malone in these words:—

> "On the day after your departure, that most friendly fellow Courtenay[97] (begging the pardon of an M.P. for so free an epithet) called on me, and took my word and honour that, till the 1st of March, my allowance of wine per diem should not exceed four good glasses at dinner, and a pint after it; and this I have kept, though I have dined with Jack Wilkes; at the London Tavern, after the launch of an Indiaman with dear Edwards; Dilly; at home with Courtenay; Dr. Barrow; at the mess of the Coldstream; at the Club; at Warren Hastings'; at Hawkins the Cornish member's; and at home with a colonel of the guards, &c. This regulation, I assure you, is of essential advantage in many respects."

Like the vow under "the solemn yew" at Mamhead, the word of honour pledged to Mr. Courtenay was soon forgotten. On the 25th February, 1791, Boswell wrote to Mr. Malone as follows:—

> "Your friendly admonition as to excess in wine has been often too applicable; but upon this late occasion I erred on the other side. However as I am now free from my restriction to Courtenay I shall be much upon my guard; for, to tell the truth, I did go too deep the day before yesterday, having dined with Michael Angelo Taylor, and then supped at the London Tavern with the stewards of the Humane Society."

In his letter of the 4th December, Boswell affirms that his promise of sobriety extended till the 1st of March; he reports on the 25th of February, that the term had closed! His melancholy had returned. On the 7th of February Mr. Temple was addressed thus:—

> "Before this time you have been informed of my having had a most miserable return of bad spirits. Not only have I had a total distaste of life, but have been perpetually gnawed by a kind of mental fever. It is really shocking that human nature is liable to such inexplicable distress. Oh, my friend, what can I do? * * * Your observation in a former letter, as to time being measured not only by days and years, but by an advancement in life, is new and striking, and is brought home to us both, especially to me, who have obtained no advancement whatever; but let me not harass you with my complaints."

In his next letter to Mr. Temple, written on the 2nd of April, Boswell further expatiates on his melancholy. He writes:—

> "Your kindness to me fairly makes me shed tears. Alas! I fear that my constitutional melancholy, which returns in such dismal fits, and is now aggravated by the loss of my valuable wife, must prevent me from any permanent felicity in this life. I snatch gratifications, but have no comfort, at least very little; yet your encouraging letters make me think at times that I may yet, by God's blessing, attain to a portion of happiness, such as philosophy and religion concur in assuring us that this state of progressive being allows. I get bad rest in the night, and then I brood over all my complaints, the sickly mind which I have had from my early years—the disappointment of my hopes of success in life—the irrevocable separation between me and that excellent woman, who was my cousin, my friend and my wife; the embarrassment of my affairs—the disadvantage to my children in having so wretched a father—nay, the want of absolute certainty of being happy after death, the *sure prospect* of which is frightful."

Within a few months after sustaining that bereavement, which he still deplored, Boswell contemplated the repair of his shattered fortunes by contracting a second marriage. While in the North he wrote Mr. Temple in July, 1790. "I got such accounts of the lady of fortune, whose reputation you heard something of, that I was quite determined to make no advances. Whether I shall take any such step I doubt much. The loss I have experienced is perpetually recurring."

Boswell resolved closely to watch his opportunity. His letter to Mr. Temple of the 2nd April, 1791, contains the following:—

> "I am to dine with Sir William Scott, the King's Advocate, at the Commons to-morrow, and shall have a serious consultation with him, as he has always encouraged me. It is to be a family party, where I am to meet Miss Bagnal (his lady's sister) who may probably have six or seven hundred a year. She is about seven and twenty, and he tells me lively and gay—a Ranelagh girl—but of excellent principles, insomuch that she reads prayers to the servants in her father's family every Sunday evening. 'Let me see such a woman,' cried I; and accordingly I am to see her. She has refused young and fine gentlemen. 'Bravo,' cried I, 'we see then what her taste is.' Here then I am, my Temple, my flattering self! A scheme—an adventure seizes my fancy. Perhaps I may not like her; and what should I do

with such a companion, unless she should really take a particular liking to me, which is surely not probable; and, as I am conscious of my distempered mind, could I *honestly* persuade her to unite her fate with mine. As to my daughters, did I see a rational prospect of so good a scheme, I should not neglect it on their account, though I should certainly be liberal to them."

Miss Bagnal's name does not reappear. But he informs Mr. Temple on the 22nd of August that his matrimonial plans were still active:—

"You must know," he writes, "I have had several matrimonial schemes of late. I shall amuse you with them from Auchinleck. One was Miss Milles, daughter of the late Dean of Exeter, a most agreeable woman '*d'un certain âge*,' and with a fortune of £10,000; she has left town for the summer. It was no small circumstance that she said to me, 'Mr. Temple is a charming man.'"

The progress of Boswell's *magnum opus* has been traced to the 4th December, 1790. On the 12th of that month the author wrote to Mr. Temple:—

"My work has met with a delay for a little while—not a whole day, however—by an unaccountable neglect in having paper enough in readiness. I have now before me p. 256. My utmost wish is to come forth on Shrove Tuesday (8th March)."

Mr. Malone was now in Ireland, and Boswell, in reporting to him the progress of his undertaking, also communicated the miserable details of his private embarrassments. In a letter to Mr. Malone, dated the 18th January, 1791, he writes thus:—

"I have been so disturbed by sad money matters that my mind has been quite fretful; £500 which I borrowed and lent to a first cousin, an unlucky captain of an Indiaman, were due on the 15th to a merchant in the city. I could not possibly raise that sum, and was apprehensive of being hardly used. He, however, indulged me with an allowance to make partial payments, £150 in two months, £150 in eight months, and the remainder, with the interests, in eighteen months. How I am to manage I am at a loss, and I know you cannot help me. So this, upon my honour, is no hint. I am really tempted to accept of the £1000 for my life of Johnson. Yet it would go to my heart to sell it at a price which I think much too low. Let me struggle and hope. I cannot be out on Shrove Tuesday as I flattered myself. P. 376 of Vol. II. is ordered for the press, and I expect another proof to-night. But I have yet near 200 pages of copy, besides letters, and *the death*, which is not yet written."

Writing to Mr. Malone on the 29th January, Boswell makes these deplorable revelations:—

"I have for some weeks had the most woeful return of melancholy, insomuch that I have not only had no relish of anything, but a continual uneasiness and all the prospect before me for the rest of life has seemed gloomy and hopeless. The state of my affairs is exceedingly embarrassed. I mentioned to you that the £500 which I borrowed several years ago and lent to a first cousin, an unfortunate India captain, must now be paid; £150 on the 18th of March, £150 on the 18th October, and £257 15s. 6d. on the 18th July, 1792. This debt presses upon my mind, and it is uncertain if I shall ever get a shilling of it again. The clear money on which I can reckon out of my estate is scarcely £900 a year. What can I do? My grave brother urges me to quit London and live at my seat in the country, where he thinks that I might be able to save so as gradually to relieve myself. But, alas! I should be *absolutely* miserable. In the meantime such are my projects and sanguine expectations, that you know I purchased an estate which was given long ago to a younger son of our family, and came to be sold last autumn, and paid for it £2500, £1500 of which I borrow upon itself by a mortgage. But the remaining £1000 I cannot conceive a possibility of raising, but by the mode of annuity which is I believe a very heavy disadvantage. I own it was imprudent in me to make a clear purchase at a time when I was sadly straitened, but if I had missed the opportunity it never again would have occurred, and I should have been vexed to see an ancient appanage, a piece of, as it were, the flesh and blood of the family in the hands of a stranger. And now that I have made the purchase I should feel myself quite despicable should I give it up. In this situation, then, my dear sir, would it not be wise in me to accept 1000 guineas for my Life of Johnson, supposing the person who made the offer should now stand to it, which I fear may not be the case; for two volumes may be considered as a disadvantageous circumstance. Could I indeed raise £1000 upon the credit of the work, I should incline to *game*, as Sir Joshua says, because it may produce double the money, though Steevens *kindly* tells me that I have over printed, and that the curiosity about Johnson is *now* only in our own circle. Pray decide for me; and if, as I suppose, you are for my taking the offer inform me with whom I am to treat. In my present state of spirits I am all timidity. Your absence has been a severe shake to me. I am at present quite at a loss what to do.... I have now desired to have but one compositor. Indeed, I go sluggishly and comfortlessly about my work. As I pass your door I cast many a longing look.... We had a numerous club on Tuesday; I in the chair, quoting Homer and Fielding, &c. to the astonishment of Jo. Warton, who with Langton and Seward eat a plain bit with me in my new house last Saturday."

On the 10th February, Boswell informed Mr. Malone that he had invested £16 8s. in a lottery ticket, and that instead of obtaining £5000 had drawn a blank. He proceeds:—

"Oh, could I but get a few thousands, what a difference would it make upon my state of mind, which is harassed by thinking of my debts! I am anxious to have your determination as to my *magnum opus*. I am very unwilling to part with the property of it, and certainly would not, if I could but get credit for £1000 for three or four years. Could you not assist me in that way, on the security of the book, and of an assignment to one half of my rents, £700, which, upon my honour, are always due, and would be forthcoming in the case of my decease. I *will* not sell till I have your answer as to this."

Mr. Malone did not reply. On the 25th Boswell made a new proposal. After referring to a severe attack of melancholy which had lately oppressed him, he proceeds:—

"I am in a distressing perplexity how to decide as to the property of my book. You must know that I am certainly informed that a certain person, who delights in mischief, has been depreciating it, so that I fear the sale of it may be very dubious. *Two quartos* and *two guineas* sound in an alarming manner. I believe in my present frame I should accept even of £500, for I suspect that were I now to talk to Robinson, I should find him not disposed to give £1000. Did he absolutely offer it, or did he only express himself so as that you *concluded* he would give it? The pressing circumstance is that I must lay down £1000 by the 1st of May on account of the purchase of land, which my old family enthusiasm urged me to make. You, I doubt not, have full confidence in my honesty. May I then ask you if you could venture to join with me in a bond for that sum, as then I would take my chance, and as Sir Joshua says, Game with my book? Upon my honour, your telling me that you cannot comply with what I propose will not in the least surprise me, or make any manner of difference as to my opinion of your friendship. I mean to ask Sir Joshua if he will join; for, indeed, I should be vexed to sell my *magnum opus* for a great deal less than its intrinsic value. I meant to publish on Shrove Tuesday, but if I can get out within the month of March I shall be satisfied."

Sir Joshua Reynolds and Mr. Malone both declined pecuniary responsibility, but Boswell was nevertheless relieved from his embarrassments. He obtained in Scotland a loan of £600 on the credit of his rents, and Dilly and Baldwin made an advance on the credit of his book. Writing to Mr. Malone on the 8th March, he excuses that gentleman's unwillingness to incur monetary risk, and elated in having overcome the pressure of his creditors, he resolves to keep the property of his book, "believing that he should not *repent* it." There is a new grievance:—

"You would observe," he writes, "some stupid lines on Mr. Burke in the 'Oracle' by *Mr. Boswell*. I instantly wrote to Mr. Burke, expressing my indignation at such impertinence, and had next morning a most obliging answer. Sir William Scott told me I could have no legal redress. So I went *civilly* to Bell, and he promised to mention *handsomely* that *James Boswell*, Esq., was not the author of the lines. The note, however, on the subject, was a second impertinence. But I can do nothing. I wish Fox, in his bill upon libels, would make a heavy penalty the consequence of forging any person's name to any composition, which in reality such a trick amounts to."

Four days after conveying to Mr. Malone the tidings of his his deliverance from pecuniary troubles, Boswell condoles with his friend, in his lottery ticket having drawn a blank, since had a prize turned up, he would have expected the accommodation of a loan! He proceeds:—

"As it is, I shall, as I wrote to you, be enabled to weather my difficulties for some time; but I am still in great anxiety about the sale of my book. I find so many people shake their heads at the *two quartos* and *two guineas*. Courtenay is clear that I should sound Robinson and accept of a thousand guineas, if he will give that sum. Meantime, the title-page must be made as good as may be. It appears to me that mentioning his studies, works, conversations, and letters, is not sufficient; and

I would suggest comprehending an account, in chronological order, of his studies, works, friendships, acquaintances, and other particulars; his conversation with eminent men; a series of his letters to various persons; also several original pieces of his compositions never before published. The whole, &c. You will probably be able to assist me in expressing my idea and arranging the parts. In the advertisement I intend to mention the letter to Lord Chesterfield, and perhaps the interview with the King, and the names of the correspondents, in alphabetical order.... Do you know that my bad spirits are returned upon me to a certain degree; and such is the sickly fondness for change of place, and imagination of relief, that I sometimes think you are happier by being in Dublin, than one is in this great metropolis, where hardly any man cares for another. I am persuaded I should relish your Irish dinners very much. I have at length got chambers in the Temple, in the very staircase where Johnson lived, and when my *magnum opus* is fairly launched, then shall I make a trial."

In his letter to Mr. Temple of the 2nd April, Boswell refers to his forthcoming work in these terms:—

"My 'Life of Johnson' is at last drawing to a close. I am correcting the last sheet.... I really hope to publish it on the 25th current.... I am at present in such bad spirits that I have every fear concerning it—that I may get no profit, nay, may lose—that the public may be disappointed, and think that I have done it poorly—that I may make many enemies, and even have quarrels. But, perhaps, the very reverse of all this may happen."

Boswell adds in reference to his professional aspirations:—

"When my book is launched I shall, if I am alone and in tolerable health and spirits, have some furniture put into my chambers in the Temple, and force myself to sit there some hours a day, and to attend regularly in Westminster Hall. The chambers cost me £20 yearly, and I may reckon furniture and a lad to attend them occasionally £20 more. I doubt whether I shall get fees equal to the expense."

On the 19th April, Boswell thus wrote to his friend Mr. Dempster:—

"We must not entirely lose sight of one another, or rather, we must not suffer 'out of sight out of mind' to be applicable to two such old friends, who have always lived pleasantly together, though of principles directly opposite.... I some time ago resigned my Recordership of Carlisle. I perceived that no advantage would accrue from it. I could satisfy you in *conversation* that I was right. The melancholy event of losing my valuable wife will, I fear, never allow me to have real comfort. You cannot imagine how it hangs upon my spirits; yet I can talk and write, and, in short, *force myself* to a wonderful degree. I enclose you a poem which I have published upon a subject on which I never heard your sentiments, but I could lay my life you are one of the pretty theorists; however, you will have candour enough to allow that I have *worked* well. I have a good house in Great Portland Street. My two eldest daughters live with me; my youngest is at a boarding-school at Chelsea; my eldest son is at Eton; my second at Westminster. I am sadly straitened in my circumstances; I can but *exist* as to *expense*; but they are so good to me here that I have a full share of the metropolitan advantages.

"My *magnum opus*, the 'Life of Dr. Johnson,' in two volumes, quarto, is to be published on Monday, 16th May. It is too great a book to be given in presents, as I gave my 'Tour,' so you must not expect one, though you yourself form a part of its multifarious contents. I really think it will be the most entertaining collection that has appeared in this age. When it is fairly launched, I mean to stick close to Westminster Hall, and it will be truly kind if you recommend me appeals or causes of any sort."

Boswell's poem on the Slave-trade, to which he refers, was either at once withdrawn from circulation, or was, on his decease, suppressed by his family. It is unknown to bibliographers. The "Life of Johnson," in two quarto volumes, was issued about the middle of May from the publishing house of Mr. Charles Dilly. The title-page, which the author had laboured to render attractive, was thus inscribed:—

"The Life of Samuel Johnson, LL.D., comprehending an Account of his Studies and numerous Works, in chronological order; a series of his Epistolary Correspondence and Conversations with many eminent persons; and various Original Pieces of his composition, never before published. The whole exhibiting a view of literature and literary men in Great Britain, for more than half a century, during which he flourished, in two volumes, by James Boswell, Esq. 2 vols., 4to.

London: Printed by Thomas Baldwin for Charles Dilly, in the Poultry, 1791."

The following passages from the Dedication to Sir Joshua Reynolds are characteristic of the writer:—

"If there be a pleasure in celebrating the distinguished merit of a contemporary mixed with a certain degree of vanity not altogether inexcusable in appearing fully sensible of it, where can I find one in complimenting whom I can with more general approbation gratify those feelings." Referring to his Tour to the Hebrides, the author proceeds: "In one respect this work will in some passages be different from the former. In my 'Tour' I was almost unboundedly open in my communications; and from my eagerness to display the wonderful fertility and readiness of Johnson's wit, freely showed to the world its dexterity even when I was myself the object of it. I trusted that I should be liberally understood as knowing very well what I was about, and by no means as simply unconscious of the pointed effects of the satire. I own indeed that I was arrogant enough to suppose that the tenor of the rest of the book would sufficiently guard me against such a strange imputation. But it seems I judged too well of the world; for, though I could scarcely believe it, I have been undoubtedly informed that many persons especially in distant quarters, not penetrating enough into Johnson's character, so as to understand his mode of treating his friends, have arraigned my judgment instead of seeing that I was sensible of all that they could observe. It is related of the great Dr. Clarke that when, in one of his leisure hours, he was unbending himself with a few friends in the most playful and frolicksome manner, he observed Beau Nash approaching, upon which he suddenly stopped. 'My boys (said he) let us be grave; here comes a fool.' The world, my friend, I have found to be a great fool, as to that particular on which it has become necessary to speak very plainly. I have therefore in this work been more reserved; and though I tell nothing but the truth, I have still kept in my mind that the whole truth is not always to be exposed. This, however, I have managed so as to occasion no diminution of the pleasure which my book should afford, though malignity may sometimes be disappointed of its gratifications."

In this manner Boswell disposes of Dr. Wolcott and the other satirists who had made merry at his "Tour." Though published at the price of two guineas, the success of the "Life" was immediate. It was eagerly sought after, and everywhere read. Even those who were indifferent about Johnson, and who despised his biographer, added the work to their library, and were amused by its *chit chat*.[98] Writing to Mr. Temple on the 22nd August, Boswell reported that twelve hundred copies were in circulation, and that he expected that the entire impression of seventeen hundred copies would be sold before Christmas. By the success of his work he was induced to cherish renovated hope; he again dreamed of professional employment. In his letter to Mr. Temple of the 22nd August he writes:—

> "I have gone the full round of the Home Circuit, to which I have returned, finding it much more pleasant; and though I did not get a single brief do not repent of the expense, as I am showing myself desirous of business and imbibing legal knowledge."

On the 22nd November he informed Mr. Temple that he kept chambers open in the Temple; and attended in Westminster Hall; but had not the least prospect of business.

After attending Westminster Hall for two years Boswell was employed in a case of appeal to the House of Peers. He had no other brief. In the autumn of 1791 he resided several weeks at Auchinleck. Returning to London in November he thus reported himself to his friend at Mamhead:—

> "I had a very unhappy time in Ayrshire. My house at Auchinleck seemed deserted and melancholy; and it brought upon my mind, with unusual force, the recollection of my having lost my dear and valuable wife. My London spirits were soon exhausted; I sank into languor and gloom; I found myself very unfit to transact business with my tenants, or, indeed, with anybody. To escape from what I felt at Auchinleck I visited a good deal, but alas! I could not escape from myself: in short, you may see that I was exceedingly ill. I hoped to be restored when I got to London, but my depression of spirits has continued, and still, though I go into jovial scenes, I feel no pleasure in existence, except the mere gratification of the senses. Oh, my friend, this is sad. I have imagined that I was quite unable to write a letter.... My spirits have been still more sunk by seeing Sir Joshua Reynolds almost as low as myself. He has for more than two months past had a pain in his blind eye, the effect of which has been to occasion a weakness in the other, and he broods over the dismal apprehension of becoming quite blind.... I force myself to be a great deal with him, to do what is in my power to amuse him.... This is a

desponding, querulous letter, which I have wished these several weeks to write. Pray try to do me some good."

Boswell's correspondence with Mr. Temple in 1792 has, one short note excepted, not been preserved. It is probable that most of his spare hours were devoted to the revision of his "Life of Johnson," of which the second edition appeared in the following year.

In October, 1792, the parish of Auchinleck became vacant by the death of Mr. Dun. Though upholding as part of his *patriotic* creed, that with negroes abroad the unlanded population at home should be denied political or other privileges, Boswell was not unwilling to obtain acceptance with the common people. As patron of Auchinleck parish he assured the parishioners that he would consult their wishes in planting the vacant cure. On this subject he thus communicated with Mr. Temple on the 26th February, 1793:—

> "I am within a few hours of setting out for Auchinleck, honest David having secured me a place in the Carlisle coach to Ferry Bridge that I may have an opportunity to stop should I be too much fatigued. It is quite right that I should now go down. The choice of a minister to a worthy parish is a matter of very great importance, and I cannot be sure of the real wishes of the people without being present. Only think, Temple, how serious a duty I am about to discharge! I, James Boswell, Esq.—you know what vanity that name includes—I have promised to come down on purpose, and his honour's goodness is gratefully acknowledged. Besides, I have several matters of consequence to my estate to adjust; and though the journey will no doubt be uncomfortable, and my being alone in that house where once I was so happy, be dreary in a woeful degree, the consciousness of duty, and being busy, will I hope support me. I shall write to you, my friend, from my seat. I am to be there only about three weeks."

Soon after his arrival in Ayrshire, Boswell presented to the vacant living Mr. John Lindsay, a probationer from Edinburgh. The appointment was not distasteful to the parishioners. Returning to the metropolis he issued, in July, the second edition of his "Life of Johnson," in three octavo volumes; it contained "eight sheets of additional matter," and was improved otherwise. In the *Advertisement* he wrote as follows:—

> "It seems to me in my moments of self-complacency, that this extensive biographical work, however inferior in the nature, may in one respect be assimilated to the 'Odyssey.' Amidst a thousand entertaining and instructive episodes, the hero is never long out of sight, for they are all in some degree

connected with him; and he, in the whole course of the history, is exhibited by the author for the best advantage of his readers:

'Quid virtus et quid sapientia possit,
Utile proposuit nobis exemplar Ulyssem.'

> Should there be any cold-blooded or morose mortals who really dislike this book I will give them a story to apply. When the great Duke of Marlborough, accompanied by Lord Cadogan, was one day reconnoitring the army in Flanders, a heavy rain came on and they both called for their cloaks. Lord Cadogan's servant, a good-humoured, alert lad, brought his lordship's in a minute; the Duke's servant, a lazy, sulky dog, was so sluggish that his Grace, being wet to the skin, reproved him, and had for an answer, with a grunt, 'I came as fast as I could;' upon which the Duke calmly said, 'Cadogan! I would not for a thousand pounds have that fellow's temper.'"

> "There are some men I believe, who have, or think they have, a very small share of vanity. Such may speak of their literary fame in a decorous style of diffidence; but I confess that I am so formed by nature and by habit that to restrain the expression of delight on having obtained such fame, to me would be truly painful. Why, then, should I suppress it? Why, out of the 'abundance of the heart,' should I not speak? Let me then mention, with a warm but no insolent exultation, that I have been regaled with spontaneous praise of my work by many and various persons eminent for their rank, learning, talents, and accomplishments, much of which praise I leave under their hands to be reposited in my archives at Auchinleck. An honourable and reverend friend, speaking of the favourable reception of my volume, even in the circles of fashion and elegance, said to me, 'You have made them all talk Johnson.' Yes, I may add, I have *Johnsonized* the land; and I trust they will not only talk, but think Johnson."

No sooner was the second edition of his work on the publisher's shelves than Boswell was again involved in the meshes of dissipation. Sauntering forth, quite drunk, he was knocked down and robbed. Some weeks after the event he communicated with Mr. Temple as follows:—

> "Behold my hand! The robbery is only of a few shillings, but the cut on my head and bruises on my arms were sad things, and confined me to my bed in pain and fever and helplessness, as a child many days. By means of surgeon Earle and apothecary Devaynes, I am now, I thank God, pretty well.

> This, however, shall be a crisis in my life. I trust I shall henceforth be a sober, regular man. Indeed, my indulgence in wine has, of late years especially, been excessive. You remember what Lord Eliot said, nay, what you, I am sorry to think, have seen. Your suggestion as to my being carried off in a state of intoxication is awful. I thank you for it, my dear friend. It impressed me much, I assure you."

In a letter to Mr. Temple, dated 31st May, 1794, Boswell again expresses his appreciation of his friend's remonstrances:—

> "I thank you sincerely for your friendly admonition on my frailty in indulging so much in wine. I do resolve anew to be upon my guard, as I am sensible how very pernicious as well as disreputable such a habit is. How miserably have I yielded to it in various years. Recollect what General Paoli said to you—recollect what happened to Berwick."

A constitution naturally robust had been severely taxed. Boswell imbibed liquor of all sorts, and like other dissipated persons, fell into bouts of drinking. When he partially abstained, he unconsciously prepared himself for inebriate practices of a more aggravated character. At length he became a victim to these social excesses. Early in the spring of 1795, Mr. Temple, junior, then an inmate of Boswell's house, wrote to his father: "A few nights ago Mr. Boswell returned from the Literary Club quite weak and languid." Such is our first intimation of an illness, which terminated fatally. About the beginning of April he commenced a letter to Mr. Temple in these words:— "My dear Temple,—I would fain write to you in my own hand, but really cannot." Boswell dropped the pen, which was taken up by his son James, who thus wrote to his dictation:—

> "Alas, my friend, what a state is this! My son James is to write for me what remains of this letter, and I am to dictate. The pain which continued for so many weeks was very severe indeed, and when it went off I thought myself quite well; but I soon felt a conviction that I was by no means as I should be— so exceedingly weak, as my miserable attempt to write to you affords a full proof. All, then, that can be said is, that I must wait with patience."

After referring to Mr. Temple's own indisposition, Boswell concludes by representing himself as "a good deal stronger," and subscribing himself "here and hereafter" his correspondent's "affectionate friend." A postscript, added by James Boswell, jun., informed Mr. Temple that his father was ignorant of his "dangerous situation." The letter was kept up, and another addition, dated 8th April, represented the patient as "in a state of extraordinary pain and weakness," but as "having a good deal recovered."

The improvement was temporary. After a few days Boswell suffered a relapse. On the 17th April, his younger son wrote to Mr. Temple as follows:—

> "My father desires me to tell you that on Tuesday evening he was taken ill with a fever, attended with a severe shivering and violent headache, disorder in his stomach and throwing up; he has been close confined to bed ever since. He thinks himself better to-day, but cannot conjecture when he shall recover. His affection for you remains the same. You will receive a long and full letter from him."

On the 4th of May, David Boswell communicated to Mr. Temple that his brother was in "the most imminent danger." On the 18th of the same month, James Boswell, jun., reported that his father was "considerably worse," and that there were "little or no hopes of his recovery." Next day David Boswell reported to Mr. Temple that the end had come:—

> "I have now," he writes, "the painful task of informing you that my dear brother expired this morning at two o'clock: we have both lost a kind and affectionate friend, and I shall never have such another. He has suffered a great deal during his illness, which has lasted five weeks, but not much in his last moments."

Boswell died in his house in Great Portland Street, on the 19th May, 1795. He had reached his fifty-fifth year. In the June number of the *Gentleman's Magazine* his friends, Messrs. Courtenay and Malone, presented estimates of his character. Mr. Courtenay wrote thus:—

> "Good nature was highly predominant in his character. He appeared to entertain sentiments of benevolence to all mankind, and it does not seem to me that he ever did or could injure any human being *intentionally*. His conversational talents were always pleasing and often fascinating. He was a Johnson in everything but *manner*; and there were few of Dr. Johnson's friends that were not very ready to dispense with *that*. His attachment to the Doctor for so long a period was a meritorious perseverance in the desire of knowledge." Admitting that his social habits had shortened his life, Mr. Courtenay adds,—"As his belief in Revelation was unshaken,

and his religious impressions were deep and recurring frequently, let us hope that he has now attained that state from which imperfection and calamity are alike excluded."

From the misrepresentations of a journalist Mr. Malone vindicated the memory of his friend in these words:—

> "The most important misrepresentation is that Mr. Boswell was convivial without being *social* or *friendly*,—a falsehood which all who knew him intimately can peremptorily contradict. He had not only an inexhaustible fund of good humour and good nature, but was extremely warm in his attachments, and as ready to exert himself for his friends as any man." After claiming for Boswell "considerable intellectual powers," he concludes,—"He will long be regretted by a wide circle of friends, to whom his good qualities and social talents always made his company a valuable accession; and by none more sincerely than by the present vindicator of his fame."

In the same number of the *Gentleman's Magazine*, a correspondent, subscribing himself "M. Green," states that Boswell contemplated the publication of a quarto volume, to be embellished with plates on the controversy occasioned by the *Beggar's Opera*. "With this particular view," he adds, "he lately paid several visits to the present truly humane 'governor of Newgate,' as he ordinarily styled Mr. Kirby."

In a subsequent number of the *Gentleman's Magazine*, Mr. Temple, under the signature of "Biographicus," denied a statement by Mr. Malone that Boswell was of a melancholy temperament; he maintained that he was quite otherwise prior to his attachment to Dr. Johnson. J. B. R., another writer in the same magazine, remarked that the deceased "had many failings and many virtues and many amiable qualities, which predominated over the frailties incident to human nature."

Boswell's Will, written with his own hand, and bearing date 28th May, 1785, was found in his repositories. It is now printed for the first time.[99] Had it earlier been made public the testator might have encountered "less obloquy," and obtained greater praise. Seldom has Scottish landlord evinced greater consideration for his tenantry and domestics. The document is as follows:—

> "I James Boswell Esquire of Auchinleck having already settled everything concerning my Landed Estate so far as is in my power as an heir of Entail, so that my mind is quiet respecting my dear wife and children, do now when in perfect soundness of mind but under the apprehension of some

danger to my life which however may prove a false alarm, thus make my last Will and Testament containing also clauses of another nature which I desire may be valid and effectual. I resign my soul to God my almighty and most merciful Father trusting that it will be redeemed by the awfull and mysterious Sacrifice of our Lord Jesus Christ and admitted to endless felicity in heaven. I request that my body may be interred in the family burial place in the church of Auchinleck. I appoint my much valued spouse Mrs. Margaret Montgomerie and my worthy friend Sir William Forbes of Pitsligo, Baronet, to be my Executors and in case of the death of either of them the office shall devolve solely to the survivor. And whereas my honoured and pious grand mother Lady Elizabeth Boswell devised to the heir succeeding to the barrony of Auchinleck from generation to generation the Ebony Cabinet and the dressing plate of silver gilt, which belonged to her mother Veronica, Countess of Kincardine, leaving it however optional to her son my father that entail thereof or not as he should think fit, and he having neglected to do so, whereby the said Ebony Cabinet and dressing plate are now at my free disposal, I do by these presents dispose the same to the heir succeeding to the barrony of Auchinleck from generation to generation. And I declare that it shall not be in the power of any such heir to alienate or impignorate the same on any account whatever. And I do hereby dispose to the said heirs of Entail in their order, all lands and heritages belonging to me, in fee simple, after payment of my debts, but under this provision, that in case any of them shall alienate the said Ebony Cabinet and dressing plate, the person so alienating shall forfeit the sum of One Thousand Pounds sterling, which shall be paid to the next heir succeeding by entail. And I declare that the heir of Entail first succeeding to these my unentailed lands, shall within six months after his succession thereto execute a deed of Entail thereof to the same series of heirs with that in the Entail executed by my Father and me, which if he fails to do they shall then go to the next heir of Entail, and it is also an express condition that he shall divest himself of the field thereof and reserve only his life-rent. I mean this to apply to the said first succeeding heir. Furthermore as my late honoured Father made a very curious collection of the classics and other books, which it is desireable should be preserved for ever in the family of Auchinleck, I do by these presents dispose to the successive heirs of Entail of the barrony of Auchinleck" [here there is a word torn off] "Greek and Latin books, as also all manuscripts of whatever kind, lying in the house of Auchinleck, under the same conditions and under the same forfeiture as I have mentioned with regard to the Ebony Cabinet and dressing plate, and all my other moveable Estate or Executory I leave equally among my other children, the furniture in the house of Auchinleck to be valued by two sworn appreazers, and the heir to keep it at that value and pay the same to my younger children, excepting however all my pictures which I dispose to the said successive heirs of Entail under the same conditions and forfeiture as above mentioned, and excepting also the furniture in my house at Edinburgh which I bequeath to my dear wife. I bequeath one hundred pounds sterling to my dear brother Thomas David Boswell Esquire banker in London, to purchase a piece of plate to keep in remembrance of me in his family and to my dear brother Lieutenant John Boswell being a batchelor, I bequeath Fifty Guineas to purchase a ring or whatever other thing he may like best to keep for my sake. To my friends the Reverend Mr. Temple in Cornwall, John Johnston Esquire of Grange, Sir John Dick Baronet, Sir William Forbes of Pitsligo, Baronet, Captain John Macbryde of the Royal Navy, and Mr. Charles Dilly of London, bookseller, Alexander Fairlie of Fairlie, Esq. and Edmund Malone Esq. of the kingdom of Ireland, The Hon. Colonel James Stewart and George Dempster Esquire, I bequeath each a gold mourning ring, and I hereby leave to the said Sir William Forbes, the Reverend Mr. Temple and Edmund Malone Esquire all my manuscripts of my own composition, and all my letters from various persons to be published for the benefit of my younger children, as they shall decide, that is to say they are to have a discretionary power to publish more or less. I leave to Mr. James Bruce my overseer Twenty Pounds yearly during his life and if he shall continue to reside at Auchinleck I leave to him the house he now possesses with his meal and all other perquisites. And to Mrs. Bell Bruce my housekeeper I leave Ten pounds yearly during her life with two pecks of meal weekly in case of her not liveing in the family of Auchinleck. Lastly, as there are upon the estate of Auchinleck several tenants whose families have possessed their farms for many generations, I do by these presents grant leases for nineteen years and their respective lifetimes of their present farms to John Templeton in Hopland, James Murdoch in Blackstown commonly called the Raw, James Peden in Old Byre, William

Samson in Mill of Auchinleck, John Hird in Hirdstown, William Murdoch in Willocks town, and to any of the sons of the late James Caldow in Stivenstown whom the ministers and elders of Auchinleck shall approve of, a lease of that farm in the above terms, the rents to be fixed by two men to be mutually chosen by the laird of Auchinleck for the time and each tenant. I also grant a lease in the like terms to Andrew Dalrymple in Mains of Auchinleck, my Baron officer. And I do beseech all the succeeding heirs of Entail to be kind to the Tenants and not to turn out old possessors to get a little more rent. And in case my nomination of Tutors and Curators to my children being written upon unstamped paper should not be valid, I here again constitute and appoint my dear wife, Mrs. Margaret Montgomerie and my worthy friend Sir William Forbes of Pitsligo, or the survivor of them, to the said office with all usual powers and with the recommendations contained in the said unstamped deed. In witness whereof, these presents written with my own hand (of which I consent to the registration in the books of Council and Session that they may have full effect and thereto constitute my procurators) are subscribed by me at London this twenty eight day of May, One thousand Seven hundred and Eighty five, before these witnesses Mr. Edward Dilly bookseller there, and Mr. John Normaville his clerk. (signed) James Boswell. Chs. Dilly witness, John Normaville witness."

The three persons nominated as literary executors did not meet, and the entire business of the trust was administered by Sir William Forbes, Bart., who appointed as his law agent Robert Boswell, writer to the signet, cousin german of the deceased. By that gentleman's advice, Boswell's manuscripts were left to the disposal of his family; and it is believed that the whole were immediately destroyed. The *Commonplace Book* escaped, having been incidentally sold among the printed books.

The following inventory of Boswell's moveable effects, presented for registration in the Commissariat Register is not without interest:

"In the first place there pertained and belonged to the said defunct at the time aforesaid of his death, the articles aftermentioned of the values underwritten, whereof the Executor herein gives up in inventary the sum of Twenty Shillings sterling of the value of each article viz., Imprimis Four hundred and eighty three pounds fourteen shillings as the amount of sales of furniture books pictures &c. in the defunct's house in London. Item, Five hundred and Seventy six pounds eight shillings and two pence as the value of furniture in the house of Auchinleck estimated by two sworn appraisers. Item, One hundred and five pounds as the value of silver plate at Auchinleck exclusive of the family plate devised to the heir estimated at or near the bullion value. Item, One hundred pounds supposed about the value of the books at Auchinleck per catalogue in the hands of the Executor exclusive of Greek and Latin classics and manuscripts there, also left to the heir. Item, Seventy seven pounds three shillings as the value of cattle and stocking at Auchinleck per estimate in the hands of the Executor. Item, Three hundred pounds as the value of the remaining copies of the Life of Dr Johnson written by the defunct and sold to Mr. Dilly bookseller. And One hundred pounds as the supposed value of manuscripts left by the defunct.

"In the second place there was indebted and owing to the said defunct at the time aforesaid of his death, the sums of money after mentioned for the reasons after specified, viz., One Pound sterling part of the sum of Ninety Seven Pounds eight shillings and Eleven pence sterling being a balance of cash in the hands of Mr Thomas David Boswell brother to the defunct per accompt. Item, One pound sterling, part of the sum of Ninety one pounds sixteen shillings and six pence being a claim Mr Alexander Boswell the heir for cash advanced to him by Mr Thomas David Boswell at the time of the defunct's death and credited to Mr Thomas David Boswell in his account with the Executor. Item, One pound Sterling part of the sum of Two hundred and twenty five pounds fourteen shillings and three pence as arrears of rent of the estate of Auchinleck for accounts transmitted by the factor. Item, One pound sterling part of the sum of Nine hundred and forty two pounds six shillings and seven pence sterling as the claim against the heirs of said estate under the Entail act for three fourths of the defunct's expenditure in improving the Entailed estate bearing interest from Martinmas seventeen hundred and ninety five. Item, One pound sterling, part of the sum of nine hundred and fifty pounds sterling as half a year's rent of said estate due to the Executor by law for the year Seventeen hundred and ninety five, being the year in which the defunct died per rental furnished by the factor. Item, one Pound sterling part of the sum of forty two pounds nine shillings and one penny being a balance of account due by Mr Dilly, bookseller. Item, One pound sterling, part of the sum of six hundred and eighty four pounds sixteen shillings and eight pence being debt due by Captn Bruce Boswell of Calcutta of Principal and Interest paid to the Executor since the defunct's death. Item, One pound sterling, part of the sum of one hundred and ninety five pounds sterling being a balance of debt due by the Trustees of the late Mr Johnston of Grange, as stated by the defunct in a holograph view of his affairs made out by him, as at the first day of January Seventeen hundred and ninety five. And One pound sterling, part of the sum of seven hundred pounds sterling and upwards of debts due from various turnpike roads in Ayrshire for money advanced by the late Lord Auchinleck."

In the terms of his Will, Boswell's remains were conveyed to Auchinleck, and there deposited in the family vault. Robert Boswell proposed that a memorial tablet should be placed at his grave and offered the following metrical inscription:—

"Here Boswell lies! drop o'er his tomb a tear,
Let no malignant tongue pursue him here;
Bury his failings in the silent grave,
And from unfriendly hands his memory save.
Record the praise he purchased, let his name
Mount on the wings of literary fame,
And to his honour say,—'Here Boswell lies,
Whose pleasing pen adorned the good and wise,
Whose memory down the stream of time shall flow
Far as famed Johnson's or Paoli's go!'"

Robert Boswell's proposal was not entertained, and the preceding epitaph was found among his papers after his own decease many years subsequently. By his descendants the memory of Johnson's biographer has not been honoured, yet the family of Boswell, with a pedigree dating from the Conquest, cannot point to a more distinguished kinsman.

The marriage of persons nearly related by blood is apt to engender cerebral weakness in the offspring. The first-born of cousins-german, James Boswell suffered from an imperfect and morbid organization. Mr. Carlyle's analysis of his mental condition we cordially accept, "The highest [quality]," writes Mr. Carlyle, "lay side by side with the lowest, not morally combined with it and spiritually transfiguring it, but tumbling in half-mechanical juxtaposition with it; and from time to time, as the mad alternative chanced, irradiating it, or eclipsed by it." Around his intellectual nature hovered a dark cloud, while there was light within; the cloud was malformation or disease, but the morbid element did not extinguish the internal fire. Boswell's perceptive power was of the highest order; he could retain and reproduce scenes and conversations with the naturalness of reality. A literary Pre-Raffaelite, his observation was acute in proportion as his reflective powers waned or slept; what he saw and heard he set forth forcibly and without embellishment. The assertion of Lord Macaulay that the "Life of Johnson" was due to the author's weakness requires no serious refutation. Boswell produced the best biography in the language, because he was the best fitted for the task. Like the astronomer who points his telescope to the heavens in a darkened room, he concentrated his mental energies on the objects of his reverence, and with photographic accuracy depicted all that he surveyed. In proportion as he failed to develop his own intellectual nature, he succeeded in delineating the intellectual character of others. A mirror true and transparent lay under the opaque cloud, and reflected outward what a healthier intellect had appropriated and transfused. If in respect of mental phenomena the figure is admissible—the reflective faculty which is ordinarily concave and thereby receptive, was in the mind of Boswell convex and radiating outwards. The cords which fettered his understanding braced his perception and nerved his memory. He showed strength in weakness. The dry rod budded. The grey ruin was mantled by the green ivy.

The fool prates unconscious of his folly; the maniac is happy in his chain. Boswell was conscious of his weakness,—hence his habitual melancholy. To Mr. Temple he early spoke of madness existing in his family, and afterwards described himself as partially insane. In his journal he compares his head to a tavern usurped by low punch drinkers, whom he could not displace. Such an unhappy consciousness might have led to reckless perversity, or hopeless inaptitude. In Boswell it stimulated to untiring effort, life-long energy. His vanity and vacillation and rashness were attendant on a distempered brain—his literary achievements were the result of a successful conflict with constitutional disorder.

Boswell lived at a period when social excesses, especially in North Britain, prevailed greatly. Into these excesses he fell, but he freely acknowledged his errors, and sincerely repented. Ambitious of personal honour, he nevertheless promoted sedulously the interests of others. A fervid patriot, he was an obliging neighbour, a generous companion, and an unfailing friend. He exercised an abundant hospitality. Angry at times he was easily reconciled, and hastened to forgive. His religious views, long unfixed, were never wholly obscured; he passed through the ordeals of credulity and scepticism, and at length returning to his old moorings, determined to know nothing but a Saviour crucified. In his Will, prepared within the retirement of his closet, he made this record of his trust,—"I resign my soul to God, my almighty and most merciful Father, trusting that it will be redeemed by the awful and mysterious sacrifice of our Lord Jesus Christ, and admitted to eternal felicity in heaven." Dr. Johnson, who knew his weaknesses, commended his piety, and Sir William Forbes, another enlightened judge of human character, has borne concerning him this testimony:—

> "I have known few men who possessed a stronger sense of piety, or more fervent devotion (tinctured no doubt with some little share of superstition, which had probably been in some degree fostered by his habits of intimacy with Dr. Johnson), perhaps not always sufficient to regulate his imagination or direct his conduct, yet still genuine, and founded both in his understanding and his heart."[100]

Of Boswell's personal aspects, the full length portrait by Langton, engraved for this volume, is understood to convey a correct representation. Rather above the middle height, and inclined to corpulency, he walked with a stately gait, and in his costume observed the latest fashion. He had a large head, and wore a powdered wig; his prominent but well set features beamed with perpetual good humour. "It was impossible," remarked a contemporary, "to look in his face without being moved by the comicality which always reigned upon it."[101] He talked much and with rapidity, but his observant faculty was not apparent to those who only met him in society.

Boswell left two sons and three daughters; James, the younger son, entered Brazenose College, Oxford, of which he was elected a fellow upon the Vinerian foundation. He was afterwards called to the English Bar, and became a Commissioner of Bankruptcy. An accomplished scholar and of industrious habits, he was by Mr. Malone appointed his literary executor. Under his care appeared Mr. Malone's enlarged edition of Shakespeare, completed in 1821, in twenty-one octavo volumes. In the first volume he defended, in an able and ingenious essay, Mr. Malone's reputation from an attack made on his statements and opinions by a writer of eminence. He inherited his father's *bonhommie* and love of sociality. He died unmarried in the Middle Temple, London, on the 24th February, 1822, aged forty-three; his remains were deposited in the Temple Church. By his elder brother his death was lamented in these lines,—

"There is a pang when kindred spirits part,

And cold philosophy we must disown;

There is a thrilling spot in every heart,

For pulses beat not from a heart of stone.

"Boswell, th' allotted earth has closed on thee,

Thy mild but generous warmth has passed away:

A finer spirit never death set free,

And now the friend we honour'd is but clay.

"His was the triumph of the heart and mind,

His was the lot which few are blessed to know:

More proved, more valued—fervent, yet so kind,

He never lost one friend, nor found one foe."

Alexander Boswell, the biographer's elder son, succeeded to the family estate. He studied at Westminster School, and the University of Oxford; and, after making the tour of Europe settled at Auchinleck. A lover of historical and antiquarian learning, he established a private printing-press, and reproduced many rare tracts preserved in the family library. Early devoted to poetical composition, he published several volumes of poetry and song. His poems abound in drollery, but are generally fragmentary. Of his songs, "Jenny's Bawbee," "Jenny Dang the Weaver," "The Lass o' Isla," and "Bannocks o' Barley Meal," have long been popular. To public affairs he devoted no inconsiderable attention. He was in the Conservative interest elected M.P. for Ayrshire, and became Colonel of the Yeomanry Cavalry, in the same county. He originated the proposal of erecting a public monument to the poet Burns, on the banks of the Doon, and raised £2,000 on behalf of the undertaking. In 1821 his patriotism and public enterprise were rewarded by a Baronetcy. His career terminated under painful circumstances. Indulging a tendency to sarcasm, he published in a Glasgow newspaper a severe pasquinade against Mr. James Stuart, younger of Dunearn, a leader of the liberal party at Edinburgh. Challenged by Mr. Stuart to mortal combat, he accepted the *cartel*, and the parties met at Auchtertool, Fifeshire. Sir Alexander fell, the bullet from his opponent's pistol having entered the middle of the right clavicle, which it severely fractured. He lingered till the following day. His death took place on the 27th March, 1822, and his remains were interred at Auchinleck. In the following verses, John Goldie, an Ayrshire poet, celebrated his obsequies:—

"O! heard you the trumpet sound sad on the gale,
  O! heard you the voice of weeping and wail?
  O! saw you the horsemen in gallant array,
  As in sorrow and silence they moved on their way.

"The people's deep wailing, the trumpet's shrill tone,
  Were the breathings of sorrow for him that is gone;

And yon dark plumes of death that did mournfully wave,
Deck'd the bier that bore on their lov'd chief to the grave.

"When the train of lone mourners arrived at the path,
That leads to the desolate mansions of death,
O! marked you each horseman lean sad on his sword,
When the corse slowly passed of the chief he adored.

"And mark'd you each manly heart heave with a sigh;
And mark'd you the tear-drop that gush'd in each eye
Of those who were robed in the garments of woe,
When they saw him in Death's dreary mansion laid low.

"Thy halls, Auchinleck! are all desolate now,
Aye! roll on in sorrow, in solitude flow;
For low lies thy bard who so sweetly did sing,—
Thy chieftain so true to his country and king."[102]

Sir Alexander married in November, 1799, Grace, fifth daughter of Thomas Cumming, banker, Edinburgh, representative of the ancient family of Erenside. By this marriage he became father of one son and three daughters. Grace Theresa, the eldest daughter, married Sir William Francis Eliott, Bart., of Stobs, and became mother of the present baronet, with other issue. Grace Jane died in childhood, and Margaret Emily, the youngest daughter, is wife of Major-General Vassall, and resides at Balhary, Perthshire. James, only son of Sir Alexander Boswell, was born in December, 1806. He studied at Brazenose College, Oxford, and after succeeding to Auchinleck resided chiefly on his estate. In 1830 he espoused his cousin, Jessie Jane, elder daughter of Sir James Montgomery Cunningham, Bart., of Corsehill; of which marriage were born two daughters. In 1850, Sir James Boswell instituted a legal process to prove the invalidity of the Auchinleck entail. He was opposed by Thomas Alexander Boswell, of Crawley Grange, next heir-male, but it was held by the judges that as the material word "irredeemably" was written upon an erasure, the entail was inoperative.[103] Relieved from the settlement of 1776, Sir James Boswell bequeathed Auchinleck to his two daughters as co-heiresses. Sir James died in 1857 when the baronetcy became extinct. Julia, his elder daughter, married George Mounsey, solicitor, Carlisle, some time mayor of that city. Emily Harriet, the younger daughter, married in 1873, the Hon. Richard Wogan Talbot, eldest son of Lord Talbot de Malahide.

The biographer's three daughters were Veronica, Euphemia, and Elizabeth. Veronica, the eldest, survived her father only four months; she died of consumption on the 26th September, 1795, aged twenty-three. Euphemia, the second daughter, inherited her father's literary tastes, combined, unhappily, with cerebral weakness. Leaving the protection of her family she fixed her abode in London, resolved on supporting herself as an operatic writer. She composed an Opera for Drury Lane Theatre, which, according to her narrative, was accepted by the manager, and was being prepared for the stage, when the theatre was in 1809 destroyed by fire. Thereafter, she made eleemosynary appeals by private letters and public advertisements. She entreated pecuniary aid from the Lord Chancellor Eldon, the Earl of Moira, Lord Lonsdale, and Lord Sidmouth. On the death of the Princess Amelia, in 1810, she composed a "Soliloquy," which she forwarded to the Prince Regent, in the belief that she would be rewarded by a pension on the Civil List. From private lodgings in Northumberland street she in 1811 despatched a missive, setting forth that being "neglected by those bound by the ties of blood to cherish her," she had "pledged her pianoforte,—though a composer is as much at a loss for an instrument as a carpenter without his tools." In another letter of the same year she writes, "If dragged to a jail, which must be my fate, I shudder at it, and implore your aid."

"Let me not suffer Otway's fate,
When Nelly's[104] tears were sent too late:
Where Genius pierced through darkest gloom,
Though hungry Death has marked his tomb."

The charge of neglect preferred against her relatives by this unhappy gentlewoman having obtained some credit, we have instituted on the subject a careful inquiry. Euphemia Boswell, we find, was the victim of a diseased imagination. By her relatives she was regarded with affectionate solicitude, while they severely suffered from her painful hallucinations and groundless complaints. She died about the age of sixty. In her Will she expressed a desire that her remains should be deposited in Westminster, Abbey near the grave of Dr. Johnson. She was buried elsewhere. She composed a small work which she dedicated to Bishop Porteous; no copy has been found.

Elizabeth, the biographer's youngest daughter, married 23rd December, 1799, her second cousin, William Boswell, advocate, who became Sheriff of Berwickshire. Of this marriage were born three sons and one daughter. Robert Cramond, the eldest son, died in 1821, shortly after being admitted advocate. James Paoli, second son, joined the army, and died in India in 1820; Bruce, the third son, also joined the army, and attained the rank of Colonel. The daughter, Elizabeth Margaret Montgomery, married November, 1849, John Williams, of H.E.I.C's. Civil Service, Bombay, who died in 1853. Mrs. Elizabeth Boswell died 1st January, 1814; her husband in January, 1841. On the death of Thomas Alexander Boswell, son of the biographer's brother, Thomas David, in March, 1852,[105] the fine estates of Crawley Grange, Buckinghamshire,[106] and Astwood, Berkshire, together worth nearly £2,000 per annum, became possessed by Colonel Bruce Boswell, who dying in

October, 1856, was succeeded by his sister, who survives. Mrs. Williams was mother of twin sons, who died in infancy; her only surviving child, Elizabeth Anne, was married in 1860 to the Rev. Charles Cumberlye, who assumed the name of Ware on the death of his grand-uncle, Mr. Samuel Ware. Mr. Cumberlye Ware died in May, 1870, and his widow in March, 1871. Their family consist of one son and three daughters. The son, Charles Edward Ware, is precluded by a family settlement from succeeding to the maternal property, and the heiress of Crawley Grange is Edith Caroline, his eldest sister, who, on succession, will assume the name of Boswell. The two younger daughters, Elizabeth Mary and Catherine Augusta, retain the family name of Cumberlye.

William Boswell, Advocate and Sheriff of Berwickshire, who married the youngest daughter of the biographer, was eldest of four sons of Robert Boswell, the biographer's cousin-german, and law agent under his will. This gentleman was born at Auchinleck House, on the 19th January, 1740; his father was Dr. John Boswell, younger brother of Lord Auchinleck, and his mother, Anne, daughter of Robert Cramond, of Auldbar, Forfarshire. Robert Boswell was a writer to the signet, in Edinburgh; he subsequently held office as Lyon Depute, and latterly removed to London. Possessed of literary tastes and unflagging industry, he qualified himself to read the Scriptures in the original tongues. He composed hymns, some of which were after his decease printed for private circulation. His metrical epitaph on his cousin, the biographer, has been quoted. Eminently pious, he exhorted publicly. He died at London in April, 1804, in his 65th year.

Alexander Boswell, writer to the Signet, second son of Robert Boswell, was father of the Rev. Robert Bruce Boswell, chaplain to the Honourable East India Company and minister of St. James's church, Calcutta.[107] The son of that reverend gentleman, John Alexander Corrie Boswell, held an appointment in the Honourable East India Company's Madras Civil Service; he died some years ago. His son, Henry St. George Boswell, now resident in London, is male representative of the house of Boswell of Auchinleck. John James, third son of Robert Boswell, was admitted advocate, but afterwards became a physician, and entered the medical service of the Honourable East India Company; he latterly sought practice in Edinburgh, where he died in August, 1839. Major John James Boswell, his only surviving son, commands the 2nd Regiment of Punjaub Infantry, at Dera Ghazee Khan, in India. John Campbell, fourth son of Robert Boswell, was a physician in India; he died at Penang, *s. p.* in October, 1841. Miss Charlotte Maria Tucker, granddaughter of Robert Boswell, is under her *nom de plume*, A. L. O. E., well known for her valuable contributions to religious literature.

Concerning James Boswell's maternal ancestors, a few particulars may be acceptable. Charles Erskine, of Alva, son of the Hon. Charles Erskine, fifth son of John, seventh Earl of Mar, was created a baronet of Nova Scotia on the 30th April, 1666. Charles, his third son, was a lord of session, with the judicial designation of Lord Tinwald, and was father of James Erskine, a lord of session, by the title of Lord Alva. Lieutenant-General Sir Henry Erskine, Bart., grandson of the first baronet, was many years M.P. for the Anstruther burghs; he composed the popular song, "The Garb of Old Gaul." He died in 1765, and was succeeded in the baronetcy by James, his eldest son, who assumed the surname of St. Clair, and on the death of his uncle, Alexander Wedderburn, first Earl of Rosslyn in 1805, became the second Earl.

Colonel John Erskine, a younger son of the Hon. Sir Charles Erskine, first baronet of Alva, and brother of Lord Tinwald, married Euphemia, daughter of William Cochrane, of Ochiltree, of the noble house of Dundonald, and his wife Lady Mary Bruce, eldest daughter of the second Earl of Kincardine. Two daughters of this marriage became memorable. Euphemia, the younger, was the first wife of Lord Auchinleck, and mother of James Boswell, who by maternal descent was great-great-grandson of John, seventh Earl of Mar.

Mary, eldest daughter of Colonel John Erskine, married in 1739 the Rev. Alexander Webster, D.D., minister of the Tolbooth Church, Edinburgh. Connected with this marriage is a romantic incident. Prior to his settlement at Edinburgh Dr. Webster was minister of Culross, Perthshire. Mary Erskine resided in that parish with her aunt Lady Preston, wife of Sir George Preston, Bart., of Valleyfield. A young gentleman of the neighbourhood was attracted by her charms, but being unsuccessful in his addresses, begged Dr. Webster to intercede on his behalf. The Doctor consented, and waiting on Miss Erskine, pled his friend's cause with energy. The lady listened patiently but expressed a decided negative. "Had you spoken as well for yourself," she added, "I might have answered differently." To his friend Dr. Webster reported the particulars of the interview, and soon afterwards presented himself at Valleyfield to plead his own suit. The lady complied, but her relations consented with reluctance. The marriage took place on the 13th June, 1737; Miss Erskine possessing a dowry of £4,000. Elated by his good fortune Dr. Webster celebrated his helpmate in a song, which, published in the *Scots Magazine* for November, 1747, became popular. It commenced thus,—

"O how could I venture to love one like thee,
And you not despise a poor conquest like me?
On lords, thy admirers, could look wi' disdain,
And knew I was naething, yet pitied my pain?
You said while they teased you with nonsense and dress,
'When real the passion, the vanity's less,'

You saw through that silence which others despise,
And while beaux we're a-talking read love in my eyes."

Through his successful wooing Dr. Webster was led to devise the Ministers' Widows Fund, so as to raise the social *status* of his clerical brethren. In 1755 the first enumeration of the people of Scotland was conducted under his superintendence. He proposed the enlargement of the city of Edinburgh by the erection of the new town. In the Highlands and islands he promoted agricultural improvement. By his wife he was energetically aided in works of active benevolence. He died in 1784, having survived his helpmate eighteen years.

BOSWELLIANA.

"MY father had all along so firm, so dry a mind, that religious principles, however carefully inculcated by his father and mother, and however constantly they remained on the surface, never incorporated with his thoughts, never penetrated into the seat of his affections. They were a dead range, not a quickset hedge. The fence had a good appearance enough, and was sufficiently strong; but it never flourished in green luxuriance, never blossomed, never bore fruit. The ground within, however, produced plentiful crops of useful exertions as a judge, and improvements as a landed ^{laird} gentleman. And let it be considered that there may be a fine fence round barren, unprofitable land."

24th Sept., 1780.

"Maclaurin[108] maintained that bashfulness was the compound effect of vanity and sensibility.[109] Nichols contended that it was quite corporeal, for the same man will be at one time bashful, and at another time quite easy. 'That is,' said Maclaurin, 'he has at one time a higher notion of himself than at another.' 'No,' said Nichols, 'it is a trick which the nerves play to the imagination.'"

23rd Sept., 1780.

"My friend Johnston[110] advised me to have our family crest, a hawk, cut upon a pebble which I found on the channel of the Lugar, which runs by Auchinleck. Said he, 'Let him perch on his native stone.'"

22nd Sept., 1780.

"It is not unusual for men who have no real freindship(*sic*) nor principle to have at the same time so sanguine an opinion of their own abilities, that they imagine they can impose on others as if they were children. They will do them an essential injury, and at the same time try to persuade them that they have done only what was fair and right. They are like determined rogues, who first rob, and then blindfold you that you may not pursue them."

24th Sept., 1780.

"Nichols said one should never dispute with a woman, for she has not understanding enough to be convinced; at least, never will own herself in the wrong, and always will be angry with you."

22nd Sept., 1780.

"Nichols said he liked better to converse with women than with men of the greatest sense and knowledge. He owned he could gain no acquisition to his intellectual stock from them, but they diverted and cheered him. I said he had them like housemaids to sweep the cobwebs from his mind and give it a polish."

22nd Sept., 1780.

"A man who wishes just to be easy will always avoid those subjects which he has discovered are hard and puzzling. Nay, he will not even take the trouble to make the selection, but like a luxurious indolent eater, wherever he finds any piece in the least degree tough he will let it alone."

23rd Sept., 1780.

"Nichols said that a man of the *ton*, as the phrase is,—of high breeding, and fashionable air, has at first an irresistible superiority over plain men, others who have not such superficial advantages. He has a shake of the head which frightens you, but when you are once used to him you laugh at the shake."

23rd Sept., 1780.

"In winter 1779, after Scotland had been exhausted by raising new levies, Sir William Augustus Cunningham[111] boasted in the House of Commons that 20,000 men might yet be raised in that country and never be missed, either from manufactures or agriculture. The Hon. Henry Ershire[112] said he believed it was true. But they must be raised from the churchyards."

From himself.

"A ludicrous recruiting advertisement was given about in Edinburgh in 1778, inviting, amongst many other denominations, all man midwives to join the King's standard (repair to the drumhead and acquire glory). Mrs. Dundas, of Melville,[113] pleasantly asked if Dr. Young, the most eminent practitioner in midwifery, would enlist. 'No, madam,' said the Hon. Henry Erskine, 'he has already right to as great a title as he could acquire in the army.' 'Ay,' said she, 'what is that?' 'Madam,' said he, 'the deliverer of his country.'"

From himself.

"In 1780 there was published at Edinburgh an account of Lord George Gordon,[114] with his head. He was then in the Tower for high treason. Harry Erskine said, 'The next thing we shall have will be an account of Lord George Gordon without his head.'"

I was present.

"When Boswell was introduced to Mr. Samuel Johnson, who had a very great antipathy at the Scotch, 'Mr. Johnson,' said he, 'I come from Scotland, but I can't help it.' 'Sir,' said Johnson, 'that I find is what a very great many of your countrymen cannot help.'"[115]

"Lord Eglintoune[116] said that the hearts of the ladies were like a looking-glass, which will reflect an image of the object that is present, but retains no trace of what is absent."

I was present.

"Doctor Blair[117] asked Macpherson[118] why he lived in England, as he certainly could not be fond of John Bull. 'Sir', said he, 'I hate John Bull, but I love his daughters.'"

DOCTOR BLAIR.

"Boswell was walking with some ladies at Ranelagh, when a large young woman passed by. 'That lady,' said Boswell, 'has a great deal of beauty; it cannot, indeed, well be exprest, but it may be *felt*.'"

"Lady Fanny Montgomerie[119] met with a very handsome woman in the highlands of Scotland, who had so much simplicity of manner that she had never seen herself but in the water. Lady Fanny showed her a little pocket mirror, which gave her a clear view of her own face, and asked her if she ever had seen anything so handsome. 'Madam,' said she, 'by your asking that question I should imagine that your ladyship had never seen such a glass as this.'"

LORD EGLINTOUNE.

"Boswell was talking away one evening in St. James's Park with much vanity. Said his friend Temple, 'We have heard of many kinds of hobby-horses, but, Boswell, you ride upon yourself.'"

"A stupid fellow was declaiming against that kind of raillery called *roasting*, and was saying, I am sure I have a great deal of good nature; I never roast any. 'Why, sir,' said Boswell, 'you are an exceedingly good-natured man, to be sure; but I can give you a better reason for your never roasting any. Sir, you never roast any, because you have got no fire.'"

"A keen Scott (*sic*) [Dr. Ogilvie][120] was standing up for his country, and boasting that it had a great many noble wild prospects. 'Sir,' said Mr. Samuel Johnson, 'I believe you have a great many noble wild prospects. Norway, too, has got some prospects; and Lapland is remarkable for prodigious noble wild prospects. But, sir, I believe the noblest prospect that a Scotchman ever sees is the road which leads him to England.'"

I was present.

"When the Duke de Nivernais was sent ambassador from France to England, at the first inn in Britain he was charged a most extravagant bill. The people of the house being asked how they could use him so ill when he was a stranger, they replied that was the very reason; for as they chose to observe Scripture rules, 'He was a stranger,' said they, 'and we took him in.'"

CAPTAIN TEMPLE.[121]

"Boswell asked Mr. Samuel Johnson what was best to teach a gentleman's children first. 'Why, sir,' said he, 'there is no matter what you teach them first. It matters no more than which leg you put first into your bretches (*sic*). Sir, you may stand disputing which you shall put in first, but in the meantime your legs are bare. No matter which you put in first so that you put 'em both in, and then you have your bretches on. Sir, while you think which of two things to teach a child first, another boy, in the common course, has learnt both.'"

I was present.

"Mr. Samuel Johnson doubted much of the authenticity of the poems of Ossian. Doctor Blair asked him if he thought any man could describe these barbarous manners so well if he had not lived at the time and seen them. 'Any man, sir,' replied Mr. Johnson,—'any man, woman, or child might have done it.'"

DOCTOR BLAIR.

"Boswell was praising the English highly, and saying they were a fine open people. 'Oh,——,' said Macpherson, 'an open people! their mouths, indeed, are open to gluttony to fill their belly, but I know of no other openness they have.'"

I was present.

"Boswell was telling Mr. Samuel Johnson how Macpherson railed at all established systems. 'So would he tumble in a hog-stye,' said Mr. Johnson, 'as long as you look at him and cry to him to come out; but let him alone, never mind him, and he'll soon give it over.'"

"Hall,[122] the author of 'Crazy Tales,' said he could not bear David Hume for being such a monarchical dog. 'Is it not shocking,' said he, 'that a fellow who does not believe[fear] in God, should believe[fear] in a king?'"

MR. DEMPSTER.[123]

"Mr. Samuel Johnson, after being acquainted with Lord Chesterfield, said, 'I see now what this man is. I thought he had been a lord among wits, but I find he is only a wit among lords.'"

DOCTOR ROBERTSON.[124]

"Mr. Samuel Johnson was once at Windsor, and dined with the mayor. But the fellow (said he) not content with feeding my body, thought he must feed my mind too, and so he told me a long story how he had sent three criminals to the plantations. Tired to death with his nonsense, 'I wish (to God),' said Johnson, 'that I was the fourth.'"

MR. SHERIDAN.[125]

"A bishop was flattering Sir Robert Walpole[126] egregiously. A gentleman asked him how he could bear such fulsome stuff. 'Sir,' said he, 'if you were as severely scourged in the House of Commons as I am, you would be glad of any dog to lick your sores.'"

MR. DEMPSTER.

"An officer on the recruiting service made his regular returns to the regiment, in which he said that he had as yet got none, but that he had a man of six foot two in his eye. 'All nonsense!' said the colonel; 'recall him immediately. He has had that fellow in his eye these six years.'"

CAPTAIN WEBSTER.[127]

"Lord Chesterfield told a half-pay lieutenant that he would bring him back to full pay in the same rank. 'My lord,' said he, 'I detest the name of lieutenant so much that I would not be made Lord Lieutenant of Ireland.'"

A Stranger.

"Boswell said that a man is reckoned a wise man rather for what he does not say than for what he says. Perhaps upon the whole *Limbertongue* speaks a greater quantity of good sense than Manly does. But *Limbertongue* gives you such floods of frivolous nonsense that his sense is quite drowned. *Manly* gives you unmixed good sense only. *Manly* will always be thought the wisest man of the two."

"Dempster, who was a great republican, was presenting an address one day at court. He was hurt to see subordination prevail so much, and was shocked to see the keen and able Lord Marchmont[128] bowing just like the rest. He said he looked like a chained eagle at a gentleman's gate."

From himself.

"Mr. Samuel Johnson said that all sceptical innovators were vain men; and finding mankind allready (*sic*) in possession of Truth, they found they could not gratify their vanity in supporting her, and so they have taken to error. Truth (said he) is a cow which will yield such people no more milk, and so they are gone to milk the bull."

I was present.

"Captain Erskine[129] complained that Boswell's hand was so large, that his letters contained very little. My lines (said Boswell) are, like my ideas, very irregular, and at a great distance from each other."

"Sir W. Maxwell[130] said he was allways affraid (*sic*) of a clever man till he knew if he had good nature. 'Yes,' said Boswell; 'when you see a clever man you see a man brandishing a drawn sword, and you are uneasy till you know if he intends only to make it glitter in the sun, or to run you through the body with it.'"

"A robust Caledonian was telling (in the Scots pronunciation) that he was born in *Embro*. 'Indeed!' said an English physician: 'upon my word, the prettiest abortion I ever saw.'"

MR. CRAWFURD,[131] ROTTERDAM.

"Boswell said that men of lively fancies seldom tell a story so distinctly as those of slower capacity, as they confound the intellect with an excess of brilliancy. It is a common expression, I cannot see for the light. It may also be said, I cannot understand you; you shine so much."

"Boswell told Mr. Samuel Johnson that a gentleman of their acquaintance maintained in public company that he could see no distinction between virtue and vice. 'Sir,' said Mr. Johnson, 'does he intend that we should believe that he is lying, or that he is in earnest? If we think him a lyar, that is not honouring him very much. But if we think him in earnest, when he leaves our houses let us count our spoons.'"

"Mr. Sheridan, though a man of knowledge and parts, was a little fancifull (*sic*) in his projects for establishing oratory and altering the mode of British education. 'Mr. Samuel Johnson,' said Sherry, 'cannot abide me, for I allways ask him, Pray sir, what do you propose to do?'"

From MR. JOHNSON.

"Boswell was talking to Mr. Samuel Johnson of Mr. Sheridan's enthusiasm for the advancement of eloquence. 'Sir,' said Mr. Johnson, 'it won't do. He cannot carry through his scheme. He is like a man attempting to stride the English Channel. Sir, the cause bears no proportion to the effect. It is setting up a candle at Whitechapel to give light at Westminster.'"

"When Mr. Trotz,[132] Professor of Civil Law at Utrecht, was at Copenhagen, he had a mind to hear the Danish pulpit oratory, and went into one of their churches. At that time the barbarous custom of making spoil of shipwrecked goods still prevailed in Denmark. The minister prayed with great fervency: 'O Lord, if it please Thee to chastise the wicked for their sins, and to send forth Thy stormy winds to destroy their ships, we beg that Thou mayest throw them upon our coasts rather upon any other, that Thy chosen people may receive benefit therefrom, and with thankful hearts may glorify Thy holy name.'"

MR. TROTZ.

"'*Tres faciunt collegium*' is the common adage. A professor of law at Utrecht came to his college one day, and found but one student. He would not have it said that he was obliged to dismiss for want of auditors. So he gravely pronounced, 'Deus unus, ergo duo in tres. Tres faciunt collegium. Incipemus.'"

An UTRECHT Student.

"An English gentleman who was studying at Geneva was introduced to Mr. Voltaire, and at one of the comedies which were given at the Delice he had the part of a stupid absurd Englishman assigned to him. The gentleman was modest and anxious, and was saying he did not know well how to do. Mr. Voltaire encouraged him: 'Sir,' said he, 'don't be affraid. Just act in your own natural way, and you'll do very well.'"

MR. TEMPLE.

"The King of Prussia asked an English gentleman why the civil law did not universally prevail in Great Britain. The gentleman replied, Because we are not Romans. 'That is true,' said the King, 'but your nation has produced many Romans.'"

M. GIFFARDIER.

"When Lord Hope[133] was presented to the King of Prussia, he told him that he made in one summer the tour of Denmark, Sweden, and Norway. 'Ay,' said the king, 'and pray, my lord, why have you not been in Siberia?'"

M. GIFFARDIER.

"Mr. Samuel Johnson said of Sheridan, 'Sherry is dull, naturally dull, but it must have cost him a great deal of pains to become so exceedingly stupid; such an excess of stupidity is not in nature.'"

MR. DEMPSTER, from FOOTE.[134]

"The Earl of Marchmont and Lord Littleton[135] differed warmly about the authenticity of Fingal. Macpherson said he should like to see them fighting a duel in Hyde Park. 'See them!' said Dempster: 'no one man could possibly see *them*, they would stand at such a distance from one another.'"

I was present.

"When Derrick was made King of Bath, Mr. Samuel Johnson said, 'Derry may do very well while he can outrun his character, but the moment that his character gets up with him he is gone.'"

I was present.

"When Dempster was at Brussels, a young gentleman of Scotland was very bad. Dempster said that the surgeons poured mercury into him as if he had been the tube of a weather-glass."

"Boswell told Mr. Samuel Johnson that Sir James Macdonald[136] said he had never seen him, but he had a great respect for him, though at the same time a great terror. 'Were he to see me,' said Mr. Johnson, 'it would probably lessen both.'"

"Mr. Samuel Johnson told Boswell that Dr. Goldsmith when abroad used to dispute in the universities, and so get prize money, which carried him on in his travels. 'Well,' said Boswell, 'that was indeed *disputing* his *passage* through Europe.'"

"Boswell was saying that Derrick was a miserable writer. 'True,' said Mr. Samuel Johnson,[137] 'but it is to his being a writer that he owes anything he has. Sir, had not Derrick been a writer, he would have been sweeping the crosses in the streets, and asking halfpence from everybody that passed.'"

"A good-natured, stupid man, at Bath, wanted to appear a man of some consequence by talking often with Mr. Quin,[138] although he had nothing earthly to say more than 'Your servant, Mr. Quin! I hope you are well.' Quin bore with him for some time, but at last he lost patience, and one day when the gentleman came up to him with a 'Mr. Quin, I hope you are well!' Quin replied, 'Yes, sir, I am very well, and intend to be so for six months to come; so, sir, till that time I desire you may not again ask me that question.'"

MR. ROSE, at Utrecht.

"Mr. Samuel Johnson and Boswell slept in one room at Chichester. A moth flew round the candle for some time, and burnt itself to death. 'That creature,' said Mr. Johnson, 'was its own tormentor, and I believe its name was Boswell.'"[139]

"Mr. Fordyce[140] said that a man of public character who falls into disgrace in England receives immediate punishment from the mob; and is a greater man than Orpheus, who only made live animals follow him, whereas the rogue makes dead cats come after him."

I was present.

"Baldie Robertson, a Scotch advocate, asked Boswell to accompany him to cheapen a couple of rooms of Lucky Rannie's. She told him, 'Sir, you shall just have them for a guinea a week, you furnishing coal and candle.' Baldie, with much emotion, cried out, 'But I tell you, woman, I have no coal and candle.'"

"Boswell said of Miss Stewart, of Blackhall,[141] 'that more brilliant beauties came armed with darts and attacked men as foes, but Miss Stewart carried no weapons of destruction, and treated with them as with allies.'"

"Lord Eglintoune said to Boswell, whose lively imagination formed many schemes, but whose indolence hindered him from executing them, 'Jamie, you have a light head, but a heavy a———.'"

"Lord Eglintoune said to Boswell, who was maintaining that by habit he would acquire the power of application to business, 'Application must be an original vigour of mind. The arm of any blacksmith may become so strong by habit that he may gain his bread; but if he has not natural strength he will never make excellent work.'"

"'The Spaniards are a noble people; at least, their gentlemen have great souls. At a famous battle there was a brave Spanish officer who had been wounded in many actions, and had but one eye left. A bullet came and struck it out as he was charging at the head of his troops, and wounded him mortally. With calm and solemn dignity he called to his men, 'Bonas noctias, cavilieros' ('Good night, my fellow-soldiers')."

MR. ROSE.

"A German baron, newly arrived at Paris in a suit trimmed with almaches—that is, small lace disposed so as to look like horns—went to the theatre just in his travelling dress, and getting behind the scenes showed himself upon the stage. The Parterre began to make a noise like the firing of cannon. One of the players begged to know what was the matter, when a gentleman replied, pointing to the baron, 'Animal, ne voys tu pas que nous attaqons cette ouvrage a corne?' 'You fool, don't you see that we are attacking that hornwork?'"

M. GIFFARDIER.

"Monsieur Chapelle satirized with much keenness the *petits maîtres* of his time. One of them who chanced to be in company with him exclaimed against these satires, and said he wished he knew the author—he would beat him heartily. He plagued the company with his threatenings, especially Chapelle, whom he sat next to and shouldered. At last Chapelle gave a spring, and turning up his back to him, cried, 'Frap et va t'en!' ('Strike, and get thee gone!')"

M. GIFFARDIER.

"When M. Voltaire was in England he had a great desire to see Dr. Clarke,[142] but the Doctor, who had heard his character, would not be acquainted with him; at last he fell in with a friend of Dr. Clarke's, who asked him to be of a party where the Doctor was. Voltaire went and seated himself next to the Doctor, in full expectation of hearing him talk, but he remained very silent. Voltaire, in order to force him to speak, threw out all the wild profane rhodomontades that his imagination could suggest against religion. At last Dr. Clarke turned about, and looking him steadily in the face with the keen eagle eyes for which he was remarkable, 'Sir,' said he, 'do you acknowledge that two and two make four?' Voltaire was so confounded by this that he said not another word."

MR. BROWN.[143]

"A dull German baron had got amongst the English at Geneva, and, being highly pleased with their spirit, wanted to imitate them. One day an Englishman came in to the baron's room, and found him jumping with all his might upon the chairs and down again, so that he was all in a sweat. 'Mon Dieu! Monsieur le baron,' dit-il, 'que faites-vous?' ('Good God! baron,' said he, 'what are you about?') 'Monsieur,' replied the baron, wiping down his temples with a handkerchief, 'j'apprens d'être vif' ('I am learning to be lively')."

MADEMOISELLE DE ZOILEN.

"Mr. Thomas Hunter,[144] minister at New Cumnock, was visiting his parish on a very cold day. At a substantial farmer's they set him down an excellent smoking *haggis*. 'Come,' said he, 'here is the grace:—O Lord, we thank Thee for this warm Providence.'"

LORD AUCHINLECK.

"When Mr. Sheridan lived at Windsor he used often to meet a very awkward fellow who did not know how to hold his arms. Mr. Sheridan said the fellow always made him imagine that he was carrying home a pair of arms that somebody had bespoke."

From himself.

"When Mr. David Hume began first to be known in the world as a philosopher, Mr. Thomas White, a decent rich merchant of London, said to him, 'I am surprised, Mr. Hume, that a man of your good sense should think of being a philosopher. Why, I now took it into my head to be a philosopher for some time, but tired of it most confoundedly, and very soon gave it up.' 'Pray, sir,' said Mr. Hume, 'in what branch of philosophy did you employ your researches? What books did you read?' 'Books?' said Mr. White; 'nay, sir, I read no books, but I used to sit you whole forenoons a-yawning and poking the fire.'"

SIR DAVID DALRYMPLE.[145]

"Pierot, the biting French satirist, had often applied to be admitted member of the Academie Royale, and still was rejected. One day, after hearing their disquisitions, a freind (*sic*) asked him, 'N'ont-ils pas beaucoup d'esprit?' 'Esprit?' replied Pierot, 'sans doute ils out beaucoup d'esprit. Ils out esprit *comme* quatre.' The society is forty-eight in number."

"Mr. Tronchin,[146] physician at Geneva, an intimate friend of Mr. Voltaire, told Mr. Brown, the English minister at Utrecht, that one time when Voltaire was very bad, he was under the greatest terror for death, and he used this strong expression to Mr. Tronchin,—'Sir, if I were put upon the rack at three o'clock in the afternoon, and had both my legs and both my arms broke, if I had my choice either to die immediately or to live till seven at night, I would choose to live till seven.' A fortnight after, when he was quite recovered, he was talking against religion with as much wildness and extravagance as ever, and seemed highly delighted with shaking the faith of all the company. Mr. Tronchin, who was present, got up with indignation, went round to Voltaire, and catching him by the breast, said, 'You pitiful wretch! are you, for a little gratification of vanity, endeavouring to destroy the only pillars which can support mankind at that awful hour which made you so lately tremble like a coward?' In contradiction to this story, see in my Journal the account which Tronchin gave me of Voltaire."[147]

MR. BROWN.

"During a hot action between the French and the allied armies, in which the former were defeated, a French grenadier was taken prisoner by an officer of the Iniskilling [Enniskillin] dragoons. He immediately demanded of the prisoner, 'Where is Marshal Broglio?' The brave grenadier replied, with the high spirit of a French soldier, 'Il est partout.' He is everywhere."

M. GIFFARDIER, from the Officer.

"As a strong picture of the difference between French and German manners, the following story will serve: An English officer in Germany during the war kept a girl. She had a great deal of spirit, and for a frolic she would pay a visit to the enemy's outpost. She first came to a French centinel, who seeing a pretty—nay, elegant lady coming towards him, immediately grounded his arms, pulled off his hat, and with all the politeness in the world saluted her with 'Ah, madame, je suis charmé,' &c. She put out her hand, which he kissed with great gallantry. She then went to a German centinel in the French service. When he observed her approaching, he looked stern and shoved her back with his hand; and when she attempted still to advance, he held out his fusil. She ran briskly off, crying, 'You brute, we have taken Cassel!'"

"After a defeat of the French in Germany by the Prussians, a French soldier got his back against a tree, and was defending himself against four or five Prussians. The King of Prussia came up himself, and called out to the soldier, 'Mon ami, croyez-vous que vous êtes invincible?' He replied, 'Oui, sire, si j'etois commandé par vous.'"

MR. GIFFARDIER.

"After another defeat of the French by the Prussians, a French soldier said to his companion while they were running off, 'Vraiment cet Roi de Prusse est un brave homme. Je crois qu'il a servi en France.'"

MR. GIFFARDIER.

"After the defeat of the French at Rosbach, there happened a ludicrous enough incident. A little French officer was taken prisoner by a tall, fierce, black hussar. After making him deliver up his sword, his watch, and his money, the hussar made him get up behind him and hold fast, and away he galloped; and all the time, with the greatest *sang froid*, he was eating apples out of his pocket, and now and then, with a humph, threw one over his shoulder to the officer, who, for fear of his displeasure, eat them every one most faithfully."

MR. GIFFARDIER, from the officer himself.

"When Boswell was a young, giddy, frolicsome dog in London, a parcel of sarcastical Scots, dining at Almack's,[148] were enlarging much on his imprudence. 'I do not know,' said Dempster, 'how Boswell may do in this world, but I am sure he would do very well in a better.'"

From Miss Dempster.[149]

"Boswell complained that he had too good a memory in trifles, which prevented his remembering things of consequence. 'My head,' said he, 'is like a tavern, in which a club of low punch-drinkers have taken up the room that might have been filled with lords who drink Burgundy, but it is not in the landlord's power to dispossess them.'"

"A gentleman was complaining that upon a long voyage their provisions were very bad, and, in particular, that their beef turned quite green. 'Very right, sir,' said Caleb Whitefoord,[150] 'you know all flesh is grass, and therefore ought to be green.'"

I was present.

"Boswell says that a man who sets out on the journey of life with opinions that he has never examined is like a man who goes a-fowling with a gun that has never been proved."

"Boswell, who had a good deal of whim, used not only to form wild projects in his imagination, but would sometimes reduce them to practice. In his calm hours he said with great good humour, 'There have been many people who built castles in the air, but I believe I am the first that ever attempted to live in them.'"

"A gentleman said of a clumsy wench that she was as hot as fire. 'Yes,' said Boswell, 'but in a very different way. The fire feels nothing, but communicates the heat to other bodies; but this wench leaves all cold around her while she herself is burning.'"

"A young lady was wishing much to be her *own mistress*. 'You are mine, miss,' said her lover, 'and that is much better.'"

"Mademoiselle de Zuyl told Boswell one day, 'Monsieur, cette après-midi j'ai voulee convaincre ma chere mere de quelque chose, mais elle ne vouloit pas m'entendre, et pour m'echaper elle a courue de chambre en chambre. J'ai la suivi pourtant et j'ai raisonnée.' 'Eh bien, Mademoiselle,' replied Boswell, 'c'etoit un raisonnement suivi.'"

"A gentleman told Boswell that one of his studious freinds used to have a bottle of wine set upon his desk in the evening, and that generally he caught himself at the end of it. 'Ay,' said Boswell, 'I suppose, sir, he took care not to catch himself before he got to the end of it.'"

"A forward fellow asked Boswell one day the character of a certain general officer. 'Sir,' said Boswell, 'the gentleman is a general, and I do not choose to enter into particulars.'"

"When Boswell had the rage of getting into the Guards, he talked of it to John Home,[151] whose poetry breathed a martial spirit, and therefore might approve his desire to be a soldier. 'Sir,' said John Home, 'the Guards are no soldiers; they are just beefeaters, only they don't eat beef.'"

"Boswell was at Leyden in the year 1764. The Hon. Charles Gordon[152] said to him with affected diffidence, in order to receive a compliment, 'Mr. Boswell, I would willingly come and see you for a day at Utrecht, but I am afraid I should tire you.' 'Sir,' replied Boswell, 'I defy you to tire me for one day.'"

"When Boswell was passing through Leyden, in the year 1764, he put up at the 'Golden Ball,' and was shown into the great parlour, which, as in all the inns in Holland, is a public room. As he was eating a sober bit of supper there entered three roaring West Indians, followed by a large dog. They made a deal of rude noise. The waiter thought it incumbent upon him to make an apology for their roughness. 'Sir,' said he, 'they are very good-natured gentlemen.' 'Yes, yes,' said Boswell, 'I see they are very good-natured gentlemen, and in my opinion, sir, the dog seems to be as good-natured as any of the three.'"

"When Mr. de Neitschutz, Grand Ecuyer du Prince d'Anhalt-Dessau was sent to the King of Prussia to treat with him, and to beg that he would not demand such great subsidies, the King used to say, 'Mon ami, il faut soutenir des armees. Je ne suis pas en etat de la faire. Vous savez que je n'ai rien. Il faut que je vole.'"

M. DE NEITSCHUTZ.

"When Voltaire was at Berlin he used to be rude to the King of Prussia. The King came into his room one day when he had before him on a table a great parcel of his Majesty's verses, which he no doubt put in order very freely. The King called to him, 'Que faites-vous, Voltaire?' He replied, 'Sire, j'arrange votre linge sale.'"

M. LESTSCH AU'DEVANT GOUVERNEUR DU P. D'ANHALT.

"After the battle of Colline, where the King of Prussia was sadly defeated, his Majesty stood in a musefull melancholy, and looked through his glass at a battery of cannon which was still playing and was within reach of him. His troops had all retired, only the Scots General Grant stood behind him at a little distance; a cannon bullet took away the skirt of his coat, and at last when he found that the King made no preparation to retire, he came up to him and said, 'Est-ceque votre majeste veut prendre la batterie tout seul?'

The King looked at him with approbation, and said, 'Allons, mon ami,' and retreated. 'Eh bien, Grant,' said he, 'c'est une triste affaire.'"

MR. SECRETARY BURNET.[153]

"During one of his campaigns the King of Prussia composed a sermon entitled 'Sermon sur le jour de jugement preché devant l'Abbé de Prade, par son aumonier ordinaire l'Incredulité.' L'Abbé de Prade was his reader. The sermon was a grave discourse, full of Scripture phrases. It might have been preached in any church in Europe."

MR. SECRETARY BURNET.

"Mr. Burnet was one day riding along with the Prussian army through a wood. He heard behind him a voice crying, 'March furt in der Deivells naam,' but did not think that the King had been near him. He turned about, however, and there was his Majesty's horse's mouth touching Burnet's horse's tail. The King had lost a battle. The weather was bad. He was muffled up in his great-coat, was in very bad humour, and looked confoundedly sulky. Burnet was anxious to make way for him, and immediately put spurs to his horse and sprung away. The wood was so thick that the branches caught hold of him and drove off his hat and wig. He had shaved his head that morning, so that there he was, he sticking with his white skull exposed to the elements. The King, notwithstanding his ill-humour, could not help being diverted, and burst out into an immense fit of laughter. He then said to Burnet, 'Monsieur, je vous demande pardon, mais je m'en vais le reparer.' He then called to a soldier, 'Geve die Heer syn Hoed en zyn peruik.'"

MR. SECRETARY BURNET.

"The King of Prussia sometimes used to amuse himself in the most extraordinary manner. After having played on his flute till he was tired, he would say to the Abbé de Prade, 'Allons, si j'etois membre du Parlement d' Angleterre voici comment je parlerais;' then he would harangue on the balance of power, &c., like a very Pitt."

MR. SECRETARY BURNET.

"The British Envoy's mail was once seized going from Berlin. It was said to have been done by the Ambassador of France. Mr. Mitchell said,[154] 'Je n'en crois rien.' 'Peut être,' said one, 'il a reçu des ordres pour le faire et qu'est ce que cela feroit,' said Mitchell. 'Monsieur,' said the gentleman, 'si vous aviéz reçu des ordres du Roi votre maître de saisir une Malle ne voudriez vous pas le faire?' 'Monsieur,' replied Mr. Mitchell, 'Premierrement le Roi mon maître ne me donnera jamais *des telles* ordres. En second lieu, assurement je ne les obeierois pas, "non," je lui ecrirois, Si vous, Sire, voulez faire des choses comme cela, il faut envoyer un voleur, et non pas tacher de faire un voleur de votre Envoye.'"

MR. MITCHELL himself.

"Boswell was presented to the Duke of Argyle,[155] at Whitton, in the year 1760. The duke talked some time with him, and was pleased, and seemed surprised that Boswell wanted to have a commission in the guards. His Grace took Boswell's father aside, and said, 'My lord, I like your son. That boy must not be shot at for three and sixpence a day.'"

"Lord Auchinleck and his son were very different men. My lord was sollid (*sic*) and composed; Boswell was light and restless. My lord rode very slow; Boswell was one day impatient to get on, and begged my lord to ride a little faster; 'for,' said he, 'it is not the exercise which fatigues, but the hinging upon a beast.' His father replied, 'What's the matter, man, how a chield hings, if he dinna hing upon a gallows?'"

"When Captain Augustus Hervey was lying in the port of Leghorn, some of the first people of the country paid him a visit aboard his ship. He ordered his men to draw up a bucket of water, and presented it to the nobles, bidding them drink that. 'Why,' said they, ''tis salt water.' 'Is it?' said he. 'Then know that wherever this water is found the King of Great Britain is master.'"

CAPTAIN WAKE.

"Mr. Burnet went once into a Presbyterian kirk. The minister lectured on these words,—'You shall take no scrip for your journey.' 'A scrip,' said he, 'my beloved brethren, was a clockbag, a portmanteau, or a wallise.'"

Himself.

"A gentleman was saying at Voltaire's table, 'J'ai lu un telle chose.' 'Monsieur,' said Voltaire, 'il ne faut pas croire tout ce qu'on a lu.' 'Monsieur,' replied he, 'j'ai pourtant lu tous vos ouvrages.'"

The Gentleman.

"Boswell said that to be a good rural poet a man must have an appetite for the beauties of nature as another has for his dinner. A man who has a poor stomach will never talk with force of a good dinner; nor will he whose taste is feeble talk with force of a fine prospect. This kind of taste must be felt, and cannot even be imagined by others."

"Boswell said that a dull fool was nothing, as he never showed himself. The great thing, said he, is to have your fool well furnished with animal spirits and conceit, and he'll display to you a rich fund of risibility. He said this at a certain court in Germany."

"A formal fellow at Paris paid a great many long-winded compliments to Mademoiselle Ameté, the Turk. When he had finished, she said to the gentleman next her, 'Je ne puis pas soutenir cet homme la; il me parle comme un Dedicace.'"

MY LORD MARISCHAL.[156]

"Boswell said that young people are often tempted to resign themselves to a warm fancy or a strong benevolent passion, because they have read that those who are thus agitated are nobler beings, and enjoy a felicity superior to that of sedate rational men. But let them consider that all these fine things have been said by the hot-brained people themselves, and that one who is drunk may and does boast as much his intoxicated situation. The impartial method of judging what state of mind is happiest is to hear the voice of the majority of sensible men, most of whom, either when young or when drunk, have felt the enticing delirium. If none approve it but such as immediately feel it, we may pronounce it a false joy. For other states, of mind, as the cool circumspection of wisdom, the moderate tenderness of affection, the solemn ardour of devotion, the noble firmness of manly honour,—these others approve of; others wish to possess."

"Boswell asked, 'Why have we not a neat phrase to express our being eager to see, equivalent to "I pricked up my ears" when eager to hear?'"

"When Sir Adam Fergusson[157] was at Dusseldorf he admired much an organ in one of the churches, and wished greatly to hear an English tune upon it. Barnard, (nephew to the great Sir John, and) a merchant at Dunkirk, was there. He begged of the organist to give him liberty to play the vespers, which he agreed to. Barnard played the solemn music very gravely, but by way of a voluntary he gave 'Ally Croaker.' He, however, adorned it with several variations, so that the organist said, 'Monsieur, en que c'est un beau morceau.'"

MR. BARNARD.

At the court of Saxe-Gotha there were two ladies of honour, Mesdemoiselles de Rickslepen, sisters, very pretty, but very little. Boswell said to a baron of the court, "Monsieur, il faut les prendre comme des alouettes, par la demi-douzaine."

"When Poniatowsky[158] was made king of Poland, anno 1764, many of the first nobles opposed his election, as they imagined that he would follow the system of the King of Prussia, and introduce arbitrary power. Le Comte de Sapia, grand Ecuyer de la Lithuanie, quitted his country in discontent. He passed some time at the court of Gotha. One of the courtiers there said to him, 'Monsieur, vous qui aimez tant la liberté vous devez aller en Angleterre.' 'Dieu m'en garde!' cried he; 'non; il faut aller en France, pour apprendre nos nouveaux devoirs.'"

LA GRANDE MAITRESSE DE GOTHA.

"Boswell showed some of his verses to a German professor, who understood English. The professor was highly pleased with them. When he laid them down Boswell said, 'I wrote some of them last night.' 'Ah,' said the professor, 'I did not know they had been yours, sir, or I should have praised them more.'"

"A prince talked of a subject of learning—a piece of history, and said, 'Je ne sais en verité.' Another prince said, 'On trouvera cela peut être dans un dictionnaire.' 'H'm, oui,' said another^{third} prince, 'ui, on le trouvera dans un dictionnaire.'"

I was present.

"Boswell said the English language was like the ancient Corinthian brass. When Corinth was burnt, the fortuitous mixture of gold, silver, and copper produced a metal more excellent than any original one. So, by the different invasions of England was produced a mixture of old British, German, and French, which makes a language superior to any original tongue. The proportions in the one case are as curious as in the other."

"Boswell compared himself to the ancient Corinthian brass. 'I am,' said he, 'a composition of an infinite variety of ingredients. I have been formed by a vast number of scenes of the most different natures, and I question if any uniform education could have produced a character so agreable'" (*sic*).

"The Dutch bourgeois generally wear coats and wigs of prodigious size, by no means made to fit them; but by way of so much cloth and so much hair Boswell said, 'Les Hollandois portent des habits et des peruques comme des Hardes.'"

"Krimberg, grand maître de madame la Marcgrave de Baden Baden, said of the Marcgrave of Baden Dourlach, 'Les autres princes s'amusent des amusements, mais ce prince s'amusa des affaires.'"

I was present.

"Boswell said that a great company was just a group of *têtes-à-têtes*."

"The father of young M. Gaio, at Strasburg, had an immense cask of prodigious fine old Rhenish. His maître d'hotel came and told him that, unfortunately, it had burst the cask and was totally lost. M. Gaio (having eat his evening soup), replied, 'Eh bien, mon vin est lu.'"

M. GAIO LE FILS.

"The uncle of young M. Gaio at Strasbourg had a set of Dresden tea china which he valued very much. As one of his servants was bringing it hastily in one day he fell and broke the whole set. His master stepped calmly forward, helped him up, and called to another servant, 'Ecoutez, donnez une verre du vin de Bourgogne a François, je crois qu'il a en peur.'"

M. GAIO LE FILS.

"Lord Eglintoune said to his brother,[159] Colonel Montgomerie, who was to be his heir, 'If I live, Archie, I'll take care of you.' 'Yes, my lord,' replied the colonel, 'and if you die I'll take care of myself.'"

LORD AUCHINLECK.

"Mr. Needham[160] went with another gentleman to call upon M. Diderot. A comely well-dressed lady opened the door to them. The gentleman said, 'Madame est sans doute la femme de M. Diderot.' She, with an air of smiling satisfaction, replied, 'Monsieur, les philosophes ne ses marient point.'"

MR. NEEDHAM.

"Mr. Needham said that Rousseau's not complying with the common established ceremonies of society was like a Quaker saying Thee and Thou, and not pulling off his hat."

I was present.

"The Syndics or Magistrates of Geneva wear prodigious periwigs. M. de Voltaire said to them, 'Messieurs, vous repandez votre poudre dans toutes les territoires voisines.'"

GRAND BAILLIF D'YUERDUN.

"Erskine[161] and Boswell were one day sauntering in Leicester Fields and talking of the famous scheme of squaring the circle. 'Come, come,' said Boswell, 'let us circle the square, and that will be as good;' so these two poets took a walk round the square, laughing very heartily at the conceit."

"Mr. Richardson, chaplain to Sir Joseph Yorke,[162] and another clergyman were walking near a village by Cambridge, where were a number of Methodists. They saw a child of four year old lying accross (*sic*) the road, and immediately ran up to lift it up, when they heard a number of people cry, 'Let it alone, let it alone, it's convicted, it's convicted.' They asked, 'Pray, how? so young a child has not been at church.' 'No, but its father and mother have, and the Lord has been dealing with their child.'"

From himself.

"Boswell said that Mademoiselle de Maasdain, at the Hague, was as black as a chimney. 'Then,' said the Rev. Dr. Maclaine, 'her husband would be a chimney-sweeper.'"

"Boswell said that Mademoiselle de Zuyl was too vivacious, and crowded her *bon mots* in conversation, so that one had not time to examine them one by one, and see their beauties. He said, she used to make people run through the Vatican, where you glance over a number of fine pictures, but have not time to look at and relish any."

"Fordyce was much scandalized at a French barber who shaved him in Paris, and having caught a fly, called it *cette machine la*. 'Why,' said Boswell, 'in England we call a machine a fly, why may not the French call a fly a machine?'"

"Andrew Stuart,[163] Nairne,[164] Colonel Scott, and Boswell went in a coach from the Hague to Rotterdam. The Dutch coachman was so heavy a blockhead that Andrew Stuart took the reins from him and drove. A mole, somehow or other, was seen upon the road. 'Well,' said Boswell, 'when Mr. Andrew Stuart drove a Dutch coach, he drove so hard that the very moles came above ground to look at him.'"

"In the year 1715 Lord Marischal observed a Highlander crying, and looking at the poor fellow he observed he had no shoes. He sent one to him, who spoke Erse, and bid him not be cast down, for he should have shoes. 'Sir,' said the Highlander, 'I want no shoes; I am crying to see a Macdonald retire from his enemy.'"

From LORD MARISCHAL.

"In the year 1715, when my Lord Marischal was preparing to leave London and join the Stuart army, Fletcher of Salton[165] came to him at seven in the morning, asked a dish of tea to get his servant out of the way, and then said, 'My lord, you are now going to join with people who will not be honest, nor so steady as yourself. I advise you, don't go.' My lord answered, 'Sir, I shall not dispute whether King James or King George has the best right to the crown. I know you are for no king. But, as things are, I think we may get rid of the union which oppresses us.' 'My lord,' replied Fletcher, 'it is a good thing to be young: when I was your age I thought as you do, and would have acted as you do; but I am now growing old, I have been sorely brought down by sickness, and I find my mind is failing with my body."

LORD MARISCHAL.

"Boswell went from Berlin to Charlottenburg while the entertainments were there on account of the betrothing of the Princess Elizabeth of

Brunswick to the Prince of Prussia; all the ladies and gentlemen pressed eagerly to get places at the windows of the palace, in order to see the royal families at supper. Boswell found this a little ridiculous, so came up to his acquaintances and said, 'Allons, allons, je vous en prie voyons la seconde table; je vous assure il vaut mieux la peine; ces gens mangent plus que les autres?' ('Come, come, pray do let us go see the second table; I assure you it is more worth while; they eat more than the others.')"

"Boswell said that Sir Joseph Yorke was so anxious lest people should forget that he was an ambassador, that he held his head as high and spoke as little as possible. As in the infancy of painting it was found necessary to write below a picture, this is a cow, or this is a horse, so from the mouth of Sir Joe cometh a label with these words—'I am an ambassador.'"

"Boswell said that the descriptions of human life which we find in books are very false, because written in retirement. When a painter would take a portrait or a landscape, he is always sure to be present, whereas a painter of human life gets away from the object, buries himself in the shade, or basks in the sunshine, and consequently gives either too black or too gay a creature of his imagination, which he calls human life."

"Two Scotch Highlanders were benighted, and lay down to sleep on the side of a mountain. After they had lain a little, one of them got up, but soon returned again. The other asked him, 'What's this, Donald? what have you been about?' Duncan replied, 'I was only bringing a stane to put under my head.' Donald started up and cried, 'H—g your effeminacy, man! canna ye sleep without a stane aneath your head?'"

MR. BURNET.

"After the Prince of Prussia had been defeated by the Austrians, the King, who was marching desperate against them, wrote to him thus:—'Mon frère, Daun vous a traité comme un petit Ecolier. Il vous a fouetté avec des verges. Un homme qui va mourir, n'a rien d'dissimuler.'"

MR. BURNET.

"Lord Auchinleck was one of the most firm and indefatigable judges that ever lived. Brown at Utrecht said that he was one of those great beams which are placed here and there to support the edifice of Society."

I was present.

"Boswell said that Berkley[166] reasoned himself out of house and home."

"An unhappy hypochondriack complained that in his gloomy hours he believed himself a fool. A hard-hearted wag was cruel enough to say to him, 'Crede quod habes et habes.'"

"Captain Bertie was in one of three English ships who advanced against seven French. The sailors were so overjoyed at this noble opportunity that they huzzaed and threw their hats overboard, and those who had no hats, their wigs. They fought and beat the French heartily."

CAPTAIN BERTIE.[167]

"If those who have no taste for the fine arts would fairly own it, perhaps it would be better. Mr. Damer and Captain Howe, two true-born Englishmen, were in the great gallery at Florence; they submitted quietly to be shown a few of the pictures, but seeing the gallery so immensely long their impatience burst forth and they tried, for a bet, who should hop first to the end of it."

THE HON. MR. HOWE.[168]

"When Boswell came first into Italy, and saw the extreme profligacy of the ladies, he said, 'Italy has been called the garden of Europe, I think it is the *Covent Garden*.'"

"Churchill,[169] in his abusive poem against Scotland called the 'Prophecy of Famine,' had the following line:—

'Far as the eye could reach no tree was seen.'

Mr. Jamieson, a true Scot, said, 'Faith, I wish I had as many Churchills to hang upon them as there's trees.'"

"Boswell had a travelling box in which he carried his hats and his papers. He was saying one day, 'What connection now have they together?' Replied Mr. Lumisden,[170] 'They have both a connection with your head.'"

"An honest Scots sailor who had been wounded in the service took up a public-house at Dundee, and on his sign had his story painted. First he was drawn with both his legs firing away, with this inscription,—'Thus I was;' then with one leg, and inscribed, 'Thus *I am*, the Fortune of war.'"

JAMES RAMSAY.[171]
MR. WILLISON.[172]

"A young fellow by chance let a china plate fall. His father asked him, 'Pray, sir, what way did you do that?' He very gravely took up another, and let it fall in the same manner: 'That way, sir.'"

COLONEL EDMONSTOUNE.[173]

"A very big man said he intended often to have spoke in the House of Commons. 'I wish you had, sir,' said Matthew Henderson; 'for if you had not been heard, you would at least have been seen.'"

CAPT. KEITH STUART.

P. 1. "April.—My father said to me, 'I am much pleased with your conduct in every respect.' After all my anxiety while abroad, here is the most perfect approbation and calm of mind. I never felt such sollid (*sic*) happiness. But I feel I am not so happy with this approbation and this calm as I expected to be. Alas! such is the condition of humanity, that we are not allowed here the perfect enjoyment of the satisfaction which arises even from worth. But why do I say alas! when I really look upon this life merely as a transient state?

P. 2. "I must stay at Auchinleck. I have there just the kind of complaining proper for me. All must complain, and I more than most of my fellow-creatures.

P. 3. "A man is but in proportion to the impressions which his power makes. I see there is variety of powers."

"Saturday, April 19th.—This morning my worthy father wak'd me early and told me of the sudden death of my Lord Justice Clerk (Lord Minto),[174] and repeated with a calm solemnity,—

'Trahimur sævo rapiente fato.'"

"A modern man of taste found fault with the avenues at Auchinleck, and said he wished to see straggling trees. 'I wish,' said Boswell, 'I could see straggling fools in this world.'"

"Boswell said that business itself helps a man on just as the chaise going down a hill helps on the horse which is in the shafts. 'When,' said he, 'I think of the fatigues of the law I tremble. But when I have once get on the harnessing of a Process, away I go without difficulty. This is just; let a man never despond as to anything, let him be yok'd, and no fear.'"

"When Boswell observed that the Lords of Session were often inattentive, he said he wished he had liberty to speak to the bench as one speaks to a company, where if any one whom one wishes to attend appears to be absent, one can rouse him by directing the discourse particularly to him. 'So,' said Boswell, 'I would say, "My Lord Sagely, your lordship must surely agree," &c.; "But besides, my Lord Doubtfull, it appears," &c.'"

"Boswell had a great aversion to the law, but forced himself to enter upon that laborious profession in compliance with the anxious desire of his father, for whom he had the greatest regard. After putting on the gown, he said with great good humour to his brother advocates, 'Gentlemen, I am prest into the service here; but I have observed that a prest man, either by sea or land, after a little time does just as well as a volunteer.'"

"Lord Auchinleck said the great point for a judge is to conduct a cause with safety and expedition, like a skillfull pilot. 'The Agents always endeavour to keep a cause afloat. But I keep my eye upon the haven, and the moment I have got him fairly in order I give one hearty push, and there he's landed.'"

"Boswell said when we see a man of eminence we desire nothing more than to be of his acquaintance; we then wish to have him as a companion; and when we have attained that we are impatient till we gain a superiority over him. Such is the restless progress of man!"

"A sailor, who had been long out at sea, was on his return asked by a companion what sort of voyage they had. 'Why,' said he, 'a very good one; only we had prayers twice. But one of the times there was no more occasion for them than if you and I should fall down and pray this minute.'"

LORD LOUDOUN.[175]

"My Lord Stair,[176] who wrote a very bad hand, sent once to my Lord Loudoun a written commission to be read to Sir Philip Honeywood.[177] Lord Loudoun received the letter at the British Coffee-house, where he was sitting after dinner with some friends taking a very hearty bottle; and whether the wine made him see double or no, so it was that he read the commission very distinctly. Next morning he went to wait on Sir Philip Honeywood, and being then quite cool and in his sober senses he could not read a word of it, and neither could Sir Philip. Lord Loudoun could not go back to Lord Stair and tell him his hand was not legible, so Sir Philip trusted to Lord Loudoun's memory of what he had read the day before, and could not then read at all, a most curious fact. When the Duke of Cumberland was told of it he said, 'Loudoun, why did you not stay and dine with Sir Philip, and then you would both have read it.'"

LORD LOUDOUN.

"Mr. Clark, uncle to Baron Clark, a most curious mortal, who had been bred a surgeon, had travelled over the greatest part of the world, and always walked. He had the misfortune to break one of his legs, and two pieces of the bone came out of it. He had them drest, and made hafts to a knife and fork of them. When he was dying he sent for Doctor Clark[178] and the Baron.[179] 'Now, gentlemen,' said he, 'this knife and fork will be the most valuable part of my executory, and I'll leave them to any of you two who shall give me the best inscription to put upon them. The Doctor, who was a fine classical scholar, tried a good many times, but at length the baron fairly got the better of him by a most elegant and well-adapted inscription,—

'Quæ terra nostri non plena laboris?'"

LORD AUCHINLECK.

"Campbell of Suckoth[180] and his son were both men of great wit. The father had been constantly attached to the Duke of Argyle, but had never got the least assistance from him, upon which the son went and paid court to the Duke of Hamilton. His dutchess (*sic*) was then of the Spencer family.[181] So young Suckoth planted a mount, which he called Mount Spencer. The dutchess made him a present of some fine foreign trees in flower-pots, so he got a cart and a couple of horses from his father to bring them home with, but most of them broke by the way. The old man was not pleased that his son had deserted his chief, so he says to him, 'Dear John, why will you pay court to the House of Hamilton, for I see naething ye get frae them but a wheen broken pigs?' 'Sir,' says he, 'broken pigs are as good as broken promises.' 'Very true,' John, 'but they're no sae dear o' the carriage.'"

LORD AUCHINLECK.

"Sir William Gordon[182] wanted a servant who could write well. 'My father,' said he, 'knew of a very clever fellow, but the most drunken, good-for-nothing dog that ever lived.' 'Oh,' said Sir William, 'no matter for that, let him be sent for.' So when he came Sir William asked him a great many questions, to which Brodie answered most distinctly. At last he asked, him, 'Can you write Latin, sir?' 'Can your honour read it?' said he. Sir William was quite fond of him, and had him drest out to all advantage. One day, at his own table, he was telling a story. 'Not so, sir,' said Brodie, who was standing at his back. 'You dog,' said he, 'how do you know?' 'Because I have heard your honour tell it before.' He lived with Sir William more than seven years."

LORD AUCHINLECK.

"Sir William Gordon was always a singular character. When he came to be eighteen it was necessary for him to choose a curator, and he chose his own livery servant, 'for' said he, 'one is plagued seeking for a curator to sign papers with you, and sometimes they refuse to sign."

LORD AUCHINLECK.

"Mr. Charles Cochrane[183] said one day to my Lord Justice Clerk (Charles Erskine[184]), 'Pray, my lord, what is the reason that there never was a gentleman a ruling elder, who was not either a knave or a very weak man?'

'Ay, Charles' said he, 'why, I'm a ruling elder myself, and what do you take me to be?' 'A very weak man, my lord.'"

LORD AUCHINLECK.

"Sir Walter Pringle,[185] afterwards Lord Newhall, was apt to be very passionate when he thought a lord did not hear him properly. One day he appeared before Lord Forglen,[186] who was very heavy. Sir Walter opened his cause. The other party answered, and among other objections which they stated, they insisted on some trifling point of form, that the cause had not been regularly put up upon the wall. Sir Walter replied to all their objections with accuracy and spirit, but took no notice of the trifling point of form. 'Lord Forglen,' said Sir Walter, 'you have pleaded your cause very well, but what do you say to the wall?' 'Indeed' said he, 'my lord, I have been speaking to it this half-hour;' and off he went in a great passion."

LORD AUCHINLECK.

"Jack Bowes, an Englishman, who was married to a noted midwife at Edinburgh, and was really mad, but had great humour, got up one day on the steps which lead up to the New Kirk (the lady's steps), and there he gathered a crowd about him, and preached to them. 'Gentlemen,' said he, 'you will find my text in the 2nd Epistle of St. Paul to Timothy, the 4th chapter, and there the 13th verse, 'The cloak that I left at Troas with Carpus, when thou comest, bring with thee, and the books, but especially the parchments.' 'We insist upon the first clause. We see, gentlemen, from these words that Paul was a presbyter, for he wore a cloak. He does not say the gown which I left at Troas, but the cloak which I left at Troas with Carpus, when thou comest bring with thee. Timothy, we all know, was a bishop. Now, my friends, the doctrine I would inculcate from this is, that a presbyter had a bishop for his baggageman.'"

LORD AUCHINLECK.

"A drover owed another ——, as the price of —— lambs. His creditor came and craved time for the money. 'John,' said he, 'let me alone for a fortnight, for I really cannot pay you sooner.' The creditor insisted, and called him before a judge and put him to his oath. He swore positively that he owed no such debt. After the court was over, the creditor asked him how he could swear against what he had owned so often. 'Because,' said he, 'you forced me, and I had nothing else for it; but, however, John, you shall lose nothing by it, for I shall give you my bill for the money payable in a fortnight,' and actually he did give his bill and paid him accordingly. A most wonderful mixture of impiety and honesty."

LORD AUCHINLECK.

"Sir William Gordon would needs make a library because my Lord Sunderland made one, but all he wanted was just dear books. He came in one day to Vanderaa's shop, in Leyden, and asked if he had got any dear new books. Vanderaa showed him the 'Thesaurus Italiæ et Siciliæ' in—— volumes. Sir William turned to Dr. Cooper and said, 'Pray, Doctor, have I got that book?' 'No, Sir William, nor do I think you have occasion for it.' 'Mr. Cooper, I cannot be without that book.' 'Upon my word, Sir William, I think you might very well be without it.' 'There, Mr. Cooper, you and I differ.—Mr. Vanderaa, let that book be packed up and sent for me to London.'"

LORD AUCHINLECK.

"Dr. Taylor, the oculist, was one evening supping at William Earl of Dumfries's, at Edinburgh. He harangued with his usual fluency and impudence, and boasted that he knew the thoughts of everybody by looking at their eyes. The first Lady Dumfries,[187] who was hurt with his behaviour, asked him with a smile of contempt, 'Pray, sir, do you know what I am thinking?' 'Yes, madam,' said he. 'Then,' replied the countess, 'it's very safe, for I am sure you will not repeat it.'"

DR. WEBSTER, who was present.

"When the first Lady Dumfries was within a quarter of an hour of her death, she showed an attention to the interests of religion, and at the same time an address equal to that of any statesman. The earl came down from her all in tears, and told it to the Rev. Mr. Webster. 'My lord,' said she, 'you have always shown a proper regard to the ordinances of religion. People have been pleased to say that you did so out of compliment to me. Providence is now giving your lordship an opportunity to show that it was entirely from yourself.'"

DR. WEBSTER.

"John Lord Hope[188] was educated at home about his father's house, full of conceit, full of petulance. His mother, the first Lady Hopetown, stood much in awe of my lord, but when he was not present was very lively and agreeable. One night at supper Lord Hope had made some figure of the crumbs of his bread, and plagued all the company to tell what it was. Many flattered him; some called it a pretty summerhouse; some, one of the ruins of Rome, and so made him exceedingly vain. He at last applied to my lady his mother. 'Madam,' said he, 'you have not told me what you think it is.' 'Well,' said she, 'if you will have what I think it, I shall tell you I think it a monument of a young lord's folly.'"

DR. WEBSTER.

"Mr. William Nairne observed that it maybe said of a well-employed barrister who lays by much money, what Horace says of the *ant*,—

'*Ore* trahit quodcunque potest atque addit acervo.'"

I was present.

"A gentleman expended immense sums of money in attempting to improve a barren soil. Boswell observed 'that the gentleman was as busy burying gold as others are in digging it up.'"

"It has often occurred to me that artificial passions are stronger than real ones, just as a wall built with good mortar is found to be harder and worse to separate than the natural rock. A passion for pageantry, and many more of the passions generated in civilized life, often influence men more than the real genuine passions natural to man."

"Cullen, the mimic,[189] had a wretched manner of his own. He was one forenoon reading Lord Mansfield's admirable speech on the Privilege Bill. Several of our brother advocates were listening to him. I could not help laughing, for I said hearing Lord Mansfield's speech read by Cullen was like hearing a piece of Handel's music played on a (trump) Jew's harp."

"I have observed that business has a different effect on the spirits of different men. It sinks the spirits of some and raises the spirits of others. To the spirits of some, a variety of affairs are like stones put into a pool of water, which make the water rise in proportion to the quantity of stones; to the spirits of others, affairs (*des affaires*) are like sponges put into a pool of water, which suck it up. Men of great firmness can retain their vivacity amidst a multiplicity of business. The King of Prussia is a distinguished example."[190]

"Mr. John Pettigrew,[191] minister of Govan, was one of the originals amongst the clergy of Scotland, of which there were many in the last age. His presbytery was once violently divided who should be moderator in the room of one Mr. Love,[192] then in the chair. While they were disputing with vast keenness Mr. Petticrew came in, and being asked his opinion, he said, 'Moderator, let brotherly love continue.' The presbytery took his advice, and so their disputes were ended in good humour."

LORD AUCHINLECK.

"Cullen, the mimick,[193] was excessively ugly, having most horrible teeth, and, upon the whole, a physiognomy worse than Wilkes's. His own manner, as has been observed, was also wretched. One morning when he was grinning and pleading a cause, I stood by and observed, 'Whom is Cullen taking off? He is taking off the devil.'"

"Sinclair, of Briggend, a Caithness laird, was telling that a gentleman with whom he had played at loo had a way of keeping Pam in the head of his boot, and bringing him out when he found him necessary. 'Ay,' said Andrew Erskine, 'it seems he played *booty* with you.'"

I was present.

"I was defending one day poor Mrs. C—— at the time when her husband was suing her for a divorce, and saying that she was no worse than the Miss V——s, for all her faults were only innocent improprieties. 'No worse!' said Andrew Erskine, 'she is ten times better; she only intrigued with certain people, but the Miss V——s did it with everybody that was near her, and would have done it with everybody at a distance had it been possible.'"

"Cullen, the mimick, as has been more than once observed, had a wretched manner of his own. I was one day to walk out with him to dine at Craig House with Mr. Lockhart,[194] the Dean of Faculty. I was saying to a lady that I wondered what characters he would give me by the road. 'Oh,' said she, 'no matter, providing you have not himself. As Sir John Falstaff said to the hostess, when she offered the fat knight a hog's countenance, "Any countenance but thy own."'"

"John Home showed the Lord Chief Baron Orde a pair of pumps he had on, and desired his lordship to observe how well they were made, telling him at the same time that they had been made for Lord Bute,[195] but were rather too little for him, so his lordship had made John a present of them. 'I think,' said the Lord Chief Baron, 'you have taken the measure of Lord Bute's foot.'"

LORD CHIEF BARON ORDE.[196]

"A very awkward fellow was dancing at the Edinburgh Assembly. Matthew Henderson[197] said, 'He looks like a professor of dislocation.'"

HON. ALEX. GORDON, [*See note, p. 254*].[198]

"A man who uses a great many words to express his meaning shows that he has no distinct idea, no neatness of speech. He is like a bad marksman, who, instead of aiming a single stone at an object, takes up a handful of stones, gravel, sand, and all, and throws at it, thinking that in that manner he may hit it."

"It sometimes happens that when a man throws out a reflection against one, he, without intending it, pays a compliment. In such a case, I think I am well entitled to take the compliment. If a man throws a snowball at me, and I find a diamond in the heart of it, surely the diamond is mine."

"One day when a company of us were dining at Mr. Foote's, in Edinburgh, and I believe I was the only man present who had any faith at all in spirits, many jokes flew around my head; but I stood my ground, and went so far as to say that I did not disbelieve the existence of witches. Matthew Henderson, who is very happy in uncommon wild sallies, cried out, 'Johnson inoculates him by moonlight.'"

"In talking of Dr. Armstrong's[199] excessive indolence to Andrew Erskine I used this strong figure, he is sometimes so that his soul cannot turn itself in its bed."

"Allan Ramsay[200] painted a portrait of David Hume, dressed in scarlet with rich gold lace. 'George III.,' said he, 'thought the picture very like, but thought the dress rather too fine. I wished,' said Ramsay, 'posterity should see that one philosopher during your Majesty's reign had a good coat upon his back.'"

"Lord President Arniston[201] was a man of uncommon fire, but at the same time of a sound strong judgement. When he was at the Bar, and his fancy sometimes ran away with him, Lord Cullen said he was a wise man upon a mad horse."

LORD AUCHINLECK.

"The first Earl of Stair[202] was a Captain of Dragoons, and when there was a comparative trial for an election to a regency, as it was called, or a professorship of the College of Glasgow, Mr. Dalrymple, afterwards known as Lord Stair, appeared in his jack-boots as a candidate, and carried the election. When he was afterwards pleading as a lawyer in the Court of Session, some ignorant fellow who was his opponent committed some gross blunders in the Latin which he quoted. 'Pray' said Stair, 'don't break Priscian's head!' 'Sir,' said the fellow, 'I was not bred a schoolmaster.' 'No' replied Stair, 'nor a scholar either.'"

LORD AUCHINLECK.

"Lord Forglen was a most curious mixture of a character. Lord Newhall, who was a grave austere judge, told my father, 'Forglen is a man of a desultory mind. I was once walking with him on that fine walk upon the river-side at Forglen, when all at once he says, "Now, my lord, this is a fine walk. If ye want to pray to God, can there be a better place? and if ye want to kiss a bonny lass, can there be a better place?'"

LORD AUCHINLECK.

"In the southern countries the warmth of the sunny climate makes the people of a due warmth without drinking, but in northern countries men's hearts are as hard as cold iron till heated by wine. In warm countries they are like the softer metals naturally; but with us there is no making any impression on the heart till it is heated by the fire of strong liquor. I look upon every jovial company among us as a forge of friendship."

"A collection of *bonmots* or lively sallies which have appeared in law papers before the Court of Session, without being expunged, would be like the pictures preserved in Herculaneum, or like mirrors saved out of the ruins after the earthquake of Lisbon."

"One of the gownkeepers to the Lords of Session had a wonderful share of natural humour. He was much given to drinking. One day the first Sir Gilbert Elliot, Lord Minto,[203] who from the political fury of the times had, when passing his trials as an advocate, been unjustly remitted to his studies, and Lord Anstruther,[204] another of the judges, who was noted for his ignorance, would needs amuse themselves with wagering so much beer that he could not walk along a certain deal in the floor of the parliament-house without going off it. The gownkeeper began; but being a good deal muddy with tippling, he soon staggered off the right line. 'You've lost,' cried Minto. 'At leisure, my Lord,' said he, 'I'll begin again. Your lordship was remitted to your studies; may not I be so too?' Anstruther gave a good laugh. The gownkeeper turned to him,—'True, my lord, he was remitted to his studies; but it was not for ignorance.'"

LORD AUCHINLECK.

"The same gownkeeper at the time when the Court of Session used to sit in the afternoon was carrying in a couple of candles. Mr. William Carmichael, advocate, who was remarkably humpbacked, and, like all deformed people, loved a little mischief, stretched out his legs as the gownkeeper passed, which made him come down with a vengeance. The Lord President flew into a great passion, calling out, 'You drunken beast! this is insufferable.' The gownkeeper gathering himself up, addressed his lordship slily: 'An't please your lordship, I am not drunk; but the truth is, as I was bringing in the candles I fell ow'r Mr. William Carmichael's back.' (This fair hit put the whole court in good humour.)"

LORD AUCHINLECK.

"Wedderburn was a little while in opposition, and then joined the court. It was said by a patriot writer, he just kissed the cause like Judas in order to betray it."

A newspaper.

"In the debate in Parliament about Falkland Island, Mr. Burke said, 'Our ministry's excusing themselves on account of its smallness puts me in mind of an unlucky country girl, who acknowledged that she had indeed a bastard child—but it was a very little one.'"

Newspapers.

"Wilkes was the ugliest fellow that ever lived, and a most notorious infidel. Boswell said he was partial as to one article, for he had too much interest to deny the resurrection of the body."

"Wilkes was one evening in company with some French *esprits forts* who were every one atheist. Wilkes opposed them with great spirit, and then said, 'Now in England Mr. Wilkes is looked upon as the most abandoned and impious fellow alive; and here am I defending the being of a God against you all.'"

From himself.

"Wilkes was one day talking of the resurrection of the body. 'For my own share,' said he, 'I would no more value being raised with the same body than being raised in the same coat, waistcoat, and breeches.'"

I was present.

"Mr. John McLaren,[205] minister of the Tolbooth Church, Edinburgh, was a man of uncommon natural genius. My father wrote the heads of his sermons for many years. His last prayer was pretty much a form, and was full of strong expressions and lively figures: 'Lord, bless Thy churches abroad in Hungary, Bohemia, Lithuania, Poland;' and 'Lord, pity Thy poor servants in France. Thou had once glorious churches there; but now they are like dead men out o' mind.' And speaking of hastening the restoration of the Jews, and in-bringing the Gentiles as a sort of joyful consummation, 'Lord, shule [shovel] awa time.' As he did not like the Union, 'Pity poor Scotland. Our rowers have brought us into deep waters [a Scripture phrase], may we have a peur [pure] ministry and peur ordinances, and let the bane o' Scotland never be a little-worth, lax, frothy ministry, that ken little o' God, less o' Christ, and are full of themselves.'"

LORD AUCHINLECK.

"When John, Duke of Argyle, came down to Scotland in all his power, the Presbytery of Edinburgh were to wait upon him. The young fashionable brethren regretted much that Mr. McLaren was moderator, as they did not think he would make a proper elegant speech. However, Mr. McLaren addressed the duke thus:—'My Lord Deuch (Duke), I am not used to make speeches to men like your Grace. All I shall say is your Grace has come of great and good men. Your Grace excels them all in greatness. I pray God you may excel them all in goodness.' The duke, who had a high value for his ancestors, was greatly pleased with this speech. He said it was the genteelest compliment he had ever heard, and most suitable from a clergyman."

LORD AUCHINLECK.

"When there was a thanksgiving day kept at Edinburgh for a victory by the Whig army over the Jacobites in the year 1715, Betty Frank, daughter to Mr. George Frank, advocate, Matthew Brown the clerk's second wife, a great Jacobite, was passing by the Talbooth Kirk in the time of publick worship, and she dropped a halfpenny into the plate, wrapped in paper with this inscription,—

'Stop, good preacher; go no further!
God receives no thanks for murther.'"

LORD AUCHINLECK.

"It was formerly the custom for the magistrates of Edinburgh on the king's birthday to get upon the Cross, which was hung with carpets and busked (drest) with flowers for the occasion, and before all the citizens to drink the health of the day, &c. The glasses used to be filled before they arrived. One day it was a very heavy rain, so that as the glasses overflowed there was at last hardly the colour of wine in them. On this occasion the same Mr. Brown wrote these lines:—

'At Cana once heaven's Lord was pleased

Amongst blithe bridle folks to dine,

And for to countenance their mirth

He turned their water into wine.

'But when for joy of Brunswick's birth

Our tribunes mounted the theatre,

Heaven would not countenance their mirth,

But turned their claret into water.'"

LORD AUCHINLECK.

"The bonnie Earl of Moray,[206] he might ha' been a queen, used to be ludicrously said of the late James, Earl of Moray. He might ha' been a queen was, however, a serious compliment to express handsomeness in Regent Moray's time, of whom it was said, 'The noble earl,' &c., and even of late date it was a serious expression in Scotland. My father told me that Taylour, the hill minister, speaking to him of Johnston of Wamphray, who was a very handsome man, said gravely, 'He might ha' been a queen.'"

"McIlvaine of Grümet (pronounced Grimmet), in Carrick, was a very great original. My father knew him well. He was a tall stately man, quite erect, with a long sword at right angles with his body, so that when he was going in or out at a door he stuck. All the old anti-revolutioners, of which number he was in a very zealous degree, were much in his style. He was offered a troop of horse at the Revolution, but refused it, as his conscience would not allow him to take the oaths to a *new* government. He had something of the old Spanish rhodomontade and a great deal of curious humour. He wrote to Mr. Charles Cochrane, with a present of solan geese, thus,—'Worthy peer, I send you four solan geese to defeat the quadruple alliance, and all alliances, leagues, and covenants that have been made repugnant to religion, honour, and honesty. What we cannot do by works let faith supply, being fortified with the juice of the generous grape, which makes a little pitiful fellow as great as any accidental forte monarch.'"

LORD AUCHINLECK.

"Grimmet lived just on the coast of Carrick, and had a little boat which he used to send out, and so had always plenty of fish. Once when my Lord Cathcart[207] had a great deal of company with him, he sent to Grimmet for some fish. Grimmet sent him some with the following letter:—'I have sent your lordship some fish, but am sorry I could not get more. The truth is, we have of late been infested with a fish called the dog-fish, from the German Ocean, which consumes our fish by sea as much as some people from that country do consume our substance by land.'"

"Bardarrock[208] was one evening drinking with a company of gentlemen. When it came to his toast he gave Miss De Hood. 'Miss De Hood,' said they, 'we never heard of her.' 'Neither,' said he, 'did I ever hear of ony o' yours.'"

LORD AUCHINLECK.

"David Hume used to say that he did not find it an irksome task to him to go through a great many dull books when writing his history. 'I then read,' said he, 'not for pleasure, but in order to find out facts.' He compared it to a sportsman seeking hares, who does not mind what sort of ground it is that he goes over farther than as he may find hares in it."

From himself.

"As it was said that French cooks will make admirable dishes of things which others throw away as useless, so the French in general can cook up a *ragoût* of vanity from the most trivial circumstances; nay, from circumstances which naturally ought to humble them. Instance the soldier running before the King of Prussia, who said, 'Ma fois, c'est un brave homme, ce Roi de Prusse. Je crois qu'il a servi en France.' And the Chevalier de Malte, who told me that if Lord George Sackville[209] had advanced at Minden, the French army would have turned, 'et il aurroit ete le plus illustre jour que la France jamais ont.'"

"Mr. William Auld,[210] the minister of Mauchline, took his Sunday's supper with me one night when I lived in the Canongate. He had provided himself with a large new wig, with the greatest number of curls in it that I almost ever saw. As he walked up the street in his way home some drunken fellows passed him, and his wig having attracted their attention, one of them called out, 'There's a wig like the hundred and nineteenth Psalm,'—a droll comparison of the number of curls in the wig to the number of verses in the psalm, very apropos (apposite) to a minister."

MR. BROWN, my clerk, who was present.

"Mr. Charles Cochrane liked to have a number of curious mortals about him at Ochiltree. Richmond of Bardarrock was one of them, but had more education and genius than most of them. One day they made a kind of butt of Bardarrock, and were all laughing at him, upon which he very gravely said, 'It's a changed world now; the lairds of this place were wont to keep hawks, but this laird has an unco' taste,—he keeps gowks.'"

LORD AUCHINLECK.

"Lord Forglen was a great original. Every Sunday evening he had with him his niece Betty Kinloch,[211] afterwards Lady Milton, Charles Forbes, who went out in the 1715, and David Reid, his clerk. He had what he called the exercise, which was singing a psalm and reading a chapter; and his form was this,—'Betsy, ye hae a sweet voice; lift ye the psalm;—Charles, ye hae a strong voice, read ye the chapter;—and, David, fire ye the plate.' This was burnt brandy for them. Accordingly all went on, and whenever the brandy was enough, David blew out the flame, which was a signal; the exercise stopped, and they took their pint."

LORD AUCHINLECK.

"When Lord Forglen was dying my grandfather went and visited him, and found him quite cheerful. 'Come awa, Mr. Boswell,' said he, 'and learn to dee (die), man. I'm ga'n awa to see your old friend Cullen[212] and mine. He was a gude honest man! but his walk and yours was nae very steady when you used to come in frae Maggy Johnston's[213] upo' the Saturday afternoons.'"

LORD AUCHINLECK.

"Old Dr. Clark told my father that he came in to see Lord Forglen when he was dying. 'Weel, Doctor' said he, 'what news?' 'I canna say I hear any,' said the Doctor. 'Dear man,' said he, 'wha do they say's to succeed me?' 'It's time enough,' said the Doctor, 'to speak o' that, my lord, when ye're dead.' 'Hoot, daft body,' said Forglen, 'will ye tell us?' Upon which the Doctor mentioned such a man. 'What's his interest?' 'So-and-so.' 'Poh, that 'ill no do. Wha else?' 'Sic a man.' 'What's his interest?' 'So-and-so.' 'Poh, that 'ill no do either.' Then the Doctor mentioned a third man and his interest. 'I'll lay my siller on his head against the field.'"

LORD AUCHINLECK.

"Old Dr. Clark told my father the day Lord Forglen died he called at his door, and was met by David Reid, his clerk. 'How does my lord do?' 'I hope he's weel.' So the Doctor knew he was dead. David conducted him into a room, and when he looked beneath the table there was (sic) two dozen of wine. In a little in came the rest of the Doctors. So they all sat down, and David gave them some of my lord's last words, at the same time putting the bottels (sic) about very busily. After they had taken a glass or two they arose to go away. 'No, gentlemen,' said David, 'not so; it was the express will o' the dead that I should fill you a' fou, and I maun fulfil the will o' the dead.' All the time the tears were running down his cheeks. 'And indeed,' said the Doctor, 'he did fulfil it, for there was na ane o' us able to bite his ain thumb.'"

LORD AUCHINLECK.

"———[214] was a very religious young woman. She refused Mr. James Dundas,[215] of Arniston, because he was a rake. Some years afterwards she married Mr. Alexander Leslie,[216] brother to the Earl of Leven, who at length was Earl of Leven himself, but had very little when she married him. Upon which Monypenny, of Pitmilly, wrote these lines:—

'Celia, who cast her eyes to heaven,
Now turns them back and looks to Leven;
Her former coyness she repents,
And thinks of men of lower rents,
Which makes it true what old folks says—
There's difference of market days.'"

LORD AUCHINLECK.

It is curious that Pitmilly's[217] sister was second wife to Mr. Leslie after he came to be earl.

"The old laird of Blair[218] was a man of singular humour. He and the laird of Baidlin were once visiting at Eglintoune. When they were coming away, Blair says, 'Baidlin, we have been very kindly entertained in this house. I think we'll leave a crown, the price o' drink-money.' 'I think so too,' said Baidlin. Blair contrived to let Baidlin go before him, who gave his crown. In a little after Blair came down, and he says to the butler, 'Heark'ye! did Baidlin gie you the crown I gied him to gie you?' 'Yes, an't please your honour,' said the butler, and bowed to the ground; so that Blair got all the honour. He was a man, however, who used to brag of his tricks, so Baidlin got notice of this, and was determined to be evens with him. The next time he was at Blair the laird had got a kind of threatening letter from Mr. William Blair,[219] one of the regents of the College of Glasgow, craving him for the annual rent of £500 which the laird of Blair owed him, and a letter of apology from Blair, with entreaties of delay, was lying open on the table. Mr. William Blair was married to a daughter of Orbistoun's,[220] with whom he got a good deal of money, and both he and she squinted a good deal. When the laird went out of the room Baidlin wrote a postscript to the letter,—

'Glee'd Will Blair has gotten a wife,

And Orbistoun defraud it;

Their eyes are in continual strife,

Similis simili gaudet.'

"The laird without looking into his letter again seals it and sends it off; upon receiving it, Mr. William Blair was in a most horrid rage, and immediately sent him a charge of horning. The laird got upon his horse, came to Mr. William, and begged to know why he used him so severely. 'Used!' said he, 'after writing to me in that impertinent manner!' The laird desired to see what he had written; and on being shown the postscript, 'Oh,' said he, 'that has been Baidlin.'"

LORD AUCHINLECK.

"I have often remarked how strongly people's faults are painted when once we are exasperated against them. The faults of indifferent people are, as it were, written in invisible ink; we scarcely perceive them, and only know where they exist. But the moment our resentment is kindled against these same people their faults appear black like the characters written in invisible ink when held to the fire."

"Pope told Lord Marchmont of his intention to have Warburton[221] write notes upon his works. 'Well said, my lord; it will be a very good trial of the strength of your genius to see how much nonsense you can carry down to posterity when you have Warburton on your back.'"

DAVID HUME, Esq., who had it from LORD MARCHMONT.

"Warburton was a prodigious flatterer of Lord Mansfield, and consequently a favourite. David Hume was one day speaking violently against him to his lordship, who said, 'Upon my word, Mr. Hume, he is quite a different man in conversation from what he is in his books.' 'Then, my Lord,' said Hume, 'he must be the most agreeable man in the world.'"

MR. DAVID HUME.

"David Hume was one day observing to me that he could not conceive what satisfaction envious people could have by saying that a work of genius such as the 'Gentle Shepherd' was not written by its reputed author, but by some other person, as one should imagine that they must be equally hurt by one person's being admired as by another. I accounted for it in this way: that by ascribing it to another person than its reputed author, they raise doubts whether the praise is due to the one or the other, and so the admiration, instead of being fixed to one, is kept *in equilibrio*, like Mahomet's coffin between the two loadstones."

"The celebrated Mr. Banks[222] before he set sail on his first expedition was in love with a Miss Blosset; when he returned he found himself so enthusiastically fond of roving in search of unknown regions, that he could not think of matrimony. At the same time he had shown such an attachment to the lady that it was matter of great doubt in the world of private news whether he would think himself bound in honour to marry her. General Paoli asked Mr. Richard Owen Cambridge, 'Pray, do you think Mr. Banks will marry Miss Blosset?' 'Oh no, sir,' said Mr. Cambridge, 'his thoughts are all *beyond* Cape *Horn*.'"

GENERAL PAOLI.

"Dempster said that Cullen the mimick was to men's characters like wax to intaglios—to seals cut inwards: That men had particularities, but that we did not perceive them till the impressions of them were shown, reversed, bold, and prominent (or words to that purpose), by Cullen's mimickry."

I was present.

"In the spring, 1772, Dempster gave me the following lively representation of Sir William Meredith.[223] 'He is no longer with us,' said he, 'nor has he yet joined the ministry. He is like a wart round which there is a string tied. All circulation is stopped between him and us; and he is ready to be cut off whenever the ministry please.'"

"I was one of Mr. Ross[224] the player's counsel as a friend. His spouse, the celebrated Fanny Murray, made me a present of some very pretty straw mats for setting dishes on. Lord Auchinleck observed to me, 'Well, James, she cannot say that then she does not value your advice a *straw*.'"

"Mr. C. F. told a story in a company in a very confused manner, and then said he told it in confidence, and then begged they would not repeat it. 'Pray,' said Dempster, 'do you think any of us can repeat this story'?"

"A Jew having been brought before Lord Mansfield as Lord Chief Justice of the King's Bench, applied to be admitted to bail. He was dressed in very rich lace clothes. The counsel against him disputed for a considerable time, alleging that the bail which he offered was not good. My lord was tired and in a hurry, and looking at the Jew's rich clothes, 'Why, sir,' said he, 'he will burn for the money.'"

COUNCILLOR VANSITTART, who was present.

"At the exhibition of the Royal Academy at London in 1772 there was a picture of Lord Clive renouncing Meer Jaffier's legacy in favour of the East India Company, for the support of invalids. Dempster did not perfectly believe the story of this picture. He was dining at Sir George Colebrooke's,[225] and Lady Colebrooke would needs expatiate upon this picture, and on the subject of it. 'Madam,' said Dempster, 'I take it that affair won't bear to be *canvassed*.'"

MR. DEMPSTER.

"On Monday, the 2nd November, 1772, I dined at Fortune's in company with Mr. Banks, Dr. Solander,[226] and several more, at an entertainment given by Mr. Hamilton, of Bangour,[227] when the following good things passed:

"Lord Kelly[228] said of a Mr. Wright who was present, 'He has been in several parts of the world, and I expect to see him in Otaheite before he dies.' 'So then, my lord,' said David Hume, Esq., 'you expect to be there yourself.' My lord, in order to retort upon Hume for this catching at his word, set himself in a steady posture, and said, 'My dear David, if you were to go there you would be obliged to retract all your essays on miracles.' 'Oh no, my lord,' said Hume, 'everything there is in nature.' 'Aye,' said the Earl, '(but) there are different natures.'"

"Mr. Hamilton of Bangour's lady, was that morning delivered of a son, who was not yet baptized. Lord Kelly proposed his health; but addressing himself to Principal Robertson, said, 'Doctor, this is not a safe toast for you, for he's not a Christian.' 'My lord,' said the Principal, 'there are good hopes.'

Hume laughed. Said the Earl, 'David, if there are hopes, I am afraid it will be worse for you.'"

"Somebody observed that Lord Elibank[229] was constantly reading Lucretius; another asked, 'Has he given up Tacitus?' Said Lord Kelly, 'It's long since he gave up Tacitus; for he never can hold his tongue a minute, and he has taken to Lucretius because he feels himself grown so old that he would make but a poor figure with Lucretia.' At saying this the earl laughed, as if in scorn, and cried, 'Such nonsense!'"

"Our frame and temper of mind depends much on the state of our bodies. The human body is often called a machine, and a wonderful machine it is. The blood is like quicksilver, the veins like feathers, the nerves like springs. The soul sits in the machine. As one who in a chaise when driving hard cannot hear or give attention, I have been conscious of the corporeal machine running on with such rapidity that I felt to apply seriously to anything was in vain for me while that continued."

"Mr. Crosbie,[230] the advocate, when he once took up an idea retained it most obstinately, even after there was convincing evidence against it. On occasion of the great cause between Nabob Fullerton[231] and Orangefield,[232] where he and I were on opposite sides, he persisted in thinking Fullerton in the right, when every one else was clear against him. I said Crosbie's head was like a Christmas-box with a slit in the top of it. If once a thing has got into it, you cannot get it out again but by breaking the box. 'We must break your head, Crosbie,' said I."

"It's a good thing for Scotland that we can appeal to the House of Lords. I look upon that court, the House of Lords, as a great rolling stone, which by going over a cause effectually smooths it at once, when our fifteen lords, who have been breaking the clods with their mallets for a long time, may have left some parts rough; or sometimes may have found large masses which they have not been able to break at all. The rolling stone can never do harm. If the cause is smooth, it will make it more firmly so; if rough in whole or in part, will smooth it."

"Banks and Solander were telling of a monstrous crater which they had found in Iceland, which threw up prodigious quantities of hot water to an amazing height. The story, I believe, was true. But I had my joke on them as travellers; I said they had found a kettle to boil Pontopidan the Bishop of Berghen's wonderful fish."

"I have observed that the Lords of Justiciary in Scotland, though they proceed with strong common sense and in general with material justice, yet have not studied criminal law as a science, though it is a very extensive, important, and nice one. Being lords of session, their attention is chiefly taken up with civil affairs, and they take criminal matters only by the bye. They are like barber-surgeons, who shave—and bleed—upon occasions."

"There are a variety of little circumstances in life, which, like pins in a lady's dress, are necessary for keeping it together, and giving it neatness and elegance."

"A man of fame and acknowledged judgment as an author giving his opinion to a bookseller in favour of a literary work, the copy of which is offered for sale, when he does not sincerely think as he says, is a piece of real dishonesty, quite different from those commendations which a good-natured though not strictly honest flattery bestows. It is like a goldsmith, to whom suspicious metal is referred, certifying that it is gold when he knows it to be brass or a bad mixture."

"Dr. Johnson had a very high opinion of Edmund Burke. He said, 'That fellow calls forth all my powers;' and once, when he was out of spirits and rather dejected, he said, 'Were I to see Burke now 'twould kill me.'"

MR. LANGTON.[233]

"Mr. Johnson used to laugh at a passage in Carte's 'Life[234] of the Duke of Ormond,' where he gravely observes 'that he was always in full dress when he went to court; too many being in the practice of going thither with double lapells.'"

MR. LANGTON.

"——, who translated 'Ariosto,' had a dispute with Tom Wharton[235] as to some passages of it. —— knew the subject perfectly, but could not express himself. Wharton knew it very superficially, but wrote with ease and vivacity. Johnson said 'the one had ball without powder, and the other powder without ball.'"

"Johnson had a sovereign contempt for Wilkes and his party, whom he looked upon as a mere rabble. 'Sir,' said he, 'had Wilkes's mob prevailed against Government, this nation had died of *phthiriasis*.' Mr. Langton told me this. The expression, *Morbus pediculosus*, as being better known, would strike more. *Lousy disease* may be put in a parenthesis."

"Mr. Ilay Campbell[236] spoke with admirable good sense and ingenuity, but had a very weak voice and a diminutive appearance and manner. I said his pleading was like Giardini's playing on a child's fiddle."

"The extracts of a book given in the review often please us much more than the book itself does. The extracts are embellished and illustrated with criticism. It is like collops well-seasoned and served up with a good sauce, which are better eating than the sirloin or rump from whence they are cut. (Or, thus one eats with greater relish slices or collops well seasoned and served up with a good sauce, than one does the sirloin or rump from whence they are cut)."

"I said the Court of Session was much more quiet and agreeable when President Dundas[237] was absent. 'When he is there,' said I, 'you feel yourself as in a bleachfield with a large dog in it. He is chained and does not bite you. But he barks *wowf, wowf,* and makes you start; your nerves are hurt by him.'"

"Mr. Alexander Murray,[238] said that the President Dundas upon the bench was like Lord Kelly playing in a concert—very quick, loud, and rumbling. Nothing can be a more lively representation of his manner than this, when you harangue a little with the president's blustering tone and bounces of voice at intervals—'I cannot agree to give you this cause against the Duke of Gordon, sitting here as judge on great revolution principles,' &c."

"I said that Mr. Charles Hay[239] and I, who studied Scotch law together, used to go to Mr. McLaurin,[240] when we found any difficulty, as to a mill to get it ground. 'Yes,' said Crosbie, 'and he made you twenty difficulties out of one.' 'The observation,' said I, 'is just and witty. It reminds me of the fable of the lady, who when she was not pleased with her looks dashed the mirror in pieces, and so saw a multitude of ugly faces instead of one.'"

"26th June, 1774.—At a Sunday's supper at Dr. Webster's, when I was finding fault with a lady for going to visit a relation who had married a low man, the Doctor said that treating such people with mere civility was the best way to get the better of them. I answered, 'I don't want to get the better of them, I want to get rid of them: you may get the better of a sow by going into the mire and boxing it; but who would do it?' My wife, who wanted to support Dr. Webster, though she had not much attended to the dispute, said something which was of pretty much the same import with my remarks. 'Well,' said I, 'this is good enough. She thinks she is opposing me, and yet she agrees with me; she thinks she is riding a race with me and getting the better, and all the time she is behind me.'"

"My father told me that when he got his gown upon the resignation of the worthy Lord Dun,[241] he went and waited upon him, and said, 'My lord, as I am to be your lordship's unworthy successor I am come to ask your blessing.' 'Sir,' said Lord Dun, 'I held that office too long, for I was come to be but half a judge. Nay, what do I say? I was come to be worse, for I was able to give corporal presence but one-half of the year, and when I was present I could not have given that attention which every man ought to have who decides on the property of others. But to tell you the truth, I held my office from an apprehension that they might put in a man even worse than half a judge. However, sir, since you are to be my successor,'—(he then paid my father some genteel compliments); he added, 'I have no title to give a blessing, but if my prayers can be of any service to you, while I live they shall never be wanting.'"

"29th June, 1774.—I said the business of the Court of Session went on as fast without the President[242] as with him, though with less noise, when he was absent the court was a plain girr (hoop), which ran smoothly and quietly; when he was there, it was a girr with jinglers.'"

"When Charles Townshend[243] read some of Lord Kames'[244] 'Elements of Criticism,' he said, 'This is the work of a dull man grown whimsical,'—a most characteristical account of Lord Kames as a writer."

MR. GEORGE WALLACE.[245]

"Mr. Andrew Balfour[246] said of Lord Kames, 'He has the obstinacy of a mule and the levity of a harlequin.'"

MR. CHARLES HAY.

"Mr. Alexander Lockhart, Dean of the Faculty of Advocates, very readily shed tears when he pleased, whether from feeling or from a weakness in his eyes was disputed. He was also very fond of getting his fees. I applied to him a *part* of a fine passage in Shakspere,—

> 'He hath a *tear* for pity, and a *hand*
> Open as the day.'"

"When Andrew Stuart declared himself a candidate as member of Parliament for Lanarkshire after being stigmatised so severely by Thurlow and Lord Camden for his conduct in the Douglas cause, Sir John Douglas, who was very keen in the great cause, and had admirable extravagant sallies, said, 'What think you of this fellow? He has brass indeed! why, you may make ten dozen of tea-kettles out of his forehead.'"

I was present.

"I always wished to go to the English bar. When I found I could labour, I said it was pity to dig in a lead mine when I could get to a gold one."

"In 1774 there came on before the Court of Session a cause at the instance of a *black*[247] for having it declared that he was free. I was one of the counsel. We took no fees; and I said I knew one thing, that he was not a Guinea *black*."

"General Scott[248] was a man of wonderful good luck. He married Lady Mary Hay, a very fine woman. She ran off with Captain Sutherland, but was catched at Barnet, and the General got a divorce with the utmost ease. He then married Miss Peggy Dundas, who proved an admirable wife. Everything turned out well for him. Sandie Murray[249] said he was like a cat, throw him as you please he always falls on his feet. Nairne,[250] on hearing this, quoted the motto of the Isle of Man,—

'Quocunque jeceris stabit.'"

"General Scott and General Grant,[251] two noted gamesters, were one day driving upon the sands of Leith at the races in a post-chaise together. Nisbet,[252] of Dirleton, pointing to them, said very significantly from Prior, 'An honest, but a simple pair.'"

"June 18th, 1774.—I said in a dispute with Sir Alexander Dick,[253] on the different estimation to be put on sons and daughters, that sons are truly part of a family; daughters go into other families. Sons are the furniture of your house; daughters are furniture in your house only for sale. No man would wish to have his daughters fixtures. Such of them as are well looked are like pictures in the catalogues of the exhibition, those marked thus are for sale. (Or thus, daughters are like certain pictures in the exhibition, those marked thus, &c.)"

"June 18th, 1774.—Cosmo Gordon and I were talking of David Moncrieffe,[254] whose vanity was consummate, and who was flattered prodigiously by those whom he entertained, Cosmo mentioned a company of some of them, and said he would be embalmed. 'Yes' said I, 'David gets himself made a mummy in his own lifetime.' Said Cosmo, 'Like Charles V., who went into his own coffin.'"

"I said Moncrieffe entertained people to flatter him, as we feed a cow to give us milk. The better the pasture, the more plentiful and richer will the milk be. Moncrieffe therefore feeds his *pecora ventri obedientia* in clover. Other comparisons may be made. He feeds people like silkworms, for their silk, or like civet cats, for their perfume."

"Mr. Brown,[255] merchant in Edinburgh, who, from his stiffness of temper and manners went by the name of *Buckram Brown*, was a violent American; and when it was said that the king's army had defeated and dispersed General Washington's army near New York, 'That is nothing,' said he; 'for there will start up new armies of twenty, thirty, forty thousand men.' The Hon. Captain Archibald Erskine[256] on being told this said very pleasantly, alluding to Falstaff's fictitious foes and Mr. Brown's nickname, yes, men in Buckram.'"

I was present.

"There was a woman called Mrs. Betty Kettle, who lived with Mr. Thomson of Charleton,[257] and was exceedingly ill-tempered and troublesome. Lady Anne Erskine[258] said, 'Mrs. Betty Kettle kept all the house in hot water.'"

HONBLE. CAPT. ARCHIBALD ERSKINE.

"The writers who attacked David Hume before Beattie[259] took the lash in hand, treated him with so much deference that they had no effect. He was cased in a covering of respect. But Beattie stripped him of all his assumed dignity, and having laid his back bare, scourged him till he smarted keenly, and cursed again. David was on very civil terms with his former opponents, being treated by them as Dr. Shebbeare was in the pillory, who was being allowed to wear a fine powdered flowing wig. But he was virulent against Beattie, as I have witnessed, for Beattie treated him as an enemy to morals and religion deserved."

"I said that Dempster and Crosbie were different: thus Dempster had elegant knowledge of men and books, with vivacity to show it; Crosbie solid stores of learning and law and antiquities and natural philosophy. Dempster resembles a jeweller's shop, gay and glittering in the sun; Crosbie, the warehouse of an opulent merchant, dusky somewhat, but filled with large quantities of substantial goods."

"I am for most part either in too high spirits or too low. I am a grand wrestler with life. It is either above me, or I am above it; yet there are calm intervals in which I have no struggle with life, and I go quietly on.—February, 1777."

"Sir Adam Fergusson,[260] who, by a strange coincidence of chances, got in to be member of parliament for Ayrshire in 1774, was the great-grandson of a messenger. I was talking at Rowallan[261] on the 17th March, 1777, with great indignation that the whole families of the county should be defeated by an upstart. Major Dunlop[262] urged the popular topick, that the other candidate, Mr. Kennedy,[263] was supported by noblemen who wanted to annihilate the influence of the gentlemen, and he still harped on the coalition of three peers. 'Sir,' said I, 'let the ancient respectable families have the lead, rather than the spawn of a messenger. Better three peers than three *oyeses*.'"

"Mr. David Rae,[264] advocate, when he pleaded in appeals at the bar of the House of Lords, used to speak a strange kind of English by way of avoiding Scotch. In particular he pronounced the termination, *tion*, as in petition, very open, that he might not sound it *shin*, as is done in Scotland. Mr. Nairne, advocate, said Mr. Rae has shone—*tion*—more in the House of Lords than any man."

I was present.

"Mr. David Rae, advocate, one day pleaded a cause in the Court of Session with a great deal of extravagant drollery. Mr. John Swinton[265] said of him upon that occasion, he was not only Rae, but *Outré*."

MR. MACLAURIN.

"Swift says, 'No man keeps me at a distance, but he keeps himself at as great a distance from me.' This has the appearance as if the man of dignity suffered something, whereas it is just what he wishes. He wishes to be at a distance from vulgar disagreeable people."

"A friend and neighbour of mine, Mr. H———n, of S———m,[266] is like a fire of a certain species of coal which has a deal of heat but no flame. He is warm, but wants free expression."

"Lord Monboddo[267] was urging with keen credulity that the Patagonians were really at a medium above eight feet high. 'Nay,' said General Melville,[268] 'I can believe anything great, as I happened in my youth to see a whale cast on shore.' 'A whale,' said I, 'is a good cast to the imagination.'"

MONBODDO, 22nd November, 1778.

"The good humour of some people must be supplied by external and occasional aids, like a pond which depends for water on the rain which falls. Others have a constant flow of good humour within themselves, like a spring well."

"The beautiful Lady Wallace[269] said in a company that she had had a dream, which from her way of expressing herself was suspected to be a little wanton. She said she could not tell it to the company. She could tell it but to one gentleman at a time. She told it to Mr. Crosbie. 'It seems,' said I, 'you take Mr. Crosbie to be a Joseph, that you tell your dream to him.' A witty allusion to Joseph's character, both for interpreting dreams and for chastity.—11th December, 1779."

"Few characters will bear the examination of reason. You may examine them for curiosity, as you examine bodies with a microscope. But you will be as much disgusted with their gross qualities. You will see them as Swift makes Gulliver see the skins of the ladies of Brobdignag."

"A poor minister who had come to Edinburgh had his horse arrested. He upon this gave in a petition to the Lords of Session, praying to have his personal estate sequestrated and his horse delivered up to him. The lords granted his petition. George Fergusson[270] found fault with them for giving him his horse. 'Come, come,' said I, 'you need not be angry; there is no kindness in it, for you know the proverb, 'Set a beggar on horseback, and he'll ride to the devil.'" 1779.

"I have not an ardent love for parties of pleasure; yet if I am once engaged in them no man is more joyous. The difference between me and one who is the promoter of them is like that between a water-dog and an ordinary dog. I have no instinct prompting me; I never go into the water of my own accord; but throw me in, and you will find I swim excellently."

"Sir Joshua Reynolds observed that a little wit seemed to go a great way with the ancients, if we might judge from the instances of it which Plutarch has collected. Edmund Burke upon this observed that wit was a commodity which would not keep. Said his brother Richard,[271] 'If there had been more *salt* in it, it would have kept.'"

SIR JOSHUA REYNOLDS, London,

25th April, 1776.

"The difference between satire in London and in Scotland is this:—In London you are not intimately known, so the satire is thrown at you from a distance, and, however keen, does not tear and mangle you. In London the attack on character is clean boxing. In Scotland it is grappling. They tear your hair, scratch your face, get you down in the mire, and not only hurt but disfigure and debase you.

"A company were talking of Dr. Johnson. Dr. Armstrong, who had a violent prejudice against him, and was in the habit of saying and being praised for saying odd things, was present. Being asked if his dictionary was not very well done, 'Yes,' said he, 'for one man; but there should have been four-and-twenty—a blockhead for every letter.'"

MR. DEMPSTER.

"Burke, talking to Mr. Dempster of——, a member of Parliament who had deserted his party for court advantages, asked if he had not fallen. 'Yes,' said Dempster, 'on his feet.'"

MR. DEMPSTER.

"Talking of the great men whom the resistance or rebellion in America had produced, Dempster said, 'It costs a great deal to raise heroes; they must be raised in a hotbed.' 'Yes,' said I, 'these have cost a great deal of bark of royal oak, and a good deal of dung too.'"

London, 23rd April, 1779.

"The conversation having turned on Andrew Stuart's[272] artful defence of the treacherous conduct of his brother to Lord Pigot,[273] I said, 'He has laid on a thick colouring upon his brother's character. It would not clean; he has died (*sic*) it.'"

London, 23rd April, 1779.

"Mr. Seward[274] once mentioned to me, either as a remark of his own or of somebody else's, that the most agreeable conversation is that which entertains you at the time, but of which you remember no particulars.' I said to-day I thought otherwise, 'as it is better both to be entertained at the time and remember good things which have passed. There is the same difference as between making a pleasant voyage and returning home empty, and making a pleasant voyage and returning home richly laden.'"

23rd April, 1779.

"I wrote to Dempster from Edinburgh, 13th December, 1779. I am in good spirits, but you must not expect entertainment from me. The most industrious bee cannot make honey without flowers. But what are *the flowers of Edinburgh*?"

"Showing Dr. Johnson slight pretty pieces of poetry is like showing him fine delicate shells, which he crushes in handling."

"In the debate concerning Sir Hugh Palliser[275] in the House of Commons, when it was proposed to address the king to dismiss him, Mr. Wedderburne said, 'Stained as that gentleman's flag has been, I should be very sorry to see it hoisted over him as an acting admiral; but I can see no reason why for one unfortunate spot he should be deprived of the last consolation of its waving over his grave.'"

Public Advertiser.

"My wife was angry at a silk cloak for Veronica being ill-made, and said it could not be *altered*. 'Then,' said I, 'it must be a *Persian* cloak,' alluding to the silk called Persian and the unalterable *Persian* laws." 1780.

"I told Paoli that Topham Beauclerck[276] found fault with Brompton's[277] refreshing the Pembroke family picture by Vandyck, and said he had spoiled it by painting it over (which, by the way, Lord Pembroke assured me was not the case). 'Po, po' said Paoli (of whom Beauclerc had talked disrespectfully), he has not *spoiled* it; Beauclerc scratches at everything. He is accustomed to scratch [scratching his head in allusion to Beauclerc's lousiness], and he'd scratch at the face of Venus.'"

London, 1778.

"Bodens was dining at a house where a neck of roast veal was set down. After eating a bone of it, he was waiting for something else. The lady of the house told him it was their family dinner, and there was nothing else. 'Nay, madam,' said Bodens, stuttering, 'if it be n-neck or n-othing, I'll have t'other bone.'"

EARL PEMBROKE,[278] London,
26th April, 1778.

"Spottiswood[279] asked me what was the reason I had given up drinking wine. 'Because,' said I, 'I never could drink it but to excess.' Said he, 'An excessive good reason.'"

Dining at Paoli's,
28th April, 1778.

"When a man talks of his own faults, it is often owing to a consciousness that they cannot be concealed, and others will treat them more severely than he himself does. He thinks others will throw him down, so he had better lye down softly."

London, April, 1778.

"I can more easily part with a good sum at once than with a number of small sums—with a hundred guineas rather than with two guineas at fifty different times; as one has less pain from having a tooth drawn whole than when it breaks and is pulled out in pieces."

London, April, 1778.

"When Wilkes was borne on the shoulders of the unruly mob, Burke applied to him what Horace says of Pindar,—'Fertur numeris legibus solutus.'"

MR. WILKES, London, April, 1778.

N.B.—"Dr. Johnson[280] thought this an admirable double pun; and he will seldom allow any vent to that species of witticism."

"General Paoli was in a boat at Portsmouth at the naval review in 17—. He seated himself close to the helm. They wanted to steer the vessel, and in the hurry of getting to the helm they overturned the general. He said, very pleasantly:—'Darbord que je me metts au gouvernail ou men chasse.'"

GENERAL PAOLI, London, 1778.

"At the regatta on the Thames, Sir Joshua Reynolds said to Dunning,[281] 'I wonder who is the Director of this show?' Dunning, who delights in the ludicrous in an extreme degree, pointed to a blackguard who was sitting on one of the lamps on Westminster Bridge, and said, 'There he is.' Sir Joshua observing a fellow on a wooden post nearer the water answered, 'I believe you are right, and there is one who has a post under him.'"

SIR JOSHUA REYNOLDS, London,

April 25th, 1778.

"Colman[282] had a house opposite to a timber yard. The prospect of logs and deals was but clumsy. Colman said it would soon be covered by some trees planted before his windows. Sir Joshua Reynolds upon this quoted the proverb, 'You will not be able to see the *wood* for *trees*.'"

SIR JOSHUA REYNOLDS,

25th April, 1778.

"At Sir Joshua Reynolds' table —— observed that in the Germanick politicks at present the King of Prussia was a good attorney for the ——. 'Yes,' said I, 'and he has a good power.'"

2nd May, 1778.

"In London you have an inexhaustible variety of company to enjoy with superficial pleasure, and out of these you may always have a few chosen friends for intimate cordiality. While you have a wide lake to sport in, you may have a stewpond to fatten, cherishing to high friendship, affection, and love, by feeding with attention and kindness. One must have a friend, a wife, or a mistress much in private; must dwell upon them, if that phrase may be used; must by reiterated habits of regard feel the particular satisfaction of intimacy. There must be many coats of the colour laid on to make a body substantial enough to last, for the colour of ordinary agreeable acquaintance is so slight that every feather can brush it off. One should be very careful in choosing for the stewpond. Horace says, '*Qualem commendes etiam atque etiam respice.*' Such a recommendation is useful to put us on our guard to preserve our character for discernment. It is as much so to make us preserve our own comfort in friendship."

London, April, 1778.

"If you wish to be very happy with your friend, or wife, or mistress, be with them in London or Bath, or some place where you are both enjoying pleasure; not in the country, where there is dulness and weariness. You may, perhaps, bear up your spirits even in dreary cold darkness in their company, but it is too severe trial to make the experiment. There may be love enough, yet not of such a supreme degree that warms amidst external disadvantages. It is not giving them fair play. Be with them in the sunshine; let mutual gladness beam upon your hearts; and let the ideas of pleasure be associated with the ideas of your being together. If pity be akin to love, it is so to melancholy love. Joy is the fond relation of delightful love of the sweet passion."

London, April and May, 1778.

"General Paoli one day asked me to read to him something good out of my journal of conversations, which he found me busy recording. I was running my eye over the pages, muttering and long of bringing forth anything, upon which the general observed with his usual metaphorical fancy, *finesse d'esprit*, 'Reason says I am a deer lost in a wood. It is difficult to find me.' I had nothing to answer at the time, but afterwards—I forget how long—I said, 'The wood is crowded with deer. There are so many good things, one is at a loss which to choose.'"

London, April, 1778.

"Mr. Crosbie was the member of several clubs. I said to him, 'Crosbie, you are quite a club sawyer.'"

"Dr. Webster was rather late in coming to a dinner which I gave at Fortune's, 9th July, 1774. His apology was, that just as he was coming out a man arrived who had money to pay him, and he stayed to receive it. 'You was very right,' said I, 'for money is not like fame, that if you fly from it, it will pursue you as your shadow does.'"

"Harry Erskine[283] was observing that a certain agent would take it amiss to have it mentioned that his grandfather was a bellman. 'I don't think it,' said I. 'A bellman is a respectable title,' said Peter Murray;[284] 'it is at least a sounding title.'"

"'I was wondering one day how many times a lawyer walks backwards and forwards in the outer house[285] in a forenoon,' said Cosmo Gordon. 'You must take a compound ratio of his idleness and his velocity.'"

"My wife said it would be much better to give salaries to members of Parliament than to let them try what they can get off their country by places and pensions. Said she, 'They are like ostlers and postillions, who have no wages, and must support themselves by vails.'"[286]

"One day when causes were called in the Inner House in an irregular manner, and not according to the roll, I said to Crosbie, 'The English courts run straight out like a fox; ours double like a hare.'"

"The pleasure of seeing Italy chiefly depends on the ideas which a man carries thither. Take an ignorant mechanick or an unlearned country squire to the banks of the Tiber. Show him Mount Soracte, the ruins of Rome, and drive him on to Naples, he will have little enjoyment. But a man whose mind is stored with classical knowledge feels a noble enthusiasm. His ideas uniting with the objects before him catch fire, and a flame is produced as in a chemical process by the mingling of certain substances, while others remain quite tame. A man must have his imagination charged with classical *particles*."

"The severe measures taken against the Americans united them firmly by a cement of blood."

A. BRITON, *Pub. Advert.*, 16th Sept., 1775.

"Parliament is now, instead of being the representative of the nation, the echo of the Cabinet; and its acts are only wrappers to the ready prepared pills of the court laboratory for the people to swallow—if they do not stick in their throats."

A. BRITON, *Pub. Advert.*, 16th Sept., 1775.

"I said of a rich man who entertained us luxuriously, that although he was exceedingly ridiculous, we restrained ourselves from talking of him as we might do, lest we should lose his feasts. Said I, 'he makes our teeth sentinels upon our tongues.'"

"I said that a drunken fellow was not honest. 'A stick,' said I 'kept allways moist becomes rotten.'"

"If a man entertains his company himself, it is a great fatigue. It is blowing a fire with his own breath. Whoever can afford it should have a led captain of strong animal spirits, who may, like perpetual bellows, keep up the social flame."

"I told Nairne one afternoon that I had been taking an airing with our solicitor-general. Said he, 'Was you *learning* to be solicitor?' 'No no,' said I; 'solicitors-general are *non docti, sed facti*.'"

1777.

"Poor David Hamilton of Monkland, on account of his vote in Lanarkshire, was made one of the macers of the Court of Session. He had a constant hoarseness, so that he could scarcely be heard when he called the causes and the lawyers, and was indeed as unfit for a crier of court as a man could be. I said he had no voice but *at an election*."

"Sandie Maxwell, the wine merchant, told a story very well, and used to heighten it by greater and greater degrees of strong humour, according to the disposition of the company. I said he *blew* a story to any size, as a man blows figures in a glasshouse. A satirical fellow would say, I warrant he shall not blow his own bottles to too large a size."

"Lady Di Beauclerk[287] said to me she understood Mrs. V—— was an idiot. I said I was told so too; but when I was introduced to her did not find it be true. 'Or perhaps,' said I, 'her being less an idiot than I had imagined her to be may have made me think she was not an idiot at all.' 'I think,' said Lady Di, 'she is bad enough, if that be all that a lawyer has to say for her, that she is only less an idiot than he imagined.' Said I, 'There are different kinds of idiots as of dogs, water idiots and land idiots, and so on.' 'I think,' said Lady Di, 'that is worth writing down.'"

Richmond, 27th April, 1781.

"Lady Di Beauclerk told me that Langton had never been to see her since she came to Richmond, his head was so full of the militia and Greek. 'Why,' said I, 'madam, he is of such a length, he is awkward, and not easily moved.' 'But,' said she, 'if he had laid himself at his length, his feet had been in London, and his head might have been here *eodem die.*'"

"Lord Chesterfield could indulge himself in making any sort of pun at a time. Dr. Barnard, now Bishop of Killaloe, was standing by his lordship in the pump-room at Bath, when the late Duchess of Northumberland's father was brought in a chair very unwieldy. The musick was playing. My lord said to Barnard, 'We have a new sort of instrument this morning—a dull Seymour[288] (dulcimer).'"

From DR. BARNARD, London, 1781.

"Parnell[289] was miserably addicted to drinking. He could not refrain even the morning that Swift introduced him to Lord Oxford.[290] My lord pressed through the crowd to get to Parnell. But he soon perceived his situation. He in a little said to Swift, 'your friend, I fear, is not very well.' Swift answered, 'He is troubled with a great shaking.' 'I am sorry,' said the Earl, 'that he should have such a distemper, but especially that it should attack him in the morning.'"

From DR. BARNARD, Bishop of Killaloe,
who had it from DR. DELANY.

"In spring, 1781, Dr. Franklin[291] wrote from Paris to a freind in London, with indignation against one who had been entrusted with money belonging to the American prisoners, and had run off with it. One expression in his letters was singularly strong, and indeed wild:—'If that fellow is not damned, it is not worth while to keep a devil.'"

MR. SUARD.[292]

"Lord Foley,[293] whose extravagance frequently brought his creditors upon him so as to have executions in his house, was rallying George Selwyn on his particular curiosity for spectacles of death. 'You go,' said he, 'I understand, to see all executions.' 'No my lord,' answered George, 'I don't go to see your executions.'"

MR. SUARD.

"The Honourable Mrs. Stuart[294] was one day talking to me with just severity against drunkenness (the sin which doth most easily beset me). I attempted to apologise, and said that intoxication might happen at a time to any man. 'Yes,' said she, 'to any man but a Scotsman, for what with another man is an accident is in him a habit.'"

"At Sir John Dick's, Sunday, 8th May, 1785, I made the gentlemen sit and drink out some capital old hock after the ladies left us. When I came into the drawing-room, and was seated by the lady of Sir Matthew White Ridley,[295] she said to me, 'We ladies don't like you when you have drunk a bottle of hock, because you then tell us only plain truth.' 'Bravo!' cried I; 'Lady Ridley, this shall go into my *Boswelliana*. It is one of the best *bon mots* I have heard for a long time. It goes deep into human nature.'"

"M. D'Ankerville (9th May, 1785) at General Paoli's paid me the compliment that I was the man of genius who had the best heart he had ever known."

"The king cannot give to Langton because he is not in the political sphere. He cannot take a handful of the gold upon the faro table, and give it to any man, however worthy, who is only looking on or stalking round the room. Let him play, let him part, and take his chance. The king is but the marker at the great billiard-table of the state. He can mark a man three, four, or five, or whatever number according to his play, and if he goes off the table into opposition, can rub out the chalk; like the marker, he can give what money he has for himself as he pleases, and employ his own tailor or shoemaker, and buy his own snuff and ballads, take a walk or a ride at his idle hours where he pleases."

"The first time Suard saw Burke, who was at Reynolds's, Johnson touched him on the shoulder and said, 'Le grande Burke.'"

"My journal is ready; it is in the larder, only to be sent to the kitchen, or perhaps trussed and larded a little."

"Mrs. Cosway[296] said she had often expressed a wish to see me. General (Paoli) did not tell me this. He has been affraid of making me too vain and turning the head of his friend. No, he knows the value of things—it was not worth telling."

"At Mr. Aubrey's, 19th April, Wilkes and I hard at it. I warm on monarchy. 'Po, your'n old Tory.' *Boswell.* 'And you're a new Tory. Let that stand for that.'"

"I mentioned my having been in Tothill Fields Bridewell; how the keeper had let me in, &c. *Wilkes*, 'I don't wonder at your getting in, but that you got out.' *Bos.* 'O no, I have no propensity to be a jail-bird; I never had the honour you have had'[297] [he looking a little disconcerted, as the pill rather too strong]—I mean being Lord Mayor of London; I mean the golden *chain*. I never had the honour to have a chain of any sort.'"

"'I'll have some of the other soup too. Were there a hundred soups, I should eat of them all.' *Mrs. Aubrey* (very pleasantly): 'I am sorry ours comes so far short of your number.'"

"Old Hutton[298] talked of men of phlegm and men of fancy. Said H., 'Men of phlegm punish the beef, the solid parts of dinner; men of fancy, the dessert.' 'Sir,' said I, 'men of fancy would have nothing to work upon were there not men of phlegm. Men of phlegm perform the actions, compile the histories, discover the arts and sciences upon which poetry is founded.'"

"Dr. Burney[299] said he hoped I was now come to plant myself in London. 'I'll bring the watering pan,' said he."

"I told Lord Galloway,[300] April, 1785, that I called Lord Daer Darius.[301] 'What,' said he, 'do you think him the son of Cyrus?' laughing at Lord Selkirk. I did not think he'd have said this, though a distinguished law lord."

"When Pitt the second made his first appearance in the House of Commons in opposition to Fox, Gibbon[302] said, 'There is a beautiful painted pinnace just going to be run down by a black collier.' He never was more mistaken. Pitt has more forcible indignation in him than Fox."

WILKES.

"As a playful instance of the proverb, I said, 'Every man has his price. Lord Shelburne[303] has his price [meaning Dr. Price],[304] whom I love and call *Pretium affectionis.*'"

Monday, 18th April, 1785, at

DR. BROCKLESBY'S.[305]

"General Paoli said more good things than almost anybody, yet he talks of them with contempt. I told him he had always *bon mots* about him, which he used like footballs—he threw them down and gave them a kick." 24th April, 1785.

"April, 1785, at Mr. Osborne's. Sir Joseph Banks told me he was sure he had a soul. He felt it high within him, as a woman does a child."

"25th April, 1785. Dining on guard with Colonel Lord Cathcart,[306] Cataline was mentioned. 'Who was he?' said George[307] Hanger, 'for I know no ancient history.' 'I'll tell you what he was,' said Colonel Tarleton. '*Alieni cupidus, sui profusus.*' 'Very fair!' said Hanger. In a little talking of fellows going carelessly to execution, Tarleton said, 'We're told Sir Thomas More smiled all the way.'"

"Mrs. Heron[308] being at her parish church, the name of the minister being Stot,[309] as it was a very bad day, and the wind and rain were driving through the windows, a lady observed that it was like a *guarde mange*. 'I think so too, madam,' said she; 'but if that were the case I should think it would be better to have a dead stot than a living one.'"

From herself.

"Houstoun Stewart[310] was one night in Drury Lane playhouse very shabbily dressed. A surly-looking, boorish fellow comes up to him: 'Pray, sir, whose seat do you keep?' Houstoun replied with an ironical complaisance, 'Yours, sir.' As he was rising the fellow observed his sword, was much confused, and asked ten thousand pardons. 'From this,' says Stewart, 'we see the value of a sword. Had I wanted it I might have been taken for a real footman.'"

MR. G. GOLDIE.

"A comical fellow was telling that Raploch sat upon turkey eggs and brought out birds, which made the company laugh extremely. 'Stay, stay, gentlemen!' says Harry Barclay;[311] 'you don't know that these turkeys are all my cousins german, for Raploch is my uncle.'"

LADY KAMES.[312]

"A gentleman was one night talking of the Nile. An ignorant boobie who was present asked him with great eagerness, 'Pray, what fellow was that?' 'Why, troth, sir,' says he, 'it was a fellow that took a conceit to hide his head so that it could not be found again.'"

MRS. HERON.

"A dog one day jumped upon Miss Bruce[313] of Kinross's lap at a tea-table. 'I wonder,' says she, 'if dogs can see anything particularly agreeable about me?' 'Indeed, madam,' replied a gentleman, 'he would be a very sad dog that did not.'"

MRS. G. GOLDIE.

"Mr. Heron[314] was one day reproving a servant at table for negligence. 'What have you been thinking of, Peter, that you have forgot spoons?' 'I suppose, my dear,' says his lady, 'that he has been thinking of knives and forks.'"

I was present.

"We are apt to imagine that the Turks are a brutal sort of people, totally given up to gross sensuality, and altogether void of gay fancy or the finer feelings. As an instance to the contrary, my Lord Galloway tells that he was sitting at Constantinople with a Turkish gentleman, who, although a true Mussulman, took a glass of wine. The custom there is not for a company to drink all at once, like a regiment going through their evolutions, but as the intention of drinking is to cheer the spirits, they take a cup of the liquor which stands before them just as they feel themselves in need of it. This Turk, after having taken three or four bumpers of champagne, pointed to a lamp which hung above their heads, as they never use candles. 'This,' says he, 'my lord, is to me as the oil is to that lamp.' A pretty allusion, as if it lighted him up."

LORD KENMORE.[315]

"My lord having shown to the same gentleman a picture of Lady Garlies,[316] he looked at it a long time very attentively, and then asked my lord, with a good deal of emotion, whose picture it was. My lord answered that it was the picture of his lady, who had died just before he left his native country. 'My lord,' said the Turk, 'you have the strongest constitution, and have a chance to live longer than any man I ever met with.' And being asked his reason for saying so, 'Because, my lord, you have been able to survive so fine a woman.' A noble expression of a feeling heart."

LORD KENMORE.

"Silinger, a gentleman of Ireland, remarkable for humour and spirit, had got himself drunk one night, and had broke windows in St. James's Street. Next morning at White's they were all talking of and abusing him most confoundedly. Lord Coke,[317] a most worthless fellow, stood up with great warmth for Mr. Silinger, who a little after came in! 'Silinger,' cried my lord, 'you are much obliged to me this morning, for I have been losing my character in defence of yours.' 'Have you so, my lord?' says he, 'then you are much obliged to me, for you have lost the worst character in all England.'"

MR. MURRAY, of Broughtoun.

"Colonel Chartres,[318] who knew mankind too well to be ignorant of the power of flattery, said to John,[319] Duke of Argyle, 'Good heaven, my lord, what would I give to have your character! I would give ten thousand pounds.'

'Indeed, Chartres,' replied the duke, 'it would be the worst bargain you ever made, for you would lose it again in a day.'"

LORD KAMES.

"A gentleman was one day making that common serious reflection, 'Time runs.' 'Very well,' replied Boswell, 'let it run there, for I am sure I shall never try to pursue it.'"

"Lady Katie Murray[320] having shown her full-length portrait to Lord Eglintoune, 'O such vanity, such vanity!' cried he, 'do you really take that for you?' 'Indeed, my lord,' says she, Mr. Reynolds says that it is me; so I can't help it.'"

From herself.

"Colonel Folly came to wait upon old Jerviswood,[321] who was very deaf; and being very finically dressed, the old gentleman asked with great curiosity, 'Who's that? who's that?' and being answered, Colonel Folly, 'I see,' says he, 'he's a fool, but what is his name?'"

LORD AUCHINLECK.

"Sir Alexander Dick passed an evening at Rome with a number of gentlemen, who had been obliged to fly Scotland on account of the rebellion, 1715. One of them sung 'The Broom of the Cowdenknowes,'[322] with which the whole company were so much affected as to burst into tears and cry with great bitterness."

From himself.

"When John McKie[323] was in Prussia, one of the sentinels petitioned him and some other gentlemen who were with him for their charity to a poor Briton, who had been seized by the advanced guards while in the Dutch service, and had now but very poor pay. 'Pray, sir,' said Mr. McKie, 'what is your name?' 'John McKie, sir,' said he, 'from the Laird of Balgowan's estate, in the parish of Monigaff, in Galloway.' Surprised and pleased at the discovery, they collected all the silver they had about them and threw to him."

SIR ROBERT MAXWELL, 3rd hand.

"Jerviswood carried his whole family to travel with him through Italy. The first night of their being in Rome they went to an assembly, and were surprised to find them dancing to the tune of 'The Lads of Dunse.' The history of the thing was this:—the Italians have no country dances; but Miss Edwin, sister to Lady Charlotte's husband, was very fond of the Scots country dances, and as her family were opulent people when they were abroad, she had influence enough with the Italians to introduce these dances, which they still remain fond of."

LORD KAMES.

"It is a tradition believed in the family of Carnwath[324] that one of the old earls, who was a very zealous Catholic, took it into his head to make a pilgrimage to the Holy Sepulchre. As he was entering one of the gates of Constantinople he saw a woman sitting on a balcony spinning and singing, 'O the broom,' &c."

LORD KENMORE.[325]

"A man had heard that Dempster was very clever, and therefore expected that he could say nothing but good things. Being brought acquainted, Mr. Dempster said to him with much politeness, 'I hope, sir, your lady and family are well.' 'Ay, ay, man,' said he, 'pray where is the great wit in that speech?'"

LADY ANN ERSKINE.

"A gentleman was complaining that he had done good to another who had made him no grateful return. 'Well, well,' said Boswell, 'you are so far lucky, that if you did good to your neighbour you have your reward, whether he will or not.'"

"Boswell and John Home met with a man in their walk one morning, who said that he was a hundred and three. 'What a stupid fellow,' said Boswell, 'must that be who has lived so long!'"

"Boswell was one day complaining that he was sometimes dull. 'Yes, yes,' cried Lord Kames, *'aliquando dormitat Homerus'* (Homer sometimes nods). Boswell being too much elated with this, my lord added, 'Indeed, sir, it is the only chance you had of resembling Homer.'"

"A countryman came one day and told Lady Machermore,[326] 'Oh, madam, you have lost a great enemy this morning—the auld bear of Kirouchtree's dead.' 'Ay, ay,' says she, 'the auld Heron dead? give the honest man a dram.' The fellow took his dram very contentedly, and then said, 'Na, God be thanked, madam, Heron's not dead, for I mean the old boar-sow that used to destroy your potatoes.'"

MR. HERON.

"At an execution in the Grass Mercat, Boswell was observing that if you will consider it abstractly there is nothing terrible in it. 'No doubt, sir,' replied Mr. Love, 'if you will abstract everything terrible that it has about it, nothing terrible will remain.'"

"When Lord Galloway was in Constantinople, an old Turk of sixty was dining one day with a company of the English, with whose ease and freedom and mirth he was so much transported as to exclaim, 'Good God, am I come to this age, and have lived but one day!'"

LORD GALLOWAY.

"Lord Mark Ker[327] was playing at backgammon with Lord Stair in a coffee-house in London; an impudent fellow was saying some rude things against Scotland. 'Come, my Lord Stair,' said Lord Mark, 'let us have a throw of the dice, which of us two kicks this scoundrel down-stairs.' Lord Stair had the highest throw, and accordingly used the fellow as he deserved. 'Well,' said Lord Mark, 'I allways am unlucky at play.'"

LORD AUCHINLECK.

"Montgomerie,[328] of Skermorly, was Provost of Glasgow. A vain, haughty man, Jacobie Corbet,[329] a merchant, and a noted man for humour, accosted him one day in the familiar style of 'How are you, Hugh?' 'Hugh, sir?' said he, 'is that a proper way of talking to the Lord Provost of Glasgow?—Officer, take this fellow to prison directly.' It was accordingly done. Some time after commissions for justices of the peace came down, and amongst the rest was one for —— Montgomerie, of Skermorly. 'Ay,' said he, 'this is pretty odd. I should think the Queen might have been better acquainted with my name.' 'Indeed,' replied Corbet, 'I dare say she remembered your name, but she knew that if she called you Hugh she would have got the Tolbooth.'"

LORD AUCHINLECK.

"When Campbell,[330] of Shawfield, returned with all his riches to Glasgow, everybody flocked about him to pay their respects except Corbet, with whom he had served his apprenticeship, who never troubled his head or went near him. Shawfield, concerned at this, and willing to ingratiate himself with everybody, came up to him as he was walking before his shop. 'Oh, my good old friend, Jacobie Corbet, I rejoice to see you. I protest I know no odds upon you these twenty years.' 'Say you so, Daniel?' cried he, 'but I know a very great odds upon you; you came here at first wanting bretches, and now you are riding a coach and six.'"

LORD AUCHINLECK.

"Colonel Irwin[331] was dancing down a country dance at Bath, when somebody said, 'I hope Mrs. Irwin is well.' The colonel, dancing on, bowed and smiled and replied, 'Dead a fortnight,—dead a fortnight.'"

LORD KELLY.

"Sanderson, the Quaker, and Lady Galloway, had a violent dispute about religion. 'Well, well, Catherine,'[332] said he, 'you have but an Act of Parliament for your religion; I have the same for mine.'"

LORD GALLOWAY.

"Lady Garlies[333] was making a cap to herself one evening. Says old Galloway, with much slyness, 'If you were a milliner, madam, you would have plenty of business.' 'Yes,' said Garlies, one way or t'other.'"

I was present.

"A young extravagant dog had contrived to swell his bills prodigiously, and among other articles he had this:—'To an entertainment to my friends the night before I left Oxford, £40.' 'My dear Tom,' said his father, 'I rejoice to find you so fortunate a man, for by what I can see you have a greater number of friends than any man in England.'"

MR. ALLAN WHITEFOORD.[334]

"A company of strolling players were rehearsing 'Macbeth,' and singing the chorus of 'We fly by night.' 'Oh,' cried the landlord, who overheard them, 'I'll take care of that;' and immediately called a constable to lay hold of them."

MR. LOVE.

"As Lord Mark Ker was going one night to pay a visit, one of his chairmen jostled a gentleman upon the street, who immediately knocked him down. Lord Mark came out of his chair, and as the fellow recovered himself, he desired the gentleman to chastise him for his insolence, which he declined. 'Why, then, sir,' said Lord Mark, 'you will excuse me for taking notice of you for knocking down my chairman,' and caned him most heartily."

LORD GALLOWAY.

"Sir William Maxwell of Springkell[335] said that Lord Fife[336] and Miss Willy[337] Maxwell resembled one another, for they had both bought their titles dear enough."

I was present.

"Whenever a young man was recommended to old Lord Stormont[338] for one of his kirks, he used allways to ask, 'Is he good-natured in his drink?' and if that was the case he said he should be his man."

SIR JOHN DOUGLAS.

"Lady Elibank[339] was regretting that old families should sink. Sir William Baird of Newbyth,[340] an ugly-looking dog, was there, who laughed and said, 'What is all that stuff about old families? All nonsense! I should be glad to know who is the representative of Nebuchadnezzar's family?' This Lord Elibank, then a boy, replied, 'You, sir, and he got you when he was eating grass with the beasts of the field.'"

SIR WILLIAM MAXWELL.

"At a hunters' meeting at Dumfries, Mr. Riddle[341] of Glenriddle came up to the Duke of Hamilton,[342] with his hand in his coat pocket. 'Will your Grace crack any walnuts?' The duke, who had lost his teeth, took it as an affront, and was very sulky."

SIR WILLIAM MAXWELL.

"When this story was told, somebody said, 'That's nuts for B[oswell].'"

"When Sir Peter Frazer of Dores[343] brought home his lady to the Highlands, he said to his English coachman, 'All these hills are mine, John.' 'Indeed, sir,' said he, 'they're all not worth a groat. I would not take off my hat and thank God Almighty for all this part of the creation.' Just as he spoke the coach overturned."

SIR WILLIAM MAXWELL.

"When Lord Hyndford[344] was ambassador at the court of Berlin, the King of Prussia said to him one morning at the levee, 'Do you know, my lord, that two of my soldiers have this morning died of the English distemper? they have hanged themselves.' 'True, sire,' replied Lord Hyndford; 'but it was for a very different reason. Suicide amongst our people is occasioned by an over-fulness; but I am told that these fellows hanged themselves because they were dying of hunger.'"

LORD AUCHINLECK.

"Lord Dunmore[345] was telling Lord Cassillis[346] that his little child was beginning to speak, and could allready say Dun. 'Well, my lord,' said he, 'it will say *more* by and by.'"

From himself.

"Colonel Murray was imposing on some ignorant young fellow at play. Lord Mark Ker said nobody but a scoundrel and a villain would do so. Murray came to Lord Mark, and asked him if he had said so. 'Sir,' said he, 'to the best of my remembrance these were my words. I am not sure but I likewise added rascal.'"

SIR W. MAXWELL.

"A fellow was swearing most terribly in a coffee-house. Colonel Forrester came up to him. 'Pray sir, what entitles you to swear and blaspheme at this rate?' 'Eh, colonel,' said he, 'What! are you reproving me for it? I'm sure you used to swear as much as any man.' 'Yes sir,' said he, 'when it was the fashion. But now it is only practised by porters and chairmen. I left it off as below a gentleman.'"

MR. GOLDIE, of Hoddam.

"Cosmo Alexander[347] the painter, upon a slight acquaintance with a Roman Catholic lady, took her out to dance in the Edinburgh assembly, and as he was figuring away in black velvet with various gesticulations, 'Lord Elibank,' asked Sir William Maxwell, 'who's that who dances?' Being told Mr. Alexander the painter, 'Upon my word,' said his lordship, 'a very picturesque minuet.'"

SIR WILLIAM MAXWELL.

"The Duke of Newcastle[348] had a very mixed character, was not deficient in parts, but was remarkable for being inattentive, confused, and hurried. Lord Chesterfield said he was like a man who had lost half an hour in the morning and was running about all the day, in order to find it again."

LORD KAMES.

"Lady———, a woman of low birth, whose father and uncle had both been strung at Tyburn, asked George Selwyn[349] to come and see an elegant room which she was fitting up at her house in Pall Mall. George, observing some vacant places for pictures, inquired what she was to put there. She said she intended to hang some family pictures there. 'O, madam' replied he, 'I thought all your ladyship's family had been hanged already.'"

CAPTAIN ERSKINE.

"The Laird of Macfarlane[350] was maintaining one day that the highlands was much better country than Fife, and that Kelly Law would make no figure among the hills in his country. 'I grant you,' said Captain Erskine, 'it would make but a contemptible figure as a hill, but it would make an admirable plain.'"

From CAPTAIN ERSKINE.

"An Irish servant told his master that his best horse had fallen over a precipice. 'Well,' said he, 'there is no help for it; let us at least save something; go directly and skin him, and come quickly back.' The fellow, being very long of returning, was asked what he had been about. 'An't please your honour,' said he, 'the horse run so fast, that it was three hours before I could overtake him to get the skin off.'"

LADY BETTY MACFARLANE.[351]

"The same gentleman sent his servant one dark night with a friend to conduct him through a bad step in the road. His friend fell into the very middle of the mire. The servant being asked upon his return if he had shown the gentleman the hole, 'Indeed sir,' said he, 'he did not need to be shown it, for he found it himself.'"

LADY BETTY MACFARLANE.

"A countryman was carrying a hare over his shoulder in the streets. A waggish young fellow accosted him thus:—'Pray sir, is that your own hare, or a wig?'"

CAPTAIN ERSKINE.

"When Mr. Love was engaged for Drury Lane, he went to Covent Garden and saw Shuter[352] play Falstaff the night before he appeared in that character himself. After the play was over, Mr. Shuter said, 'He has satisfied me very much—because he satisfied nobody else.'"

From himself.

"The Duke de Nivernois[353] is a man of fine parts and address, but a very diminutive figure. When he made his appearance in London in the year 1762, Charles Townshend said, 'It is impossible this can be an ambassador, for he has not even the preliminaries of a man.'"

LORD KELLY.

"Eating supper is nothing. 'Tis drinking supper hurts a man."

29th May, 1783.

"Mr. Burke said at Chelsea College dinner, a poor French cook was persecuted by the mob at Edinburgh as a Papist. Said young Burke, 'They had taken him for a *frier!*'"

"At Chelsea College dinner, 29th May, 1783, Sir George Howard,[354] the Governor, drank to the memory of Charles the Second, the founder; and then to the glorious and immortal memory of William the Third, its last royal benefactor. Mr. Burke, who used to joke with Mr. Boswell as a friend to the House of Stewart, observed that no notice had been taken of James the Second, whose name is still inscribed upon the college as a benefactor. Mr. Boswell then said, merely from the connection of the word *medio* with that prince as the *middle* king who had promoted that institution, 'Sir George, you are unmindful of *medio tutissimus ibis*.' Sir George answered, very justly, 'That is a maxim I think he did not understand.'"

"My friends are to me like the cinnamon tree, which produces nutmeg, mace, and cinnamon; not only do I get wisdom and worth out of them, but amusement. I use them as the Chinese do their animals; nothing is lost; there a very good dish is made of the poorest parts. So I make the follies of my friends serve as a dessert after their valuable qualities."

"It is very disagreeable to hear a man going about a subject and about it, and hesitating, while one perceives what he means to say. Mental stammering hurts one as much as a stammering in speech."

Mrs. Boscawen,[355] 17th May, 1784.

"I was observing at Mr. Dilly's how terrible an idea it was when Mr. Perry was going to the East Indies for ten years in quest of languages. Dr. Johnson said, with his wonderful shrewdness, 'He went *to* the East Indies. The question is, what did he go *from*?'"

"My only objection to living in London is that there is too much space and too little time."

27th May 1784.

"I said Suard had a feeble venom spit-spit."

1784.

"I told General Paoli that Dr. Johnson said Langton was first a talking man—then he would be a silent man. 'All upon system, to be distinguished,' said the General. 'He wanted to go into the cave of Trophonius, and he went into that of Polyphemus' (alluding to his being a disciple of Dr. Johnson)."

1784.

"My son Alexander,[356] one day in December [1783], when in a passion at his sister Phemie for something she had said, used this strong expression,—'Phemie, if your tongue be not cut out, it will soon be full of lies.'"

1784.

"January 7. He understood that there was a violent opposition to the king; and he imagined Sir Philip Ainslie[357] was on that side. He said the king should send messengers to discover all that are against him. That would soon turn Sir Philip Ainslie's brain right."

"January 10. He complained that his brother James beat him. Grange said he should not mind him, as he was but a child. 'Ay,' said he, 'but he must not be a big man to me' (alluding to the weight of his blows)."

"The difference between an ancient family is sometimes not visible. Above the ground the tree may be the same. The ancient has only deeper roots, which only antiquarian diggers observe. Yet from the deep roots there are plants of a more stately air, so that in general the difference appears even in the stem and branches; sometimes, indeed, by rich and happy culture, the new ones will look almost as well."

"In a book of science or of general information, one may introduce an eloquent sentence, if not too flighty; or, when an elevated thought occurs stand on tiptoe, but not rise from the ground. I made this remark to Mr. Lumsden, while reading a passage of higher tone in his account of Rome. It will also apply to Sir John Pringle's[358] Discourses before the Royal Society."

"A man begged sixpence from a gentleman and was refused. With a melancholy look he said, 'Well, then, I know what to do.' The gentleman struck with this, and dreaming the poor man meant to kill himself, gave him the sixpence, and then asked him, 'What would you do?' 'Why, sir,' said he, 'I should be obliged to work.'"

DR. WEBSTER.

"Peter Boyle[359] has so much milk of temper one can hardly be angry with him. But even milk will offend, when it goes down the *wrong throat*."

"Asparagus is like gentility; it cannot be brought to the table till several generations from the dunghill."

"The arsenic sophistry of Gibbon—sweet and poisonous."

"The minds of some men are like a dark cellar—their knowledge lies concealed; while the minds of others are all sunshine and mirror, and reflect all that they read or hear in a lively manner."

"Sir John Wemyss[360] calling on R. Colville[361] in the abbey a few weeks after losing £500 by him, was offered by him a tune on the fiddle. 'Stay,' said Sir John, 'till the rest of your creditors get a share.'"

"'Who's there?' said the Lord President Arniston, one morning at breakfast, in winter, 1782-3; 'I dinna see.' John Swinton, then a candidate for a gown, courteously said, 'The light is in your lordship's eyes.' 'No, John,' said he, 'the light's out of my e'en.'"

"Burke said that it was of great consequence to have a British peerage, for each generation is born in a great theatre where he may display his talents. I told this to General Paoli, who was of a different opinion. 'It is true,' said the general, he is born in a great theatre, but he is applauded before he acts.'"

"When it was asked in India why Sir Thomas Rumbold's[362] acquisition of wealth made more noise than that of others, a black man said, 'Others pluck one feather, and one feather from the fowl, and the fowl do not make noise; but Rumbold tear all the feathers all at once, and the fowl cry Zua, Zua.'"

MR. DEMPSTER.

"General Paoli said of Sir Joshua Reynolds, whose deafness made him use a trumpet, 'He has a horn only at one ear; if he had one at both he would be a Jupiter.'"

6th May, 1781.

"I told young Burke that Wilkes said he was an enemy to General Paoli from the natural antipathy of good to bad. 'Which *is* the bad?' said Burke."

6th May, 1781.

"General Paoli described a blue-stocking meeting very well:—Here, four or five old ladies talking formally, and a priest (Dr. Barnard, Provost of Eton), with a wig like the globe, sitting in the *middle*, as if he were confessing them.'"

May, 1781.

"Mrs. Thrale spoke slightingly of Paradise.[363] She said, 'I never heard him say anything, but my fader vos not a Greek, but my moder was a Greek.' Young Burke and I thought her too severe; 'but,' said young Burke, 'it seems she does not find the tree of knowledge in Paradise.'"

6th May, 1781.

"Lady Preston[364] had catched cold by going to some meeting. Capt. Brisbane[365] wrote to Lady Maxwell,[366] 'Some ladies have a zeal, I do not say without knowledge, but without constitution to support it.'"

"When Wilkes and I sat together, each glass of wine produced a flash of wit, like gunpowder thrown into the fire—Puff! puff!"

"Lord Mountstuart said at J. R. McKye's, 30th April, 1783, that it was observed I was like Charles Fox. 'I have been told so,' said I. 'You're much uglier,' said Col. James Stuart, with his sly drollery. I turned to him, full as sly and as droll: 'Does *your wife* think so, Colonel James?' Young Burke said, 'Here was less meant than meets the ear.'"

"Mr. Charles Cochrane[367] was applied to requesting freestone to erect a monument at Falkirk to Sir Harry Monro,[368] who was killed at the battle there, fighting against Prince Charles in 1745. Mr. Cochrane very readily granted the request, and said he should be very glad to give stones for burying all the Whigs in Scotland."

From MR. STOBIE, Mr. Cochrane's agent.

"One who boasted of being an infidel said to Mr. Allan Logan that he wished much to see a spirit, but had in vain visited churchyards and every other place where he had the best chance. Mr. Logan, who was a very serious and even superstitious and credulous believer, answered, 'Why, man, you was a great fool for making the experiment, and you would have the devil to be as great a fool as yourself. He is sure of you at present, and you would have him to appear to you, that you might be convinced of a future state and escape him? No, no; he is too wise for that.'"

1st Oct., 1780, from the Rev. Mr. ROLLAND[369] of Culross.

"The Earl of Dumfries,[370] in Charles the Second's time, was a hard-hearted, unfeeling father. His son, Lord Crichton, had gone to Edinburgh, foolishly, as he thought. He died there, and his corpse was brought home to be buried in the family vault. As the earl saw the hearse from his window he said, 'Ay, ay, Charles, thou went to Edinburgh without an errand; I think thou hast got one to bring thee back again.' My father, who was always averse to my going to London, often told this story before me. I said one day of the earl, 'What a barbarian!'"

"Mr. Beauclerc told Dr. Johnson that Dr. James[371] said to him he knew more Greek than Mr. Walmsley.[372] 'Sir,' said he, 'Dr. James did not know enough of Greek to be sensible of his ignorance of the language. Walmsley did.'"

MR. LANGTON.

"A certain young clergyman used to come about Dr. Johnson. The Doctor said it vexed him to be in his company, his ignorance was so hopeless. 'Sir,' said Mr. Langton, 'his coming about you shows he wishes to help his ignorance.' 'Sir,' said the Doctor, 'his ignorance is so great, I am afraid to show him the bottom of it.'"

MR. LANGTON.

"To account for the common remark that the more a man advances in knowledge, the less he seems to himself to know, Mr. Burke said that what is in itself infinite, there is a larger circle without the first, and a larger without the next, and so on."

                                                                             Young MR. BURKE.

"Dr. Johnson desired me to tell Sheridan[373] he'd be glad to see him and shake hands with him. I said Sheridan was unwilling to come, as he never could forget the attack —— half told him. 'But it was wrong to keep up resentment so long,' said the Doctor; 'the truth is, he knows I despise his character; 'tis not all resentment; partly out of habit, and rather disgust, as at a drug that has made him sick.'"

"Lady Townshend[374] sent to Mr. Winnington for his coach and six horses one day. He asked her afterwards if they came in proper time, and her ladyship was pleased with them. 'Oh,' said she, 'I only invited them to dine. I wished they should have one good dinner, so I ordered them plenty of hay and straw.'"

                                                                                MR. LANGTON.

"I said it was a strange thing that Short,[375] the famous telescope maker in London, left a legacy of a thousand pounds to Lady Mary Douglas, who had no need of money, when he had a number of poor relations. Thomas Earl of Kelly said upon this, 'He was not a reflecting telescope maker.'"

"It was mentioned at Lady Colville's[376] that Mrs. C., of S., whose husband was a very big man, had once been very fond of Colonel M., and had suffered much from his forsaking her. 'What!' said a lady; 'she seems to like her husband so well, that I could not believe she was ever fond of any other man.' 'She *was* very fond of another man,' said I. 'But her husband *smothered* that passion.'" 1783.

"At a dinner at Mr. Crosbie's, when the company were very merry, the Rev. Dr. Webster told them he was sorry to go away so early, but was obliged to catch the tide, to cross the Frith of Forth to Fife. 'Better stay a little,' said Thomas Earl of Kelly,[377] 'till you be half seas over.'"

                                                                     Rev. DR. WEBSTER.

"Harry Erskine and another advocate, had written papers in a cause before Lord Westhall.[378] They thought them very good papers. But a clerk came to Mr. Erskine with a message that 'My Lord had read the papers, and could not *understand* them, and he would send a note of what he *wanted*.' 'Make my compliments to his lordship,' said Erskine, 'and tell him (pointing to his forehead) I have none to spare.'"

                                                          From MR. ERSKINE himself.

"On the 2nd December, 1782, I went to dine at Walker's tavern with a committee of the Presbytery of Edinburgh, who were taking evidence in a criminal process—the heritors of Carsphairn[379] against Mr. Affleck, who had a presentation to that parish. The agent for the heritors was the entertainer. I was asked to take the head of the table thus:—'Mr. Boswell, you'll take this end.' 'No,' said I, 'the Moderator will sit there.' 'Then you'll take this end,' the foot of the table. 'No,' said I, pointing to the agent. I placed myself about the middle of the table, and said, 'I have no end in view but a good dinner.' Said the Rev. Mr. Brown,[380] of Edinburgh, 'The end is lawful if the means be good.'"

"Miss Leslie, General Leslie's[381] daughter, had a pretty necklace, she obligingly took it off, and let me look at it. I said, 'It is pretty, even when it's off.'"

12th Nov., 1782.

"Sir James Johnstone[382] asked me if turning off nominal and fictitious voters now upon the roll would not be an act of violence. 'Yes,' said I, 'it would be an act of violence. But it would be an act of violence like turning thieves out of your house.'"

12th Nov., 1782.

"Mr. Keith,[383] the envoy, was in company with a good Highland lady, some of whose sons had been successful in the army. The company were talking of putting their sons to different professions. Said she, with great earnestness, 'If I had twenty *sons*, I would put them all to the *sword*.'"

From his eldest daughter, 12th Nov., 1782.[384]

"I said Lord Monboddo chose to vary Horace's *Mens sana in corpore sano*, and to have *mens insana incorpore sano*; for his endeavour is to keep his mind wild and his body robust."

12th Nov., 1782.

"Langton said he could not laugh at Burke's wit. The Bishop of Killaloe said, 'I'll tell you a story: Colonel Lutterel was at the house of a gentleman who insisted on his drinking more than he chose, and locked the door on him. The colonel fell upon a contrivance to get off which succeeded. "Come," said the gentleman, "fill your glass, you must drink;" "Sir," said the colonel, "I don't like your wine." The gentleman had nothing to say.'"

27th May, 1783.

"Langton said Burke hammered his wit upon an anvil, and the iron was cold. There were no sparks flashing and flying all about. Said the Bishop of Killaloe,[385] 'I don't think the iron is cold, but Burke is not so much a smith as he is a chymist, he analyzes a word, he decomposes it, and brings out all its different^{meaning} senses.'"

27th May, 1783.

"I said to General Paoli, it was wonderful how much Corsica had done for me, how far I had got in the world by having been there. I had got upon a rock in Corsica and jumped into the middle of life."

27th May, 1783.

"It was observed by somebody that Lord Dundonald attended to the church very ill. Miss Preston said that their two black servants were generally there every Sunday,—'Ay,' said Mr. Charles Preston, 'but two blacks don't make a white.'"

Valley Field, 17th October, 1778.

UXORIANA.

"When I was warm, telling of my own consequence and generosity, my wife made some cool humbling remarks upon me. I flew into a violent passion; I said if you throw cold water on a plate of iron much heated it will burst into shivers."

"She recommended reading the 'Arabian Nights Entertainments' to one in bad health and low spirits; 'not,' said she; 'to be taken into the mind, but to keep out disturbing thoughts; let them be like a sentry, whom we do not admit into the chamber of a sick person, but place at the door to prevent noisy intruders.'"

"She disapproved of my inviting Mr. M———sh, a man of ability but of violent manners, to make one in a genteel party at our house one evening. 'He is,' said she, 'like fire and water, useful, but not to be brought into company.'"

"Dr. Grant asked if Mr. Macadam of Craigengellan had but one daughter. I said he had properly speaking but one—one beautiful daughter, the other poor girl was very ugly. My wife said that it was hard that want of good looks should make her not be reckoned his daughter; she was more a daughter on that account, as being more likely to continue with him."

APPENDIX.

Page 52.—In his "Life of Garrick" (Lond., 1868, vol. I., p. 422) Mr. Percy Fitzgerald presents the following narrative of Boswell's appearance at a dinner in Guildhall. The date 1759 assigned to the occasion is evidently erroneous. It is not improbable that it took place shortly after the interchange of letters between him and Mr. Pitt. "The Grocer in London" was probably composed in the manner of the "Song of the Barber," quoted at page 36.

"At a Guildhall dinner, when Mr. Pitt was present with Sir Joshua [Reynolds] and other celebrities, Mr. Boswell contrived to be asked to sing; then, standing up, he delivered a short speech referring to himself, in which he said that he had had the good fortune to be introduced to most of the crowned heads and distinguished characters in Europe, but with all his exertions had never attained the happiness of being presented to a gentleman, who was an honour to his country, and whose talents he held in the highest esteem. All the company understood the allusion, but Mr. Pitt remained perfectly cold and impassive. Then Mr. Boswell gave his song, which was a sort of parody on Dibdin's 'Sweet Little Cherub,' and called 'A Grocer in London.' The minister was a member of the Grocers' guild, and this absurdity was in his honour. So far this was ludicrous enough, but Boswell, half volunteering and half pressed by the company, and no doubt much affected by the wine, sang this song over no less than six times, until Mr. Pitt's muscles at length relaxed, and he was obliged to join in the general roar. Mr. Taylor, who was present, walked home with the author of the song, and recollected that they roared 'Grocer of London' all through the streets."

Pages 49 and *110.*—Boswell was wont to attend public executions, both in Edinburgh and London, but the propensity of witnessing such spectacles was in his mind unassociated with an indifference to suffering. His love of excitement overcame his natural sympathies, and obscured his judgment. In June, 1790, he induced Sir Joshua Reynolds to accompany him to Newgate, to witness the execution of five convicts. One of these, an old servant of Mrs. Thrale, recognised Boswell among the crowd, and bowed to him from the scaffold. Some persons having censured Sir Joshua for being present at such a revolting spectacle, he justified his procedure in a letter to Boswell. An extract follows:—

"I am obliged to you for carrying me yesterday to see the execution at Newgate of the five malefactors. I am convinced it is a vulgar error; the opinion that it is so terrible a spectacle, or that it in any way implies a hardness of heart or cruelty of disposition, any more than such a disposition is implied in seeking delight from the representation of a tragedy. Such an execution as we saw, when there was no torture of the body, or expression of agony of the mind, but when the criminals, on the contrary, appeared perfectly composed, without the least trembling, ready to speak and answer with civility and attention any question that was proposed, neither in a state of torpidity nor insensibility, but grave and composed,—I am convinced from what we saw, and from the report of Mr. Ackerman, that it is a state of suspense that is the most irksome and intolerable to the human mind, and that certainty, though of the worst, is a more eligible state; that the mind soon reconciles itself even to the worst, when that worst is fixed as fate.... I consider it is natural to desire to see such sights, and, if I may venture, to take delight in them, in order to stir and interest the mind, to give it some emotion, as moderate exercise is necessary for the body."

Page 136.—When he was passing through the press his "Tour to the Hebrides," Boswell conceived the idea of sitting for his portrait to Sir Joshua Reynolds. The following letter which he addressed to the great artist is peculiarly characteristic:—

"MY DEAR SIR,—The debts which I contracted in my father's lifetime will not be cleared off by me for some years. I therefore think it unconscientious to indulge myself in any expensive article of elegant luxury. But in the meantime you may die, or I may die; and I should regret very much that there should not be at Auchinleck my portrait painted by Sir Joshua Reynolds, with whom I have the felicity of living in social intimacy. I have a proposal to make to you. I am for certain to be called to the English Bar next February: will you now do my picture? and the price shall be paid out of the first fees which I receive as a barrister in Westminster Hall. Or if that fund should fail, it shall be paid at any rate five years hence by myself or my representatives. If you are pleased to approve of this proposal, you signifying your concurrence underneath upon two duplicates, one of which shall be kept by each of us, will be a sufficient voucher of the obligation. I ever am, with very sincere regards, my dear sir, your faithful and affectionate humble servant,

JAMES BOSWELL.

"London, 7th June, 1785."

This letter was endorsed by Sir Joshua thus:—"I agree to the above condition.—London, September 10th, 1785." Boswell's portrait, in *kit-cat* size, was painted by Sir Joshua some time afterwards. Whether a price was named or paid does not appear, but it is certain the biographer and the great painter remained in terms of the closest friendship. Sir Joshua died in 1792; he bequeathed to Boswell the sum of £200, to be expended, if he thought proper, in the purchase of a picture at the sale of his paintings, to be kept for his sake. Boswell's portrait by Reynolds is now in the collection of Sir Robert

Peel, Bart. ("Life and Times of Sir Joshua Reynolds," by C. R. Leslie, R.A., and Tom Taylor. Lond., 1815, 2 vols.)

FOOTNOTES:

[1] I happened however to be present on an occasion when a quotation from Dr. Johnson served as a special illustration of the infallible memory and rapid intuition of a man of letters in whose distinction Scotland has a considerable share. It was in the house of a lady of literary and social importance in her day, who was fond of displaying her disregard of religious decencies. At one end of the table the party were talking of a remarkable fall of some fronts of houses in Tottenham-court-road, leaving the rooms open to the street in all their usual conditions. At the other the hostess was tracing resemblances between Mormonism and Christianity, with peculiar application to their founders. Mr. Macaulay, seated in the middle, leant over to Dean Milman opposite, and said in a low tone, "You remember Johnson's London,—

'Here falling houses thunder on your head,
And here a female Atheist talks you dead.'"

[2] This opinion receives an accidental confirmation of its events by the publication of the Life of Sir Gilbert Eliot—a work highly honourable to a Scottish house by the dignity of its records and the talent of their reproduction. This cannot be better expressed than in the words of Lady Minto, writing from Edinburgh, February 21, 1802:—

"This country has arrived at the true pitch of comfort and happiness. The people are full of information, are natural, unassuming, and social, but with a great mixture of occupation. People meet together to be pleased, cheerful, and easy; even the Scotch pride has its uses by putting the poor often on an equal footing with the rich. A Douglas or a Scott would consider himself on a par with persons of the highest title and rank; their education is equally good, their society the same, their spirit and love of their country possibly much greater. Almost every family can boast of heroes in some generation, which excites emulation; and nothing is so uncommon as to see idle men and listless manners. All is energy, and every one has some object in view to exercise his faculties and talents. I must say, at the present time I think the race very superior to the English, who are too far gone in luxury and dissipation to be agreeable or happy. *Morals* here are certainly very good, and yet the manners are much more free, and one scarcely ever meets with affectation and airs. People meet like friends, and not with a cold bow and a distant curtsey."

[3] In reference to Thomas Boswell the following entries appear in the Treasurer's books:—May 15th, 1504. "Item, to Thomas Boswell he laid downe in Leith to the wife of the kingis innis and to the boye ran the kingis hors 18s." Aug. 2, 1504. "Item, for twa hidis to be jakkis to Thomas Boswell and Watte Trumbull, agane the Raid of Eskdale [an expedition against the Border thieves], 56s." January 1, 1504-5. "Item, to Thomas Boswell and Pate Sinclair to by thaim daunsing geir, 28s." December 31, 1505. "Item, to 30 dosane of bellis for dansarris, delyverit to Thomas Boswell, £4 10s." In his "Collection of Criminal Trials," Mr. Pitcairn, who quotes these entries, supposes that Thomas Boswell held the position of royal minstrel. In this office he was probably the successor of Sir William Rogers, chief musician to James III. Rogers, like Boswell, obtained from his sovereign a grant of lands in guerdon of service. He suffered a violent death in 1482. ("Traquair Papers," quoted in Chambers' "History of Peeblesshire," Edinb., 1861, 8vo., pp. 81-86.)

[4] Lord Balmuto was a large coarse-looking man, with black hair and beetling eyebrows. Though not vulgar he was passionate, and had a boisterous manner. My mother and her sisters gave him the nickname of the "black bull of Norr'away," in allusion to the northern position of Balmuto.—"Personal Recollections of Mary Somerville," Lond., 8vo., 1873, p. 55.

[5] In a MS. commonplace-book of Lord Hailes, preserved at New Hailes, near Edinburgh, occurs the following entry in his lordship's handwriting:—"1754, Feb. 14. My friend Mr. Alex. Boswell, of Auchinleck, admitted a Lord of Session. He has told me that it was by the interest of the Duke of Newcastle. For once at least his Grace judged right." The Duke of Newcastle was Prime Minister.

[6] This lady's eldest sister was wife of the celebrated Dr. Alexander Webster, of Edinburgh (see *postea*).

[7] Dr. Stevens' "History of the High School of Edinburgh," pp. 100, 135.

[8] In Lord Hailes' Commonplace-book, preserved at New Hailes, is the following entry:—"1755, April 1.—I began my office of Advocate Depute at Stirling—a ridiculous day of the year. At that time I was very ignorant of criminal law, but good intentions have, I hope, atoned for my defects."

[9] Letter of Dr. Jortin, preserved at New Hailes.

[10] Letter to Mr. Temple, dated 1st May, 1761.

[11] "Letter to the People of Scotland," Lond., 8vo., 1785.

[12] This person is entitled to more than a passing notice. Long before the modern publication of cheap literature by W. and R. Chambers and Charles Knight, Alexander Donaldson opened a shop in London for the sale of what were termed "spurious editions" of popular books. The London booksellers endeavoured to check his enterprise, but were defeated in the courts of law. Latterly he was unfortunate. His nephew, James Donaldson, also a printer at Edinburgh, founded and endowed the hospital in that city which bears his name. For that purpose he bequeathed the sum of £200,000.

[13] Boswell has appended this note. "Who has not heard of '*Every man soap his own beard*'—the reigning phrase for 'Every man in his humor'? Upon this foundation B—— instituted a jovial society, called the SOAPING CLUB."

[14] An Edinburgh tavern.

[15] The name of this Soaper has not been discovered.

[16] Throughout his whole career Boswell entertained the idea that his mind was imperfectly balanced.

[17] Letters between the Honourable Andrew Erskine and James Boswell, Esq. London, 1763, 8vo.

[18] "Archibald Constable and his Correspondents." Edinburgh, 1873, 8vo, vol. I., p. 32.

[19] Mrs. Davies was originally an actress, and was celebrated as a beauty.

[20] Boswell's letter at New Hailes.

[21] Boswell's "Life of Johnson."

[22] Original letter at New Hailes.

[23] Original letter preserved at New Hailes.

[24] "Autobiography of the Rev. Dr. Alexander Carlyle." Edinburgh, 1860, 8vo., p. 322.

[25] Of this society, styled the Lunan and Viney Water Farming Club, the Rev. James Roger, of Dunino, father of the writer, was on Mr. Dempster's nomination elected perpetual secretary. The minute-book is in the writer's possession.

[26] In 1765 Mr. Dempster obtained the patent office of Secretary to the Order of the Thistle, with a salary of £500 per annum.

[27] Cards.

[28] Letter of Boswell preserved at New Hailes.

[29] "Institutes of the Law of Scotland," by John Erskine, of Carnock. A standard book of reference in the law courts of Scotland.

[30] This account of the quotation from Johnson's poem of "London" is contained in a letter addressed by Boswell to Sir David Dalrymple. In the "Life of Johnson" Boswell states that the quotation was made by himself.

[31] "I could give you pages of strong sense and humour which I have heard from that great man, and which are treasured up in my journal. And here I must inform you that he desired me to keep just the journal that I do; and when I told him that it was already my practice, he said he was glad I was upon so good a plan."—*MS. letter from Boswell of 13th July, 1763, preserved at New Hailes.*

[32] Dutch for "our envoy."

[33] The meaning here is defective.

[34] "Memoirs and Papers of Sir Andrew Mitchell, K.B., Envoy Extraordinary and Minister Plenipotentiary from the Court of Great Britain to the Court of Prussia, from 1756 to 1771," edited by Andrew Bisset, Esq., vol. ii., p. 381.

[35] Boswell's "Account of and Tour to Corsica," London, 1769, 8vo., p. 288.

[36] Boswell's "Corsica," 3rd edition, p. 349.

[37] "Life of Johnson."

[38] "Private Correspondence of David Hume." Lond. 1820, 4to., p. 131.

[39] "Chatham Correspondence," vol. ii., p. 388.

[40] Richard Owen Cambridge, author of "The Scribleraid" and other works. A gentleman of opulence, he entertained in his villa at Twickenham the literary celebrities of his time. He died in 1802, aged eighty-five.

[41] In his letters to Mr. Temple of 9th September, 1767, and 14th May, 1768, Boswell evinces a particular desire to possess Mr. Gray's opinion of his work, and to obtain his personal acquaintance. It is hoped that he remained uninformed of the poet's sentiments concerning him.

[42] "The Works of Thomas Gray. Edited by the Rev. John Mitford." London: 1816, 2 vols., 4to, vol. ii., p. 498.

[43] Boswell's servant.

[44] Sir Alexander Gilmour, Bart., of Craigmiller, M.P., Boswell's supposed rival in the affections of Miss Blair, died *unmarried* in France, on the 27th December, 1792.

[45] Miss Dick was eldest of the three daughters of Sir Alexander Dick, Bart., of Prestonfield. Mr. Temple met her during his visit to Scotland on the Adamtown expedition.

[46] Letter to Mr. Temple, written from Auchinleck, 24th August, 1768.

[47] Letter from Boswell to Mr. Temple, dated Edinburgh, 9th December, 1768.

[48] "The Carron Company has furnished me them very cheap; there are two 32-pounders, four 24's, four 18's, and twenty 9-pounders, with one hundred and fifty ball to each. It is really a tolerable train of artillery." (Letter from Boswell to Mr. Temple, dated 24th August, 1768.)

[49] See Correspondence between the Rev. N. Nicholls and the poet Gray, *passim*.

[50] Boswell's "Tour to the Hebrides."

[51] John, fifth Duke of Argyll, married Elizabeth, relict of James, sixth Duke of Hamilton, and daughter of John Gunning, Esq., of Castle Coote, co. Roscommon. The Duchess was a celebrated beauty.

[52] Life of Johnson.

[53] John, Lord Mountstuart, eldest son of John, third Earl of Bute, and afterwards first Marquess of Bute. He was born 30th June, 1744, and died 16th November, 1814.

[54] This lady was Margaret, daughter of Sir David Cunninghame, of Milnecraig, and his wife, Lady Mary Montgomery, daughter of Alexander, ninth Earl of Eglinton. She married, in 1767, the Hon. James Archibald Stuart, second son of John, third Earl of Bute. This gentleman was one of Boswell's most attached friends.

[55] Afterwards Viscount Melville.

[56] A forcible rendering of what he meant by styling Dr. Johnson "Ursa major."

[57] Letter dated 6th June, 1775.

[58] Boswell's "Life of Johnson," London, 1818, 10 vols., 12mo., vol. vi., p. 34.

[59] From the Register of Tailzies, preserved in the General Register House, Edinburgh, vol. xix., folio 233.

[60] The Rev. Thomas Barnard, D.D., Dean of Derry, was elected a member of the Literary Club in December, 1755. Son of William Barnard, D.D., successively Bishop of Raphoe and Derry, he was educated at Westminster School. Obtaining orders, he was appointed Dean of Derry in 1769. He was consecrated Bishop of Killaloe in 1780, and translated to the see of Limerick in 1794. He died at Wimbledon, Surrey, on the 7th June, 1806. He was a cherished friend of Dr. Goldsmith, and an associate of Johnson, Burke, and Sir Joshua Reynolds.

[61] "Life of Johnson."

[62] The negro gained his plea.

[63] Correspondence of the Right Hon. Edmund Burke, edited by Charles Earl Fitzwilliam. Lond., 4 vols., 1844, vol. ii, p. 207.

[64] "Life of Johnson."

[65] Mr. Croker relates the anecdote on the authority of the Marquess of Wellesley, who received it from Mr. Thomas Sydenham. That gentleman got the story from Mr. Knight, to whom it was communicated by Sir Joshua Reynolds.

[66] "Life of Johnson."

[67] Throughout these papers Boswell adopts his peculiar system of orthography, presenting *judgement* for judgment, *authour* for author, *empannael* for empannel.

[68] The Honourable Mary Monckton was youngest daughter of John, first Viscount Galway. She married, on the 17th January, 1786, Edmund, seventh Earl of Cork; she died in 1840.

[69] "Life of Johnson."

[70] This gentleman was, we believe, father of Mr. John Murdoch, the first and most efficient instructor of the poet Burns.

[71] A Mr. Twamley invented a kind of box-iron for smoothing linen.

[72] Lord Lowther was son-in-law of the Earl of Bute, and brother-in-law of Boswell's friend, Colonel Stuart. Boswell's relations with this

influential nobleman will form a prominent feature in the subsequent narrative.

[73] Life of Edmund Malone, by James Boswell, jun., contributed to the *Gentleman's Magazine*, and reprinted for private circulation.

[74] Mr. Malone published in 1778 his "Attempt to ascertain the order in which Shakespeare's Plays were written."

[75] A Poetical Review of the Literary and Moral Character of the late Samuel Johnson, LL.D., with Notes by John Courtenay, Esq. Lond.: C. Dilly, 1786.

[76] The celebrated Flora Macdonald.

[77] The pseudonym of Dr. John Wolcott, the eminent satirist.

[78] From the Hebrides Dr. Johnson wrote to Mrs. Thrale in these terms:—"We had a passage of about twelve miles to the point where Sir Alexander Macdonald resided, having come from his seat, in the middle of the island, to a small house on the shore, as we believe, that he might with less reproach entertain us meanly. If he aspired to meanness, his retrograde ambition was completely gratified; but he did not succeed equally in escaping reproach. He had no cook, nor I suppose much provision; nor had the lady the common decencies of her tea-table; we picked up our sugar with our fingers. Boswell was very angry, and reproached him with his improper parsimony.... I have done thinking of Sir Alexander Macdonald, whom we now call Sir Sawney; he has disgusted all mankind by injudicious parsimony, and given occasion to so many stories, that Boswell has some thoughts of collecting them, and making a novel of his life." (Letters to Mrs. Thrale, vol. i., p. 137.)

[79] Lady Macdonald, *née* Elizabeth Diana Bosville, was a member of the eldest branch of the Boswell family, and was one of those gentlewomen to whom early in life Boswell thought of offering his hand (see page 67). Daughter of Godfrey Bosville, Esq., of Gunthwaite, Yorkshire, she married Sir Alexander Macdonald in 1768.

[80] Sir Alexander Macdonald, Bart., was raised to the peerage, as Baron Macdonald of Slate, on the 17th July, 1776.

[81] See *postea*.

[82] In the Library of the British Museum is contained a copy of the pamphlet which belonged to Mr. Wilkes. In Boswell's handwriting it is thus inscribed:—

> "Comes jucundus in via pro vehiculo est.
> "To John Wilkes, Esq., as pleasant a companion as ever lived.
>
> From the Author.
>
> ". . . Will my Wilkes retreat,
> And see, once seen before, that ancient seat," &c.

[83] This satirical allusion to Lord Monboddo is conceived in the very worst taste. His lordship had shown marked attention to Boswell in his youth, and had entertained him and Dr. Johnson at Monboddo, during the progress of their tour. Latterly his lordship and Dr. Johnson had differed, and probably on this account Boswell considered himself entitled to make this offensive allusion to his philosophical opinions.

[84] Boswell's motion in Court, *quare adhæsit pavimento*, is preserved as a jest in the courts of Westminster.

[85] Letter from Boswell to Mr. Temple.

[86] Letter to Mr. Temple of 22nd May.

[87] Letter to Mr. Temple.

[88] Henry Seymour Conway, a General in the army, was brother of the first Marquess of Hertford. He was under the Rockingham administration Secretary of State for Ireland, and leader of the House of Commons. He died in 1795.

[89] Pitt was brought into Parliament for the close borough of Appleby by Sir James Lowther, afterwards Lord Lonsdale.

[90] Letter to Mr. Temple.

[91] Mrs. Piozzi's Anecdotes of Dr. Johnson. London: 1785.

[92] Boswell called on Sir John Hawkins, and complained of being slighted in his book. "I know what you mean," said Sir John; "you would have had me to say that Johnson undertook this tour with *the* Boswell." *Miss Hawkins' Johnsoniana.*

[93] Malone's Edition of Shakspere, in ten volumes, was published in 1790.

[94] Lord Chancellor Thurlow.

[95] Boswell's Life of Johnson, edited by the Right Hon. John Wilson Croker and others, London, 1848, 12mo., vol. x., pp. 209-220.

[96] "Sermons, in two volumes, by John Dun, V.D.M. Kilmarnock, 1790," 8vo.

[97] John Courtenay, Esq., was born in Ireland in 1741, and died in 1816. He composed the "Poetical Review of Dr. Johnson" and other works. He was, when Boswell knew him, Surveyor of the Ordnance and M.P. for Tamworth. He was a warm friend and pleasant companion.

[98] See "Life of William Wilberforce," Lond., 1838. Vol. iii., pp. 63, 70.

[99] From the Commissariat Register of Glasgow, preserved in the General Register House, Edinburgh, vol. 74, p. 194.

[100] "Life of James Beattie, LL.D.," by Sir William Forbes, of Pitsligo, Bart., Edinb. 1807, 3 vols., vol. iii., p. 378.

[101] Statement of Mr. William Macfarlane, of Edinburgh, to Robert Chambers. "Traditions of Edinburgh," 1869, 12mo., p. 74.

[102] See the Poetical Works of Sir Alexander Boswell, Bart., with memoir, by Robert Howie Smith, Glasgow, 1871, 12mo.

[103] Decisions of the Court of Session, 20th March, 1851.

[104] The celebrated Nell Gwynne, who is believed to have transmitted a benefaction to the starving poet, which did not reach till after his decease.

[105] The only son of Thomas Alexander Boswell, of Crawley Grange, died in India in his 18th year.

[106] Births Register of Auchinleck.

[107] The Rev. Robert Bruce Boswell published in 1842 a volume of "Psalms and Hymns, chiefly selected," dedicated to Daniel, Lord Bishop of Calcutta.

[108] John Maclaurin, eldest son of Colin Maclaurin, Professor of Mathematics in the University of Edinburgh, was admitted advocate in August, 1756. After a period of successful practice at the bar, he was raised to the bench by the title of Lord Dreghorn in January, 1789. He died at Edinburgh 24th December, 1796. Maclaurin was one of Boswell's early associates; he contributed several poems to the first volume of Donaldson's "Collection," Edinburgh, 1760. Three dramas from his pen, entitled, "Hampden," "The Public," and "The Philosopher's Opera," are of very ordinary merit. His collected works were published in 1798 in two octavo volumes.

[109] John Nichols, printer, the celebrated author of the "Literary Anecdotes," was born in 1744 and died in 1826. A person of ripe and varied scholarship, he enjoyed the esteem of Dr. Johnson.

[110] John Johnston, of Grange, was one of Boswell's early and more confidential associates. Professionally a writer to the signet, he owned the small estate of Grange, Dumfriesshire, which brought him a rental of about £100 per annum. In a letter to the Hon. Andrew Erskine, dated 8th May, 1762, Boswell alludes to Johnston in these terms:—"I shall be at Dumfries soon, when I hope to see my friend Johnston. We will talk much of old Scotch history, and the memory of former years will warm our hearts. Johnston is a very worthy fellow. I may safely say so, for I have lived in intimacy with him more years than the Egyptian famine lasted." In his reply Erskine desires to be kindly remembered to "honest Johnston." He inquires whether "his trees are growing well at his paternal estate of Grange; if he is as fond of Melvil's Memoirs ["Memoirs of Sir James Melvil, of Halhill," London, 1752, 8vo.] as he used to be; and if he continues to stretch himself in the sun upon the mountains near Edinburgh." Johnston fell into bad health. He predeceased Boswell, who became a creditor on his estate. At Boswell's death the trustees on Johnston's estate were indebted to his representatives in the sum of £195. (See *supra*, p. 188.)

[111] Sir William Augustus Cunynghame, fourth baronet of Milncraig, Ayrshire, was eldest son of Lieutenant-General Sir David Cunynghame and his wife, Lady Mary Montgomery, only daughter of Alexander, ninth Earl of Eglinton. For many years he represented the county of Linlithgow in the House of Commons; he also held several important offices in the public service. He died 17th January, 1828.

[112] The Hon. Henry Erskine, a celebrated humorist, was second son of Henry David, tenth Earl of Buchan, and brother of Lord Chancellor Erskine: he was born at Edinburgh, in November, 1746. He passed advocate in 1768, and soon attained professional eminence. He was appointed Lord Advocate on the accession of the Coalition Ministry in 1783, and three years afterwards was chosen Dean of Faculty. On the return of the liberal party to power he was reappointed Lord Advocate, and was at the same time elected M.P. for the Dumfries burghs. After a period of broken health, he died on the 8th October, 1817. Many of his sparkling witticisms and humorous sallies are included in popular collections of *bonmots*.

[113] Mrs. Dundas, of Melville, was daughter of David Rennie, Esq., of Melville Castle, and first wife of Henry Dundas, subsequently Viscount Melville. She died about 1790.

[114] On the 2nd June, 1790, Lord George Gordon, M.P., a younger son of Cosmo George, third Duke of Gordon, led 100,000 persons in procession to the House of Commons, to present a petition against a measure for relieving Roman Catholics from certain disabilities and penalties. The procession was followed by a riot, which continued several days, and was attended with the destruction of Catholic chapels and private dwellings. The prisons of London, too, were thrown open by the rabble, and the mansion of the chief justice thrown down. Lord George Gordon was tried for high treason, but acquitted. Afterwards convicted of libelling Queen Marie Antoinette of France, and presenting a petition reflecting on the laws and administration of criminal justice, he was committed to Newgate, where he died on the 1st November, 1793. Lord George Gordon evidently laboured under mental aberration, and ought to have been placed in a lunatic asylum.

[115] This anecdote is included by Boswell in his "Life of Johnson."

[116] Alexander, tenth Earl of Eglinton, was a friend of the Auchinleck family, and one of Boswell's early patrons. Born in 1726, he succeeded his father in his third year. A zealous promoter of agriculture, he was much beloved by his tenantry and neighbours. He was mortally wounded by a poacher, whom he sought forcibly to deprive of his firelock: he died on the 25th October, 1769.

[117] Dr. Hugh Blair, the celebrated preacher and rhetorician, was a central figure in the literary society of Edinburgh. He was collegiate minister of the High Church, and professor of rhetoric in the University. The first volume of his "Sermons" was published by Strahan, on the recommendation of Dr. Johnson. Dr. Blair was an early patron of Burns, and to his encouragement and active assistance Macpherson was much indebted in producing his first specimens of Ossianic poetry. Dr. Blair died at Edinburgh on the 27th December, 1800, aged eighty-two.

[118] James Macpherson, the editor of Ossian, established his residence in London in 1766, in his twenty-eighth year. In 1780 he was elected M.P. for Camelford. He died at Belleville, Inverness-shire, on the 17th February, 1796, aged fifty-eight. Boswell's allusion to John Bull is explained by the attacks made on Macpherson by Dr. Johnson and other English writers, in reference to the authenticity of Ossian's poems.

[119] Lady Frances Montgomerie was daughter of Alexander, ninth Earl of Eglinton, and sister of the tenth and eleventh earls. She died unmarried.

[120] Dr. John Ogilvie, was minister of Midmar, Aberdeenshire. He composed many volumes of poetry, and several of his lyrics have obtained celebrity. He died in 1814, at an advanced age.

[121] Captain Robert Temple was younger brother of Boswell's intimate friend, the Rev. William Johnson Temple, rector of Mamhead. (See *supra*, pp. 36, 47.)

[122] John Hall-Stevenson was a relative of Laurence Sterne, and the "Eugenius" of his "Tristram Shandy." His "Crazy Tales," which appeared anonymously in 1762, are described by Sir Walter Scott as "witty and indecent." Bishop Warburton describes Hall-Stevenson as "a monster of impiety and lewdness." He died in 1785. He is noticed in Dr. Alexander Carlyle's Autobiography.

[123] George Dempster, M.P. (See *supra*, pp. 32-34.)

[124] Dr. William Robertson, the historian, was son of a Scottish clergyman, and claimed descent from the Robertsons of Struan, an important family in the Highlands. Born in 1721, he was appointed minister of Gladsmuir in 1743; he was translated to one of the city churches of Edinburgh in 1758, and three years afterwards was appointed Principal of the University. He became historiographer royal for Scotland, and received other offices attended with honours and emoluments. His "History of Scotland during the Reigns of Mary and James VI." appeared in 1759, and at once attracted attention. His other historical works sustained his reputation. He died on the 11th June, 1793, aged seventy-one. His sister, Mrs. Syme, was grandmother of Henry, Lord Brougham.

[125] Thomas Sheridan, father of Richard Brinsley Sheridan, whose acquaintance Boswell formed at Edinburgh early in life. Mr. Sheridan was a lecturer on elocution, and author of a pronouncing dictionary. He was latterly at variance with Dr. Johnson. He died in 1788.

[126] Sir Robert Walpole, latterly Earl of Orford. This eminent statesman was born in 1676, and died 18th March, 1745.

[127] Captain Webster, only son of the Rev. Dr. Alexander Webster, minister of the Tolbooth church, Edinburgh, was Boswell's maternal cousin. Captain Webster attained the rank of colonel; he fell in the American war.

[128] Hugh Home, third Earl of Marchmont, was celebrated for his elegant learning and remarkable powers of debate. He enjoyed the esteem of Chatham and Walpole. Lord Cobham placed his bust in the

temple of worthies at Stowe; and Pope, who enjoyed his intimacy, has thus celebrated him in the grotto at Twickenham,—

"There the bright flame was shot through Marchmont's soul."

Dr. Johnson entertained a prejudice against him, but was induced by Boswell to wait on him for his recollections of Pope. Johnson was received by the earl with much cordiality, and at the close of a long interview he remarked to Boswell that he "would rather have given twenty pounds than not have come." Lord Marchmont died on the 10th January, 1794, aged eighty-six.

[129] Captain Andrew Erskine (see *supra*, pp. 19-24).

[130] Sir William Maxwell, fourth Baronet of Monreith, Wigtonshire. He died 22nd August, 1771.

[131] Mr. Crawfurd succeeded the Rev. John Home in 1770, as Conservator of Scots Privileges at Campvere.

[132] C. H. Trotz, the great German jurisconsult, whose lectures on civil law Boswell attended at Utrecht in 1763. Professor Trotz was born in 1701, and died in 1773.

[133] James, Lord Hope, subsequently third Earl of Hopetoun, was born in 1741; he entered the army in 1758, and was present at the battle of Minden the following year; he left the army in 1764 to accompany his elder brother on a Continental tour; he succeeded to the earldom in 1781, and was afterwards elected a representative peer. He died on the 29th May, 1816, aged seventy-five.

[134] Samuel Foote, the celebrated comedian, was born in 1720, at Truro, in Cornwall; he belonged to a respectable family, but he soon wasted his inheritance and his wife's fortune by a course of dissipation. Compelled by necessity, he became a player, making his *début* in the Haymarket Theatre in 1747. From a grotesque imitation of leading persons he attained popularity, accompanied with a rancorous feeling on the part of those whom he subjected to ridicule. He was an entertaining companion, but possessed few amiable qualities. He died in October, 1777, and was buried in Westminster Abbey.

[135] George Lyttleton was born in 1709. As a commoner he entered Parliament in his twenty-first year. He opposed Walpole, and in 1732 was appointed secretary to Frederick, Prince of Wales. On Walpole's retirement he obtained a succession of offices, culminating in the Chancellorship of the Exchequer; in 1759 he was raised to the peerage. Henceforth he cultivated letters, producing various works in prose and

verse. He was inclined to indolence, but was much esteemed for his high principle and moral worth. He died 22nd August, 1773.

[136] Boswell has inserted this anecdote in his Life of Dr. Johnson. Sir James Macdonald, Bart., the "Scottish Marcellus," was eighth baronet of Sleat, and male representative of the Lords of the Isles. Born in 1741, he early distinguished himself at Eton by the variety of his accomplishments, and high hopes were entertained of his career. He was unhappily seized with a complication of disorders, of which he died on the 26th July, 1766, at the age of twenty-five.

[137] This anecdote is included by Boswell in his "Life of Johnson."

[138] James Quin, the player, was extremely pugnacious; he fought two duels, in one of which he killed his antagonist. His latter years, on his partial retirement from the stage, were spent at Bath. He died on the 21st January, 1766, aged seventy-three.

[139] Boswell has published this anecdote in his "Life of Johnson."

[140] Boswell was on terms of friendship with the Rev. Dr. James Fordyce, author of "Addresses to the Deity." He died at Bath on the 1st October, 1796. His nephew, Dr. George Fordyce, an eminent physician in the metropolis, became in 1774 a member of the Literary Club. He published numerous professional works, and died 25th May, 1802.

[141] Miss Margaret Stewart, eldest daughter of Sir Michael Stewart, Bart., of Blackhall, married in 1764 Sir William Maxwell, Bart., of Springkell. She had a younger sister, Eleanora, who died unmarried.

[142] Voltaire visited England in 1724, when Dr. Samuel Clarke was in the zenith of his fame. His "Evidences of Natural and Revealed Religion" appeared in 1705, and was followed by other theological and philosophical works. Dr. Clarke was born at Norwich in 1675, and died in 1729. He displayed a playful humour among his ordinary associates, but was grave and circumspect in the presence of strangers, especially of forward or eccentric persons.

[143] With the Rev. William Brown, minister of the Scottish Church at Utrecht, Boswell became acquainted during his residence in that city. Mr. Brown had a personal history, not uneventful. Son of the Rev. Laurence Brown, minister of Lintrathen in Forfarshire, he rescued when a theological student several officers captured by the rebels at the battle of Prestonpans. The rescue took place at Glammis, the captors being followers of Lord Ogilvie, a zealous adherent of the Prince. Soon afterwards Mr. Brown was ordained minister of Cortachy,

a parish inhabited by Lord Ogilvie's tenantry. Reports to his disadvantage soon spread, and in 1748 he demitted his charge on account of "the odium of the disaffected, the prejudices of the people, and his life being attacked by a ruffian." Through the influence of the Duke of Cumberland he was appointed chaplain to a British regiment stationed in Flanders, and was subsequently admitted pastor of the Scottish church at Utrecht. In 1757 he received a commission from the Crown as Professor of Church History at St. Andrews, but he did not obtain induction for several years; his appointment, on account of the rumours at Cortachy, being resisted both by the university and the presbytery. He was at length admitted by decree of the General Assembly. His lectures were composed in Latin, but his theological attainments were less conspicuous than his patriotism. He died on the 10th January, 1791, aged seventy-two. His son was the celebrated William Laurence Brown, Principal of Marischal College, Aberdeen.

[144] The Rev. Thomas Hunter, minister of New Cumnock, Ayrshire, from 1706 to 1757, died in 1760, in his hundredth year.—*Dr. Scott's "Fasti."*

[145] Sir David Dalrymple, Bart., a judge in the Court of Session by the title of Lord Hailes, was one of Boswell's earliest patrons. Admitted advocate in 1748, he was raised to the bench in 1766. He employed a portion of his time in literary and historical researches. He died on the 29th November, 1792, aged sixty-six (see *supra* p. 10).

[146] Theodore Tronchin belonged to an eminent Protestant family at Geneva. On the mother's side he was related to Lord Bolingbroke. Born on the 14th May, 1709, he studied medicine, and settled at Amsterdam in 1736. He attained eminence in his profession, chiefly as a promoter of inoculation. In 1757 he published "De Colica Pictorum." He died 30th November, 1781.

[147] Boswell's Journal was probably destroyed by his family. (See *supra*, p. 186.)

[148] Almack's Hotel was thus originated: A sister of Dr. Cullen, the celebrated physician, was waiting-maid to the Duchess of Hamilton. She married the duke's valet, whose name was Macall. They were both favourites of the duke and duchess, who resolved to establish them comfortably. As they inclined to open an hotel in London, the duke secured eligible premises. Macall was deemed a name unsuited for a London landlord, and on the duke's suggestion it was changed to Almack.

[149] Helen Dempster, only sister of George Dempster, M.P., married General Burlington. On the death of her brother without issue, in 1818, she succeeded to the family estate of Dunnichen.

[150] An amiable man, but crushing satirist, Caleb Whitefoord was born at Edinburgh in 1734. He was intended for the Scottish Church, but preferring the concerns of business, settled in London as a wine merchant. He contributed satirical poems, in prose and verse, to the *Public Advertiser*, directing his shafts chiefly against Wilkes. He attracted the notice of Government, and on his recommendation Dr. Johnson was requested to prepare his pamphlet in defence of the recent negotiations respecting the Falkland Islands. He was secretary of the commissioners appointed to meet at Paris in 1782, to treat of a general peace with America on the separation of the colonies from the mother country. He latterly received a Civil List pension, and was honoured with the diplomas of the Royal and other societies. He is described by Goldsmith in his poem, "The Retaliation." He died in 1809, aged seventy-five.

[151] The Rev. John Home, author of "Douglas," was born at Ancrum, Roxburghshire, on the 22nd September, 1722. Having studied for the Church, he was in 1741 ordained minister of Athelstaneford. During the previous year he distinguished himself as member of a volunteer corps in support of Government; he was taken prisoner by the rebels at the battle of Falkirk, but contrived to escape from Doune Castle, where he was confined. In 1755 he produced his tragedy of "Douglas," which soon became popular. On account of encouraging theatricals, he was assailed by his clerical brethren: he escaped deposition by resigning his charge. He obtained a Civil List pension of £300, with the sinecure office of conservator of Scots privileges at Campvere. He died 5th September, 1808, in his eighty-sixth year.

[152] A younger son of William, second Earl of Aberdeen.

[153] Secretary to the Prussian Embassy.

[154] Mr., afterwards Sir Andrew Mitchell, was only son of the Rev. William Mitchell, minister of the High Church, Edinburgh, and who had the singular distinction of being five times Moderator of the General Assembly. After following legal pursuits at Edinburgh, Mr. Mitchell was in 1741 appointed secretary to the Marquis of Tweeddale, minister for the affairs of Scotland, and in 1747 was chosen M.P. for the Banff district of burghs. In 1751 he was sent as ambassador to Brussels, and in 1753 was created a Knight of the Bath and envoy extraordinary to the court of Prussia. He was a great favourite with Frederick the Great, whom he accompanied in his campaigns. He died

at Berlin, on the 28th January, 1771. Boswell became acquainted with Sir Andrew Mitchell during his Continental tour. (See *supra*, pp. 43-47.)

[155] Archibald, third Duke of Argyll, was born in June, 1682. As colonel of the 36th regiment he served under the Duke of Marlborough. Devoting himself to civil affairs, he was in 1705 nominated Lord High Treasurer of Scotland; in the following year he became a commissioner on the Union, and in 1710 was appointed Justice General. He was wounded at the battle of Sheriffmuir in 1715, when he held a command under his brother, the Duke of Argyll and Greenwich. He succeeded his brother as Duke of Argyll in 1743, and died 15th April, 1761. He founded the family residence at Inverary, and there established a valuable library. He was a zealous promoter of learning, and excelled in conversation.

[156] The celebrated George, tenth Earl Marischal, whom Boswell had the honour of accompanying through Germany and Switzerland in 1763. Born about 1693, Lord Marischal held a high command in the army of Queen Anne, and on her death signed the proclamation of George I. Deprived of office by the Duke of Argyll, he joined the Earl of Mar in the insurrection of 1715, and at the battle of Sheriffmuir commanded two squadrons of cavalry. In 1719 he made a second attempt on behalf of the Chevalier. In the rising of 1715 he took no part. Having by a residence in Prussia gained the favour of Frederick the Great, he became Prussian ambassador at the courts of France and Spain. In 1759 he revealed to Mr. Pitt, afterwards Earl of Chatham, the family compact of the house of Bourbon; he was, consequently, invited to the court of George II., and his attainder was reversed. On possessing himself of his forfeited estates he purposed to reside in Scotland, but on the urgent entreaty of the Prussian monarch he returned to Berlin. He died, unmarried, at Potsdam, on the 28th of May, 1778.

[157] Sir Adam Fergusson, Bart., of Kilkerran, LL.D., was elected M.P. for Ayrshire in 1774; he afterwards sat for the city of Edinburgh. He died 23rd September, 1813, at an advanced age.

[158] By the cabinets of St. Petersburg and Berlin Stanislas Poniatowski was presented to the Poles as their king in 1764: owing to the partition of his dominions he died broken-hearted at St. Petersburg in 1798.

[159] Alexander, tenth Earl of Eglinton, died in 1769, and was succeeded by his brother, Colonel Archibald Montgomery.

[160] John Turberville Needham, a priest of the Roman Catholic Church, and an eminent physiologist, was born 1713 and died 1781.

He received honours from many of the learned societies, and was sometime director of the Academy of Sciences at Brussels. In botanical science his name is perpetuated in the *genus needhamia*.

[161] The Hon. Captain Andrew Erskine.

[162] Sir Joseph Yorke was third son of Lord Chancellor Hardwicke. After serving in the army till he attained the rank of general, he was appointed ambassador at the Hague, where he remained thirty years. In 1788 he was created Baron Dover. He died on the 2nd December, 1792.

[163] Andrew Stuart was counsel on the Hamilton side of the Douglas case, and fought a duel with Edward, afterwards Lord Thurlow, the leading counsel for Mr. Archibald Douglas. He published, in 1773, "Letters to Lord Mansfield," on the Douglas case, which, as models of polished invective, have been compared with the Letters of Junius. In 1798 he issued a "Genealogical History of the Stewarts."

[164] William Nairne, son of Sir William Nairne, Bart., of Dunsinnan, was admitted advocate in 1755. He was in 1758 appointed conjunct commissary-clerk of Edinburgh, and in 1786 was raised to the bench, when he assumed the judicial title of Lord Dunsinnan. He died in March, 1811.

[165] A zealous patriot, deeply imbued with republican notions, Andrew Fletcher of Saltoun opposed the arbitrary measures of the House of Stuart, and after the revolution proved, from his irritable temper, a considerable incubus on the Government of William III. He violently opposed the union, and subsequently to that event retired from public affairs. He died at London in 1716, aged sixty-three.

[166] The celebrated Bishop Berkeley, who maintained the non-existence of matter as one of his philosophical opinions.

[167] The Hon. Peregrine Bertie, third son of Willoughby, third Earl of Abingdon, was born in 1741. He became a captain in the Royal Navy, and was sometime M.P. for Oxford. He died in 1790.

[168] General the Hon. Sir William Howe led the troops at the battle of Bunker's Hill in 1775, and was subsequently appointed commander of the British forces in America. As an officer he somewhat lacked energy, but he was much esteemed in private life. Captain Howe, mentioned in the anecdote, was Sir William's elder brother, afterwards the celebrated Admiral Earl Howe. Sir William Howe died in 1814.

[169] Charles Churchill, now nearly forgotten, enjoyed considerable reputation as a satirical poet. Bred to the Church, he abandoned the

clerical profession and embraced infidelity. He acted honourably in discharging his debts, but was in other respects profligate. He died on the 4th November, 1764, in his thirty-third year. His political satire, referred to in the text, was the most successful of his poetical writings.

[170] Andrew Lumsden belonged to an old family in the county of Berwick. After the suppression of the rebellion in 1745 he proceeded to Rome, where he became private secretary to Prince Charles Edward. He latterly returned to Britain, and established his residence at Edinburgh. He published "Remarks on the Antiquities of Rome and its Environs," a pleasing and judicious performance. He died on the 26th December, 1801, aged eighty-one.

[171] The Rev. James Ramsay, one of the earliest opponents of the slave trade, was born at Fraserburgh in 1733. A surgeon in the Royal Navy, he incurred a serious accident, and thereafter abandoned his profession and took orders. For some time he held two livings at St. Christopher's, worth £700 a year. He returned to England in 1781, and became vicar of Teston in Kent. His work against the slave trade appeared in 1786. He died on the 20th July, 1789.

[172] The Rev. John Willison ministered at Dundee from 1716 till his death, which took place in May, 1750. An eminent theologian, his numerous writings found a ready acceptance, and have been frequently reprinted. Mr. Willison was a leader in the Church courts; he was much esteemed for his urbanity.

[173] Colonel Archibald Edmonstone, of Duntreath, created a baronet in 1774, was in 1761 elected M.P. for the county of Dumbarton and the Ayr burghs. He died in July, 1807.

[174] Sir Gilbert Elliot, of Minto, Bart., Lord Justice Clerk, died at Minto, Roxburghshire, on the 16th April, 1766, aged seventy-three. His father, who bore the same Christian name, was the first baronet of Minto, and a senator of the College of Justice. His grandson was created Earl of Minto.

[175] Of John, fourth Earl of Loudoun, Boswell in his "Scottish Tour" thus writes:—"He did more service to the county of Ayr in general, as well as to individuals in it, than any man we have ever had.... The tenderness of his heart was proved in 1745-6, when he had an important command in the Highlands, and behaved with a generous humanity to the unfortunate. I cannot figure a more honest politician; for though his interest in our country was great and generally successful, he not only did not deceive by fallacious promises, but was anxious that people should not deceive themselves by too sanguine

expectations. His kind and dutiful attention to his mother was unremittent. At his house was true hospitality, a plain but a plentiful table; and every guest being left at perfect freedom, felt himself quite easy and happy. While I live I shall honour the memory of this amiable man." Boswell relates that, having sent a message that he and Dr. Johnson purposed to dine with him, the messenger reported that the earl "jumped for joy." John, fourth earl of Loudoun, was born in 1705, and died in 1782.

[176] John, fifth earl of Stair, born 1720, died 1789. Joining the army, he attained the rank of captain. He composed several pamphlets on political topics.

[177] General Philip Honywood was a cadet of the House of Honywood, Evington, baronet; he died in 1785.

[178] John Clerk, a cadet of the house of Clerk, of Pennycuik, was born in 1689, and having studied medicine, became the first physician in Scotland. In 1740 he was elected President of the Royal College of Physicians. He died in 1757.

[179] Sir John Clerk, second baronet of Pennycuik, was appointed a Baron of Exchequer in 1707. He was a patron of Allan Ramsay, and an ingenious antiquary. From his pen proceeded the song commencing, "O merry may the maid be that marries the miller." He died 4th October, 1755.

[180] The Campbells of Succoth are descended from a branch of the ducal house of Argyll, their ancestors possessing Lochow, in Argyleshire (Nisbet's Heraldry). John Campbell of Succoth, mentioned in the text, was progenitor of Archibald Campbell of Succoth, Principal Clerk of Session, and of Sir Islay Campbell, Lord President of the Court of Session.

[181] Anne, third wife of James fifth Duke of Hamilton, was daughter and co-heiress of Edmund Spencer, Esq., of Rendlesham, in the county of Suffolk.

[182] Sir William Gordon of Park, Bart., was grandson on the mother's side of the celebrated Archbishop Sharp. He joined Prince Charles Edward in 1745, and was attainted, but the attainder was afterwards reversed. He died at Douay, 5th June, 1751.

[183] Charles Cochrane, of Ochiltree, grandson of the first Earl of Dundonald, succeeded his mother in the estate of Culross. He died in 1752.

[184] Charles Erskine, of Tinwald, third son of Sir Charles Erskine, Bart., of Alva, was admitted advocate in 1711. He was elected M.P. for the county of Dumfries in 1722, and nominated Solicitor-General in 1725. Raised to the bench in 1744 by the judicial title of Lord Tinwald, he was in 1748 promoted as Lord Justice Clerk. He died at Edinburgh, on the 5th April, 1763. Lord Tinwald combined a dignified deportment with much suavity of manner.

[185] Sir Walter Pringle, of Newhall, was called to the Bar in 1687. After enjoying a high reputation as a pleader, he was raised to the bench, as Lord Newhall, in June, 1718. He died 14th December, 1736, and the judges in their robes attended his funeral. The Faculty of Advocates commended him in their records, and the poet Hamilton, of Bangor, composed his epitaph.

[186] Sir Alexander Ogilvy of Forglen, Bart., second son of George Ogilvy, second Lord Banff, was Commissioner for the Burgh of Banff from 1702 to 1707. Admitted advocate, he was in 1706 appointed a Lord of Session, when he assumed the title of Lord Forglen. He died 30th March, 1727.

[187] The first wife of William, fourth earl of Dumfries, was the Lady Anne Gordon, only daughter of William, second Earl of Aberdeen. She died in 1755.

[188] John Lord Hope succeeded his father in 1742 as second Earl of Hopetown. A nobleman of considerable parts, he was appointed one of the lords of police in Scotland, and in 1754 was nominated Lord High Commissioner to the Church of Scotland. He died 12th February, 1781, aged seventy-seven.

[189] Robert Cullen, advocate, was eldest son of William Cullen, M.D., the celebrated physician. He was called to the Scottish bar in 1764, and was early noted for his forensic talents. Contrary to the estimate formed of him by Boswell, he was held in general esteem for his courteous manners, while his powers of mimicry were of a first order. He was appointed a Lord of Session in 1796, by the title of Lord Cullen. He died at Edinburgh on the 28th November, 1810.

[190] Boswell's allusion to Frederick the Great is evidently founded on a remark of Dr. Johnson's. Conversing with Dr. Robertson, the historian, in 1778, Johnson remarked, "The true strong and sound mind is the mind that can embrace equally great things and small. Now I am told the King of Prussia will say to a servant, 'Bring me a bottle of such a wine, which came in such a year; it lies in such a corner of

the cellar.' I would have a man great in great things, and elegant in little things."

[191] The Rev. John Pettigrew, A.M., was minister of Govan, Lanarkshire, from 1688 to 1712; he died in March, 1715, in his seventy-eighth year. He was remarkably facetious; a number of his witty sayings have been preserved. (Dr. Scott's "*Fasti*," vol. ii., p. 69.)

[192] The Rev. William Love, A.M., ministered at Cathcart, Renfrewshire, from 1710 to 1738, when he died at the age of fifty-seven. He made a monetary bequest to the poor of Paisley. (Dr. Scott's "*Fasti*," vol. ii., p. 61.)

[193] A portrait of Cullen in "Kay's Portraits" (vol. ii., p. 331) does not warrant Boswell's assertion as to his extreme ugliness. He was plain-looking, as was his father before him, but his aspect was not repulsive.

[194] Son of George Lockhart, of Carnwath, and Lady Euphemia Montgomery, daughter of the Earl of Eglinton, Alexander Lockhart passed advocate in 1722. He distinguished himself in defending the unfortunate persons who were taken at Carlisle and subjected to trial for taking part in the rebellion of 1745. Elected Dean of Faculty in 1764, he was raised to the bench in 1775 by the title of Lord Covington. He died 10th November, 1782, aged eighty-two.

[195] John, third Earl of Bute, the favourite minister of George III., a munificent patron of literature, and himself an accomplished scholar and man of science. Lord Bute died 10th March, 1792.

[196] In his "Scottish Tour" Boswell thus refers to the Lord Chief Baron Orde:—"This respectable English judge will be long remembered in Scotland, where he built an elegant house and lived in it magnificently. His own ample fortune, with the addition of his salary enabled him to be splendidly hospitable.... Lord Chief Baron Orde was on good terms with us all, in a narrow country, filled with jarring interests and keen parties."

[197] A native of Ayrshire, Matthew Henderson long resided in Edinburgh, where his society was much cherished. Allan Cunningham relates on the authority of Sir Thomas Wallace, who knew him personally, "that he dined regularly at Fortune's Tavern, and was a member of the Capillaire Club, which was composed of all who inclined to be witty and joyous." When Robert Burns visited Edinburgh in 1787, Matthew Henderson was one of his chief associates; he subscribed for four copies of the second edition of his poems, and by his pleasing and beneficent manner gained a deep place in his affections. Henderson died in the summer of 1790, and his

memory was celebrated by the Ayrshire bard in an elegiac poem, of which the following stanzas are familiar:—

"O Henderson! the man—the brother!
And art thou gone, and gone for ever?
And hast thou crossed that unknown river,

    Life's dreary bound?

Like thee where shall I find another

    The world around?

"Go to your sculptured tombs, ye great,
In a' the tinsel trash o' state!
But by thy honest turf I'll wait,

    Thou man o' worth!

And weep the ae best fellow's fate

    E'er lay in earth."

In transmitting the poem to Mr. McMurdo, Burns writes from Ellisland, 2nd August, 1790, "You knew Henderson? I have not flattered his memory." In a tract by the Lord Chief Commissioner Adam, entitled "Two Short Essays on the Study of History—the gift of a grandfather," and printed at the Blair-Adam press in 1836, the author concludes a list of eminent Scotsmen, his contemporaries, with the following note:—"Besides these here enumerated, there were many others who made a respectable figure in the society of Edinburgh during the period here referred to (between 1750 and 1766), and there were some who stand more prominently forward, whose rank, whose wit, and whose taste and talent for conversation adorned the society when they joined it, such as Thomas, Earl of Kelly; Thomas, Earl of Haddington; Nisbet, of Dirleton; *Matthew Henderson, at a future period distinguished by Burns*; Sir Robert Murray, of Hillhead; George Brown, of Elliestoun, and others."

[198] The Hon. Alexander Gordon was third son of William, second Earl of Aberdeen. Born in 1739, he was admitted advocate in his twenty-first year. In 1764 he was appointed Steward Depute of Kirkcudbright, and in 1788 was raised to the bench as Lord Rockville. He died 13th March, 1792. He was much esteemed for his urbanity.

[199] John Armstrong, M.D., physician and poet, was son of the minister of Castleton, Roxburghshire. Having studied medicine at the University of Edinburgh, he became physician in 1732, and commenced practice in the metropolis. His "Art of Preserving

Health," an ingenious poem, appeared in 1744. He was appointed physician to a military hospital in London, and afterwards to the army in Germany. He subsequently resumed medical practice in the metropolis. He became notorious for his indolence; spending his time lounging in a coffee-house, where he received his letters. He died on the 7th September, 1779, about his seventieth year.

[200] Son of the poet of the same name, Allan Ramsay the painter was born at Edinburgh in 1713. Having studied his art in Italy, he became portrait-painter first at Edinburgh and afterwards in London. Introduced by the Earl of Bute to George III., he was appointed principal painter to the king. He was an associate of Dr. Johnson, who thus spoke of him:—"I love Ramsay. You will not find a man in whose conversation there is more instruction, more information, and more elegance than in Ramsay's." He died on the 10th August, 1784.

[201] Robert Dundas, of Arniston, was born 9th December, 1685, and admitted advocate in July, 1709. He was appointed Solicitor-General in 1717, and soon afterwards Lord Advocate. In 1721 he was chosen Dean of Faculty. In 1722 he was elected M.P. for the county of Edinburgh. He was raised to the bench in 1737, and in 1748 succeeded Duncan Forbes, of Culloden, as Lord President. An ingenious pleader and powerful reasoner, he was also distinguished for his sound judgment and inflexible integrity. He died on the 26th August, 1753.

[202] Sir John Dalrymple, first Earl of Stair, son of Lord President Stair, was born about 1648, and passed advocate in 1672. With his father he experienced much persecution under the rule of the House of Stewart; he afterwards made his peace at court, and in 1687 was appointed Lord Advocate. In 1688 he was raised to the bench as Lord Justice Clerk. He became Lord Advocate, and one of the principal Secretaries of State. His connection with the massacre of Glencoe brought him into odium, and compelled him to seek temporary retirement. In 1703 he was created Earl of Stair. He was a chief promoter of the Treaty of Union. He died on the 8th January, 1707.

[203] Sir Gilbert Elliot originally practised as a writer in Edinburgh, and was a vigorous supporter of the Presbyterian Church. From his adhering to the Marquess of Argyll he was found guilty of treason, and forfeited. Obtaining a remission of his sentence, he applied to be taken on trials as advocate, but was, on his first examination, rejected. He was admitted in November, 1688, and soon attained important practice. In 1700 he was created a baronet, and in 1705 was raised to the bench. He died 1st May, 1718.

[204] Sir William Anstruther, Bart., was M.P. for Fifeshire during the administration of the Duke of York in 1681, and stoutly opposed the measures of the Court. In 1689 he was appointed an ordinary Lord of Session; he afterwards obtained other offices and honours. He died 24th January, 1711.

[205] The Rev. John M'Claren was, in 1690, doctor in the Grammar School, Glasgow. He was in 1692 ordained minister of Kippen, and was translated to Carstairs in 1699. In 1711 he was preferred to the Tolbooth Church, Edinburgh. He declined the oath of abjuration in 1712, and was one of six who protested against the Seceders being loosed from their parochial charges, November, 1733. As a preacher he was most acceptable, delighting his hearers by his fertile and striking illustrations. He died 11th July, 1734.

[206] An ancient Scottish ballad, entitled "The Bonnie Earl of Murray," is founded on the murder of James Stewart, Earl of Murray, son-in-law and successor of the celebrated regent. He was slain at his own residence at Donibristle, Fifeshire, on the 9th February, 1592, by the hereditary enemy of his house, George, sixth Earl of Huntly. According to the story, the Earl of Murray, who was young and extremely handsome, attracted the admiration of Queen Anne of Denmark, who in the king's hearing described him as "a proper and gallant man." This emphatic commendation offended the king, who requested the Earl of Huntly to bring him into his presence. Huntly forthwith set fire to Donibristle Castle, and the earl in attempting to escape was slain. Lord Huntly was thrown into prison, but being released at the king's command was created a marquess. According to Boswell, James, seventh Earl of Moray, who died in 1767 was also styled "The Bonnie Earl."

[207] Charles, eighth Lord Cathcart.

[208] Mr. Richmond of Bardarrock, an Ayrshire landowner in the vicinity of Auchinleck, remarkable for his humorous sallies.

[209] Lord George Sackville, third son of the first Duke of Dorset, entered the army in 1737, and served at Dettingen, Fontenoy, and Culloden. In 1759 he was present at the battle of Minden, serving as lieutenant-general under Prince Ferdinand. Accused of disobeying orders, he was tried by court-martial, and being found guilty, was dismissed from the army. George II. caused his name to be removed from the roll of Privy Councillors. During the reign of George III. his good fortune was restored. As Secretary of State for the colonies under Lord North, he conducted the American War. In 1782 he was created

Viscount Sackville. He died in 1784, aged sixty-nine. Some have ascribed to him the Letters of Junius.

[210] The Rev. William Auld, designated *Daddy* Auld by the poet Burns, was ordained minister of Mauchline, Ayrshire, in 1742, and died 12th December, 1791, in his eighty-third year. He was a pious exemplary clergyman.

[211] Elizabeth, daughter of Sir Francis Kinloch, of Gilmerton, married Andrew Fletcher, a judge in the Court of Session by the title of Lord Milton.

[212] Sir Francis Grant, Bart., passed advocate in 1691, and was raised to the bench as Lord Cullen in 1709. A zealous loyalist and profound lawyer, he was, according to Wodrow, a man of exemplary piety. He died on the 26th March, 1726. Sir Alexander Ogilvy, Lord Forglen, died 30th March, 1727.

[213] A respectable tavern-keeper near Edinburgh.

[214] The heroine of this anecdote, whose name Boswell omits, was his relative, Mary Erskine, daughter of Colonel Erskine of Carnock, and aunt of the celebrated Dr. John Erskine of Greyfriars Church, Edinburgh.

[215] Brother of Robert Dundas of Arniston, Lord President of the Court of Session.

[216] Alexander Leslie, second son of David, third Earl of Leven, was admitted advocate in 1719. He succeeded his nephew as fifth Earl of Leven in 1729, and was appointed a judge in 1734. From 1741 to 1753 he held office as Lord High Commissioner to the General Assembly. He died in 1754.

[217] The second wife of Alexander Leslie, fifth Earl of Leven, was Elizabeth, daughter of David Monypenny, of Pitmilly, Fifeshire.

[218] Bryce Blair, of Blair, died 4th February, 1639.

[219] The Rev. William Blair was son of John Blair, burgess of Irvine, and great-grandson of Blair of that ilk; his youngest brother was the celebrated Robert Blair, minister of St. Andrews. Born in 1586, he became a regent in the University of Glasgow, and in 1620 was ordained minister of Dumbarton. He died in December, 1632, bequeathing a house for a residence to his successors.

[220] Mr. Blair's wife was Barbara Robertson, probably of the family of Orbiston.

[221] Bishop Warburton, author of "The Divine Legation of Moses," published in 1739 a series of letters in defence of Pope's "Essay on Man," against Mons. de Crousaz, who had accused the poet of favouring the doctrines of Spinoza. These letters led to a close intimacy between the poet and his vindicator. Bishop Warburton died at Gloucester on the 7th June, 1779.

[222] Afterwards Sir Joseph Banks.

[223] Sir William Meredith, M.P., published a work entitled "Historical Remarks on the Taxation of Free States." Lond., 1788, 8vo.

[224] See *supra*, p. 17.

[225] Sir George Colebrooke was chairman of the East India Company's Court of Directors. He represented Arundel in three successive parliaments. He married Mary, only daughter and heiress of Patrick Gaynor, Esq., of Antigua. Sir George Colebrooke died 5th August, 1809.

[226] David Charles Solander, the eminent naturalist, was born in Sweden in 1736. He was a companion of Sir Joseph Banks in Captain Cook's first voyage. In 1771 he received the degree of D.C.L. from the University of Oxford, and in 1773 became assistant librarian in the British Museum. He died in 1782.

[227] James Hamilton of Bangour, son of the poet, William Hamilton of Bangour.

[228] Thomas Alexander Erskine, sixth Earl of Kellie, was celebrated as a musician. Addicted to convivial pleasures, he made sacrifice of his genius, and expended in social humour talents which might have brought him eminence in the literary or political world. He died at Brussels, on the 9th October, 1781, aged forty-nine.

[229] Patrick Murray, fifth Lord Elibank, was an elegant and accomplished scholar. He studied law and passed advocate, but subsequently joined the army. In 1740 he accompanied Lord Cathcart in the expedition to Carthagena. Latterly he established his residence at Edinburgh. Dr. Johnson much enjoyed his society; in a letter addressed to his lordship he used these words:—"I have often declared that I never met you without going away a wiser man." Lord Elibank employed much of his time in classical studies. He died 3rd August, 1778, aged seventy-six.

[230] Andrew Crosbie of Holm, an eminent advocate, the original of "Councillor Pleydell" in "Guy Mannering." He met Dr. Johnson at Boswell's residence in Edinburgh, and engaged with him in keen

debate. In his "Journey" Boswell has described him as "his truly learned and philosophical friend." Crosbie attained opulence in his profession, but having made an unfortunate investment fell into poverty. He died in 1785.

[231] See *supra*, p. 74.

[232] Orangefield, an estate in the parish of Monkton, Ayrshire, now belonging to A. Murdoch, Esq.

[233] Mr. Bennet Langton, of Langton, in Lincolnshire, was an attached friend of Dr. Johnson. Many sayings of Dr. Johnson, which he preserved, Boswell has included in his great work. Mr. Langton at first sought employment as an engineer; he was an eminent Greek scholar. Possessed of an agreeable demeanour, he excelled in conversation. He died on the 10th December, 1801, aged sixty-four.

[234] 'History of the Life of James, Duke of Ormonde,' by Thomas Carte. 3 vols., fol. 1735-6.

[235] Thomas, Marquess of Wharton, a vigorous supporter of William of Orange, was on account of his peculiar manners familiarly known as Tom Wharton. He remained in favour with William III., and held high offices of state under Queen Anne and George I. He composed the celebrated "Lillibullero," and used to boast that he had sung a King out of three kingdoms. He died 12th April, 1713.

[236] Son of Archibald Campbell, of Succoth, and Helen Wallace, of Ellerslie, Ilay Campbell was admitted advocate in 1757. Obtaining distinction as a lawyer, he was appointed Lord Advocate in 1784, and was in 1799 promoted as Lord President of the Court of Session. This office he resigned in 1808, when he was created a baronet. He died on the 28th March, 1823, in his eighty-ninth year. The Most Reverend Archibald Campbell Tait, D.C.L., Archbishop of Canterbury, is his grandson.

[237] See *supra*, p. 255.

[238] Alexander Murray was admitted to the Scottish bar in 1758, and three years afterwards succeeded his father as sheriff of Peeblesshire. In 1775 he was appointed Solicitor-General, and was in 1780 chosen M.P. for Peeblesshire. He was promoted to the bench in 1783, with the title of Lord Henderland. He died 16th March, 1795.

[239] Charles Hay passed advocate in 1768, and with the title of Lord Newton was raised to the bench in 1806. By Lord Cockburn in his "Memorials" he is thus described:—"A man famous for law, paunch, whist, claret, and worth. His judicial title was Newton, but in private

life he was chiefly known as 'the Mighty.' He was a bulky man with short legs, twitching eyes, and a large purple visage; no speaker, but an excellent writer and adviser; deep and accurate in his law, in which he had extensive employment. Honest, warm-hearted and considerate, he was always true to his principles and his friends. But these and other good qualities were all apt to be lost sight of in people's admiration of his drinking. His daily and flowing cups raised him far above the evil days of sobriety on which he had fallen, and made him worthy of honours quaffed with the Scandinavian heroes. His delight was to sit smiling, quiet, and listening; saying little, but that little always sensible, for he used to hold that conversation—at least, when it was of the sort that merits admiration—spoiled good company." Lord Newton died on the 19th October, 1811.

[240] John Maclaurin, son of the celebrated Professor Colin Maclaurin, was admitted advocate in 1756. He enjoyed a high reputation as a lawyer, and was extensively consulted by his professional brethren. In 1788 he was raised to the bench, with the judicial title of Lord Dreghorn. He died on the 24th December, 1796, in his sixty-second year. His works, chiefly on judicial subjects, were published in 1798 in two octavo volumes.

[241] David Erskine, son of the proprietor of Dun, was called to the Bar in 1698. As parliamentary representative of the county of Forfar he strongly opposed the Union. In 1710 he was appointed a Lord of Session, when he took the title of Lord Dun. He died on the 26th May, 1758, in his eighty-fifth year. Lord Dun was respected for his piety.

[242] Lord President Dundas.

[243] The Right Hon. Charles Townshend, styled by Lord Macaulay "the most brilliant and versatile of mankind," was second son of the third Viscount Townshend. Entering the House of Commons in his twenty-second year, he became in Chatham's last administration Chancellor of the Exchequer and leader of the House of Commons. He died suddenly 4th September, 1767, in his forty-fifth year. A considerable humorist, he marred his reputation by a tendency to sarcasm.

[244] Henry Home, Lord Kames, author of "The Elements of Criticism" and other works, was son of George Home of Kames, Berwickshire. He passed advocate in 1723, and was elevated to the bench in 1752. He died 27th December, 1782, aged eighty-seven.

[245] Second son of the Rev. Robert Wallace, D.D., George Wallace was born at Moffat in 1730. Admitted advocate in 1754, he attained

considerable eminence in his profession. He published "A System of the Principles of the Law of Scotland," vol. i., Edinb., 1760, folio; "Thoughts on the Origin of Feudal Powers, and the Descent of Ancient Peerages in Scotland," Edinb., 1783, 4to.; "The Nature and Descent of Ancient Peerages, addressed to the Earl of Mansfield," Edinb., 1785, 8vo.; "Prospects from Hills in Fife," 3rd edit., Edinb., 1802, 8vo. The last work is composed in verse, the author remarking in the preface that the "Prospects" were mostly composed many years ago to afford their "author an occasional relief from the austerity and vexations of a profession very remote from poetry." Mr. Wallace died on the 15th March, 1805, in his seventy-fifth year. His father, Dr. Robert Wallace, successively minister at Moffat and in the city of Edinburgh, was founder of the Philosophical Society, which afterwards merged into the Royal Society of Edinburgh. An expert mathematician, he assisted Dr. Alexander Webster in making calculations connected with the establishment of the Ministers Widows' Fund. He died in 1771.

[246] Andrew Balfour was admitted advocate in 1763; he practised at the bar for nearly half a century.

[247] The negro's name was Joseph Knight. (See *supra*, p. 115.)

[248] Major-General John Scott, of Balcomie, descended from Scot of Scotstarvet, author of "The Staggering State," was one of the most noted Scotsmen of his period. About 1768 he was elected M.P. for Fifeshire. Lady Mary Hay, his first wife, was the eldest daughter of James, thirteenth Earl of Erroll. The general married, secondly, Margaret, youngest daughter of Robert Dundas of Arniston, Lord President of the Court of Session. General Scott died in December, 1775. A notorious gamester, he acquired numerous estates, and at the period of his death was regarded as the wealthiest commoner in Scotland. He is represented by the Duke of Portland.

[249] Afterwards Lord Henderland.

[250] Sir William Nairne, Bart., Lord Dunsinnan (see *supra*).

[251] General Sir Archibald Grant had served in the East Indies; he succeeded his father as third baronet of Monymusk. He died in 1796.

[252] William Nisbet of Dirleton died 1784. He was a patron of John Kay, the eminent Edinburgh caricaturist, who frequently resided at his house. His present representative is his great-granddaughter, Lady Mary Christopher Nisbet Hamilton.

[253] Sir Alexander Dick, Bart., younger son of Sir William Cuninghame of Caprington, Ayrshire, was born in October, 1703. For some years he practised as a physician in Pembrokeshire. Succeeding his brother in 1746 in the lands and baronetcy of Prestonfield, near Edinburgh, he assumed the name of Dick, and fixed his residence at the family seat. He was elected President of the Royal College of Physicians, Edinburgh, and attained other professional and scientific honours. Dr. Johnson held him in high esteem. Boswell, in his "Tour to the Hebrides," commends Sir Alexander for his amiability and culture. He died on the 10th November, 1785, aged eighty-two.

[254] David Stuart Moncrieffe, of Moredun, second son of Sir David Moncrieffe, Bart. He was an advocate at the Scottish bar, and latterly one of the Barons of Exchequer.

[255] John Brown, china merchant in Old Shakespeare Square, and sometime one of the magistrates of Edinburgh, caused to be erected at his sole expense an elegant window of stained glass in the great hall of the Court of Session known as the Parliament House. He died 13th April, 1780.

[256] Hon. Archibald Erskine was younger brother of Thomas Alexander, the musical Earl of Kellie, and succeeded him in 1781 as seventh earl. For twenty-six years he served in the army, and became lieutenant-colonel of the 104th Foot. In 1790 he was chosen a Scottish representative peer. Through his unwearied efforts the restraints imposed on Scottish Episcopalians in 1746 and 1748 were abrogated. He died at Kellie, Fifeshire, 8th May, 1797, aged sixty-two.

[257] John Thomson, of Charleton, Fifeshire.

[258] Lady Anne Erskine was eldest daughter of Alexander, third Earl of Kellie, and wife of her cousin, Sir Alexander Erskine, second baronet of Cambo, Lord Lyon King at Arms.

[259] James Beattie, LL.D., Professor of Moral Philosophy, Marischal College, Aberdeen. His essay on "The Nature and Immutability of Truth," alluded to by Boswell, was published in 1770. Dr. Beattie died on the 6th October, 1802.

[260] Sir Adam Fergusson, Bart., of Kilkerran, LL.D., was eldest son of Sir James Fergusson, Bart., a judge of the Court of Session by the title of Lord Kilkerran. Elected M.P. for Ayrshire in 1774, Sir Adam continued to represent that county for eighteen years. He afterwards sat for the county of Edinburgh. By the House of Lords he was found to be heir-general to Alexander, tenth Earl of Glencairn. He died 23rd September, 1813. That he was "great-grandson of a messenger" is not

historically borne out. His paternal great-grandfather was Simon Fergusson of Auchinwin, youngest son of Sir John Fergusson of Kilkerran, Knight.

[261] The seat of John, fourth Earl of Loudoun.

[262] Major Andrew Dunlop was second son of John Dunlop, of Dunlop, Ayrshire. He served in the American war, and afterwards commanded the Ayrshire Fencibles. He died in 1804. His mother was Frances Anne, daughter and heiress of Sir Thomas Wallace of Craigie. She was a friend and correspondent of the poet Burns.

[263] David Kennedy was admitted advocate in 1752. He was elected M.P. for Ayrshire in 1768. In 1775 he succeeded his elder brother as tenth Earl of Cassilis, and died 18th December, 1792.

[264] David Rae was called to the bar in 1751, and soon obtained reputation as a lawyer. He was appointed a judge in succession to Lord Auchinleck in November, 1782, and was promoted as Lord Justice Clerk in 1799. He was created a baronet in 1804. He died the same year, aged eighty.

[265] John Swinton, son of John Swinton of Swinton, was admitted advocate in 1743. After several professional preferments he was raised to the bench as Lord Swinton in 1782. He published an abridgment of statutes relating to Scotland, and other works. He died 5th January, 1799.

[266] John Hamilton, of Sundrum, was for thirty-six years Convener of the county of Ayr. He died in 1821 at a very advanced age.

[267] James Burnett, of Monboddo, was admitted advocate in 1737. After a brilliant and successful career at the bar, he was raised to the bench in 1767 as Lord Monboddo. He visited London every year, accomplishing the journey on horseback. Introduced at court, he was especially honoured by George III., who much relished his conversation. An accomplished scholar, he cherished some strange ideas regarding the origin of mankind. Of his several works the most notable is his "Origin and Progress of Language." He died on the 26th May, 1799, aged eighty-five.

[268] General Robert Melville was son of the minister of Monimail, Fifeshire. Entering the army in his twenty-first year, he served in the invasion of Guadaloupe and other important concerns. After the general peace he travelled over Europe, and endeavoured to ascertain the passage of Hannibal over the Alps. He traced the sites of different Roman camps in Britain. His historical and antiquarian learning were

acknowledged by several learned societies, and the University of Edinburgh granted him the degree in laws. General Melville died in 1809, aged eighty-six.

[269] Eglinton, youngest daughter of Sir William Maxwell, Bart., of Monreith, married, 4th September, 1773, Sir Thomas Wallace, sixth Baronet of Craigie. Like her elder sister, Jane Duchess of Gordon, she was celebrated for her beauty and wit.

[270] Son of Sir James Fergusson, Bart., of Kilkerran, George Fergusson was admitted advocate in 1765. Appointed a judge in 1799 he adopted the title of Lord Hermand. He retired in 1826, and died the following year.

[271] Richard Burke, collector of Grenada, was brother of the celebrated Edmund Burke, who used every opportunity of bringing him forward. He possessed some share of his brother's powers, which, however, he only displayed in the social circle.

[272] Andrew Stuart, M.P. (see *supra*), published in 1778 "Letters to the Directors of the East India Company respecting the conduct of Brigadier-General James Stuart at Madras," 4to.

[273] Sir George Pigot, Bart., Governor of Fort St. George, Madras, was created a peer of Ireland 18th January, 1766, as Baron Pigot, of Patshul, county Dublin. At his death in illegal confinement in India, 17th August, 1777, the barony expired.

[274] William Seward, F.R.S., was born at London in 1747, his father being a wealthy brewer, partner in the house of Calvert and Seward. Educated at the Charterhouse and at Oxford, he early devoted attention to literary concerns. He published "Biographiana" and "Literary Miscellanies," and edited "Anecdotes of some Distinguished Persons," in four volumes, octavo. He was much esteemed for his amiable manners. He died 24th April, 1789.

[275] Sir Hugh Palliser was born at Kirk Deighton, Yorkshire, 26th February, 1722. Joining the navy, he became lieutenant in 1742. He was posted captain in 1746, after taking four French privateers. In 1759 he led the seamen who aided in the capture of Quebec. In 1773 he was created a baronet and elected M.P. for Scarborough. He became a Lord of the Admiralty, and Vice-Admiral of the Blue. In an action off Ushant on the 27th July, 1778, a misunderstanding arose between Admiral Palliser and Admiral Keppel, which was attended with a court-martial, and brought on Palliser unmerited odium. He became Governor of Greenwich Hospital, and died 19th March, 1796.

[276] Topham Beauclerk, only son of Lord Sidney Beauclerk, third son of the first Duke of St. Alban's, was born in 1739. When a student at Trinity College, Oxford, he became acquainted with Dr. Johnson, who, though many years his senior, was partial to his society. Johnson permitted sallies from Beauclerk which others might not attempt. Beauclerk died in 1781.

[277] Robert Brompton, an artist of considerable celebrity, accompanied Lord Northampton, the English ambassador, to Venice, where he executed portraits of the Duke of York and other notable persons. He returned to London in 1767, but not meeting with sufficient encouragement he proceeded to St. Petersburg, where he died in 1790.

[278] Henry, tenth Earl of Pembroke, was lieutenant-general in the army and colonel of the first regiment of dragoons. He was born in 1734, and died 26th January, 1794.

[279] The representative of an ancient Scottish house, which produced a distinguished archbishop and a Lord President of the Court of Session, John Spottiswoode, younger of Spottiswoode, practised in London as a solicitor. His literary tastes brought him into contact with men of letters. The conversation alluded to in the text took place at Paoli's, when Dr. Johnson, Sir Joshua Reynolds, and others were present. In his "Life of Dr. Johnson," Boswell, who reported the conversation in reference to wine drinking, omits with unusual reticence his remark respecting his own habits. Spottiswoode was son-in-law of William Strahan, the printer. He died 3rd February, 1805.

[280] This anecdote is related in the Life of Johnson, the quotation from Horace being correctly given, thus:—

"Numerisque fertur

Lege solutis."

[281] John Dunning was born at Ashburton, Devonshire, on the 18th October, 1731. Called to the bar, he attained a first rank in his profession. In 1767 he was appointed Solicitor-General. In 1768 he was elected M.P. for Calne. He was in 1782 created Baron Ashburton, and appointed Chancellor of the Duchy of Lancaster. He was an occasional associate of Dr. Johnson, who styled him "the great lawyer." Informed by Boswell that Mr. Dunning experienced pleasure in listening to him, Dr. Johnson expressed appreciation, adding, "Here is a man willing to listen, to whom the world is listening all the rest of the year." Lord Ashburton died 18th August, 1783.

[282] George Colman the elder was born in 1733. While studying at Christ Church, Oxford, he was called to the bar, but he soon renounced practice as a barrister and sought fame as a dramatic author. He became joint manager of Covent Garden Theatre, and was ultimately proprietor of the Haymarket. For many years he enjoyed an annuity from Lord Bath, who married his mother's sister. After a period of mental aberration, Colman died in 1794, aged sixty-one.

[283] The Hon. Henry Erskine, second son of Henry David, fourth Earl of Buchan, was a celebrated humorist. Born in 1746, he was admitted advocate in 1768, and soon attained the foremost place in his profession. He was Lord Advocate in 1783, and again in 1806. He latterly retired from public business, residing on his estate of Amondell, Linlithgowshire, where he died 8th October, 1817. His younger brother was Lord Chancellor Erskine.

[284] Patrick Murray, an Edinburgh advocate, published, with others "Decisions of the Court of Session," from November, 1760, to November, 1764. Edinb., 1772, folio.

[285] The outer house of the court of session, where the lords ordinary formerly sat, is a spacious hall, the ancient meeting-place of the Scottish Parliament. It is now solely used as a promenade-room by advocates and others attending on the business of the court.

[286] Household servants in Scotland formerly assembled in the hall when guests were departing, doing obeisance to each, in acknowledgment of which they expected gratuities. These were termed *vails*.

[287] Lady Diana Spencer, daughter of Charles Duke of Marlborough, was born in 1734, and in 1757 married Lord Bolingbroke. She was divorced in 1768, and thereafter became the wife of Mr. Topham Beauclerk.

[288] Algernon Seymour, who succeeded his mother in 1722 as Baron Percy, and in 1748 inherited the Dukedom of Somerset. His only child, Lady Elizabeth Seymour, became Duchess of Northumberland.

[289] Thomas Parnell, D.D., author of "The Hermit" and other poems, was an Irish clergyman, and a friend of Swift, who bestowed on him a share of his patronage. Early inclined to the excessive use of wine, he latterly became an habitual drunkard. He died in July, 1718, in his thirty-ninth year.

[290] Robert Harley, Earl of Oxford, Lord High Treasurer, was a steady promoter of men of letters. His career forms an important part

of the political history of England. He died 21st May, 1724. The Harleian Collection of books and MSS. in the British Museum is a monument of his learning and industry.

[291] The great Dr. Benjamin Franklin, born 1706, died 1790.

[292] Jean Baptiste Antoine Suard published "Variétés Littéraires" and "Mélanges de Littérature." He was born 16th January, 1750, and died 20th July, 1817.

[293] Thomas, second Lord Foley, died 8th January, 1766.

[294] See *supra*, p. 97.

[295] Sir Matthew White-Ridley, Bart., M.P. for Newcastle-on-Tyne, married, 12th July, 1777, Sarah, daughter and heiress of Benjamin Colborne, Esq., of Bath. Lady White-Ridley died 3rd August, 1806.

[296] *Née* Miss Hadfield, born at Leghorn, of English parents. She married Richard Cosway, R.A., and shared her husband's reputation as an artist. Her musical *soirées*, at which she was *prima donna*, were much resorted to by persons of rank and fashion.

[297] Wilkes was in 1703 imprisoned in the Tower on the charge of sedition. In 1774 he was elected Lord Mayor of London.

[298] Probably James Hutton, M.D., author of "The Plutonic Theory of the Earth." He was born in 1726, and may have been styled *Old* Hutton to distinguish him from Charles Hutton, the eminent mathematician, who was born in 1737.

[299] Charles Burney, Mus.D., author of "The General History of Music," and other works. He was an intimate friend of Dr. Johnson, who confessedly prepared his "Tour to the Hebrides" after the model of Dr. Burney's "Continental Travels." Dr. Burney was born at Shrewsbury, on the 7th April, 1726, and died at Chelsea, 12th April, 1814.

[300] John, seventh Earl of Galloway, K.P., one of the lords of the bedchamber to George III. In 1796 he was created a peer of Great Britain by the title of Baron Stewart of Garlies. He died 13th November, 1806.

[301] John, Lord Daer, third son of Dunbar Hamilton Douglas, fourth Earl of Selkirk.

[302] The celebrated Edward Gibbon was born in 1737, and died in 1794. In conversation he was genial and elegant, but he occasionally indulged in flashes of irony.

[303] William, second Earl of Shelburne, subsequently Marquess of Lansdown, a distinguished statesman. In 1782 he succeeded the Marquess of Rockingham as Prime Minister. At one period he much frequented the society of Dr. Johnson. The Marquess died in May, 1805.

[304] Richard Price, D.D., a Dissenting minister in London, and eminent philosophical writer, was born in 1723, and died in March, 1791. Dr. Price was a friend and correspondent of Lord Shelburne. An advocate of civil and religious liberty, he supported the cause of American independence, and welcomed the early triumphs of the French Revolution.

[305] Dr. Brocklesby, an accomplished physician, and the generous friend of Edmund Burke and Dr. Johnson. He published various periodical papers on professional subjects. Dr. Brocklesby was born in 1702, and died 1797.

[306] William Schaw, tenth Baron and first Earl Cathcart, born 1755, died 16th June, 1843.

[307] Colonel George Hanger, an eccentric writer and clever humorist, served in the American war. He subsequently resided in London, where his society was cherished by the Prince of Wales, afterwards George IV. Several works from his pen are full of whimsicality. He succeeded his brother in 1814 as fourth Lord Coleraine, but refused to accept the title. He died in 1824, aged seventy-four.

[308] Mrs. Heron, of Heron, Wigtonshire.

[309] Rev. Ebenezer Stott, minister of Monigaff, Wigtonshire. He was ordained in 1748, and died 17th September, 1788.

[310] Houstoun Stewart, second son of Sir Michael Stewart, Bart., of Blackhall, succeeded to the entailed estate of Carnock, Stirlingshire, when he assumed the name of Nicolson.

[311] Harry Barclay, of Collairnie, Fifeshire.

[312] In 1741, Henry Home, Lord Kames, married Miss Agatha Drummond, only daughter of the proprietor of Blair-Drummond, Perthshire, who, on the death of her brother in 1766, succeeded to the paternal estate. Her proper designation was Mrs. Hume Drummond, of Blair-Drummond.

[313] Anne, only surviving daughter of Sir William Bruce, Bart., of Kinross, and heiress of his estates. She married, first, Sir Thomas

Hope, Bart., of Craighall; and secondly, Sir John Carstairs, of Kilconquhar, and had issue by both marriages.

[314] Patrick Heron, Esq., M.P.

[315] John, tenth Viscount Kenmure. Died 21st September, 1824. He was Vice-Lieutenant of Kirkcudbrightshire.

[316] John, seventh Earl of Galloway, had as his first wife Charlotte Mary, daughter of Francis, first Earl of Warwick. He bore by courtesy the title of Lord Garlies before succeeding his father as Earl in 1773.

[317] Edward, Viscount Coke, eldest son of the Earl of Leicester. He married Lady Mary Campbell, daughter and co-heiress of John, Duke of Argyll and Greenwich, and died *s. p.* in 1753.

[318] Pope has thus described the character of this noted libertine:—"Francis Chartres, a man infamous for all manner of vices. When he was an ensign in the army, he was drummed out of the regiment for a cheat; he was next banished to Brussels, and drummed out of Ghent on the same account. After a hundred tricks at the gaming-tables, he took to lending money at exorbitant interest and on great penalties, accumulating premium, interest, and capital into a new capital, and seizing to a minute when the payments became due. In a word, by a constant attention to the vices, wants, and follies of mankind, he acquired an immense fortune. He was twice condemned for rapes and pardoned, but the last time not without imprisonment in Newgate, and large confiscations. He died in Scotland in 1731 (February, 1732). The populace at his funeral raised a great riot, almost tore the body out of the coffin, and cast dead dogs into the grave along with it." Arbuthnot's epitaph on Colonel Chartres is celebrated for its epigrammatic force.

[319] John, Duke of Argyll and Greenwich, celebrated as a statesman and military commander, is immortalized in these lines of Pope,—

"Argyll, the state's whole thunder born to wield,
And shake alike the senate and the field."

The Duke was born in 1678, and died in 1743.

[320] Lady Catherine Murray was elder daughter of William, third Earl of Dunmore.

[321] George Baillie of Jerviswoode and Mellerstain. His great-grandson, George Baillie Hamilton, became tenth Earl of Haddington.

[322] There are several versions of this song. The oldest has this opening stanza:—

"How blithe, ilk morn, was I to see

My swain come o'er the hill!

He skipt the burn and flew to me;

I met him with good-will.

Oh the brume, the bonnie, bonnie brume!

The brume o' the Cowdenknowes!

I wish I were with my dear swain,

With his pipe and my yowes."

[323] John McKie, of Bargaly, in the stewardry of Kirkcudbright. His grandson, who bore the same Christian name, was many years M.P. for the stewardry.

[324] Probably Sir Robert Dalzell, first Earl of Carnwath.

[325] John, eighth Viscount Kenmure.

[326] Mrs. Dunbar, of Mackermore, whose estate in the parish of Monnigaff, Kirkcudbrightshire, bordered that of Mr. Heron of Heron.

[327] Lord Mark Ker was fourth son of the first Marquess of Lothian, a distinguished military officer; he was wounded at the battle of Almanza, 25th April, 1707; he acted as brigadier-general at the capture of Vigo. In January, 1745, he was appointed Governor of Edinburgh Castle. He died 2nd February, 1752.

[328] Hugh Montgomerie, a prosperous merchant in Glasgow, and Lord Provost of the city, succeeded his uncle as fourth baronet of Skermorly. He became M.P. for Glasgow, and was a commissioner for the Treaty of Union. He died in 1735.

[329] James Corbet, merchant in Glasgow, rejoiced in tracing his descent from Roger Corbet (Roger the Raven), who came from Normandy with William the Conqueror. Till lately the family of Corbet possessed lands in Clydesdale.

[330] David Campbell, first of Shawfield, second son of Walter Campbell, Captain of Skipness, made a fortune abroad, and was elected M.P. for Glasgow; he was a commissioner in the Treaty of Union.

[331] Colonel John Irving, pronounced Irwin, of the family of Irving, of Logan, served in the Madras army, and became lieutenant-colonel of the Dumfriesshire militia.

[332] Catherine, second wife of Alexander, sixth Earl of Galloway was youngest daughter of John, fourth Earl of Dundonald.

[333] This gentlewoman was second wife of John, Lord Garlies, subsequently seventh Earl of Galloway. She was daughter of Sir James Dashwood, Bart., and was married to Lord Garlies in 1764. Her ladyship died in 1830.

[334] Son of Sir Adam Whitefoord, Bart., of Blairquhan, Ayrshire. The baronetcy is extinct.

[335] Sir William Maxwell, third baronet of Springkell; born 31st December, 1739; died 4th March, 1804.

[336] The earldom of Fife was renewed in the person of William Duff of Braco, who in 1727 was elected M.P. for the county of Banff. In 1735 he was created Baron Braco of Kilbryde, and was raised to the Earldom of Fife in 1759. He died 30th September, 1763.

[337] The reference is probably to Miss Jane Maxwell, second daughter of Sir William Maxwell, Bart., of Monreith, who married, in 1767, Alexander, fourth Duke of Gordon. The Duchess was celebrated for her beauty and wit.

[338] David, sixth Lord Stormont, died 1748.

[339] Apparently the dowager of Alexander, fourth Baron Elibank, daughter of George Stirling, surgeon, Edinburgh.

[340] Sir William Baird, Bart., of Newbyth, succeeded his cousin Sir John Baird in 1746.

[341] Robert Riddell, head of an old Dumfriesshire family, was predecessor of Robert Riddell of Glenriddell, the antiquary and an active patron of Robert Burns.

[342] James, sixth Duke of Hamilton. He married Elizabeth, one of the three beautiful Misses Gunning, who on his death espoused John, fifth Duke of Argyle. The Duke of Hamilton died on the 18th January, 1758, in his thirty-fourth year.

[343] Representative of Sir Alexander Fraser of Durris, who was created a baronet in 1673. The baronetcy is extinct.

[344] John, third Earl of Hyndford, was in 1741 appointed envoy extraordinary and plenipotentiary to the King of Prussia. He died 19th July, 1767, aged sixty-seven.

[345] John, fourth Earl of Dunmore. His eldest son, George, Viscount Fincastle, was born on the 30th April, 1762. The Earl died in March, 1809.

[346] Thomas, ninth Earl of Cassilis. Died 30th November 1775.

[347] Probably a brother of John Alexander, the celebrated painter. John Alexander studied his art chiefly in Florence; he returned to Scotland in 1720, and thereafter chiefly resided in Gordon Castle, under the patronage of the Duchess of Gordon.

[348] Henry, second Duke of Newcastle. His Grace died in 1794.

[349] George Selwyn, M.P., the celebrated humorist, was born in 1719, and died 25th January, 1791. ("Sir George Selwyn and his Contemporaries," by J. H. Pope, 1843.)

[350] Walter Macfarlane, of that ilk, descended from the old Earls of Lennox, was an accomplished antiquary and ingenious genealogist. He died at Edinburgh, on the 5th June, 1767. His valuable MSS. were acquired by the Faculty of Advocates.

[351] Lady Elizabeth Macfarlane, wife of Walter Macfarlane, of that ilk, was eldest daughter of Alexander, fifth Earl of Kellie. She married, secondly, Alexander, eighth Lord Colville, of Culross, and died in 1794.

[352] Edward Shuter, comedian, died 1st November, 1776.

[353] The Duke de Nivernais, an eminent French statesman and poet, was born 16th December, 1716, and died 25th February, 1798.

[354] General Sir George Howard served under the Duke of Cumberland in suppressing the Scottish Rebellion of 1745. In a note to his "Life of Johnson," Boswell styles him "My very honourable friend."

[355] Mrs. Boscawen was daughter of William Evelyn Glanville, Esq., and wife of Admiral Edward Boscawen, a distinguished commander, and sometime a Lord of the Admiralty. In 1761 she became a widow. Her only son succeeded as third Viscount Falmouth; and of her two daughters, Frances, the elder, married Admiral John Leveson Gower, brother of the first Marquess of Stafford; Elizabeth, the younger daughter, married Henry, fifth Duke of Beaufort. In her poem entitled "Sensibility," Miss Hannah More remarks of Mrs. Boscawen that she—

"Views enamoured in her beauteous race

All Leveson's sweetness and all Beaufort's grace."

In the "Life of Johnson," Boswell, in allusion to having met the Hon. Mrs. Boscawen at dinner at Allan Ramsay's (29th April, 1778), writes: "Of whom, if it be not presumptuous in me to praise her, I would say that her manners are the most agreeable, and her conversation the best, of any lady with whom I ever had the happiness to be acquainted."

[356] See *postea*.

[357] Sir Philip Ainslie, of Pilton, Edinburghshire.

[358] Sir John Pringle, Bart., a distinguished physician. He was in 1772 elected President of the Royal Society, and six discourses delivered by him to that body were published after his decease, under the care of Dr. Kippis. These discourses form the theme of Boswell's criticisms. John Pringle died on the 18th January, 1782, aged seventy-five.

[359] The Hon. Patrick Boyle, second son of John, second Earl of Glasgow.

[360] Sir John Wemyss, Bart., of Bogie, Fifeshire.

[361] This improvident gentleman, who had sought refuge from his creditors in the sanctuary of Holyrood Abbey, was related to the family of Lord Colville, of Culross. From a dinner card pasted into the commonplace-book, the wife of Dr. Alexander Webster, of Edinburgh, formerly minister of Culross, thus entreats Boswell's support to this unfortunate bankrupt:—

"Mrs. Webster begs Mrs. Boswell would set about the collection for poor Mr. Colville, who is truly starving and has not a house to cover his head. Mr. Ely Campbell has too much humanity not to give something handsome."

[362] Sir Thomas Rumbold was created a baronet 23rd March, 1779, being then Governor of Madras and M.P. for Shoreham. He had distinguished himself at the siege of Trichinopoly and the retaking of Calcutta. He was wounded at the battle of Plassey, when acting as aide-de-camp to Lord Clive. He died 11th November, 1791.

[363] John Paradise, D.C.L., P.R.S., was son of the English consul at Salonica, by his wife, a native of Macedonia. He studied at Padua, and afterwards at Oxford. Having settled in London, he became a cherished associate of Dr. Johnson. He was distinguished for his learning and social virtues. He died 12th December, 1795.

[364] This gentlewoman, *née* Anne Cochrane, was wife of Sir George Preston, Bart., of Valleyfield. She was daughter of William, Lord Cochrane of Ochiltree.

[365] A naval captain, of the House of Brisbane, of Brisbane in Ayrshire.

[366] Katherine, Lady Maxwell of Monreith, wife of the fourth baronet. She was daughter and heir of David Blair of Adamton, Ayrshire.

[367] Charles Cochrane, Esq., of Culross, a member of the Dundonald family.

[368] Sir Robert Monro, Bart., of Fowlis (not Sir Harry Munro), is commemorated in the churchyard of Falkirk by a massive and elegantly sculptured tombstone. He fell in the engagement at Falkirk on the 17th January, 1746.

[369] The Rev. James Rolland was ordained minister of the first charge of Culross in 1758; he died 10th December, 1815, in his eighty-eighth year, and the sixty-second of his ministry. He was reputed for his amiable manners and sterling piety. (*Scott's Fasti.*)

[370] William, second Earl of Dumfries, had only one son, Lord Crichton, who reached maturity. He predeceased his father, leaving a son and daughter. The earl died in 1691.

[371] Dr. Robert James, best known in connection with the fever powder that bears his name, was born in 1703, at Kinverston, Staffordshire. After practising as a physician at Sheffield, Lichfield, and Birmingham, he removed to London, where he published his "Medicinal Dictionary." In the preparation of this work he was assisted by Dr. Johnson, who had been his schoolfellow, and who regarded him as a skilful practitioner. Dr. James produced several other medical works. He died at London on the 23rd March, 1776.

[372] Mr. Gilbert Walmsley, an early friend and patron of Dr. Johnson. He was an elegant scholar, and contributed many translations in Latin verse to the *Gentleman's Magazine*. He died on the 3rd August, 1751. A monument to his memory has been reared in Lichfield Cathedral.

[373] Thomas Sheridan, father of his more celebrated son, Richard Brinsley Sheridan (see *supra*).

[374] *Née* Lady Charlotte Compton, daughter of James, Earl of Northampton, and wife of Field-marshal George, fourth Viscount Townshend.

[375] James Short, the eminent optician, was a native of Edinburgh, and studied at the university of that city. In 1736 he became mathematical tutor to the Duke of Cumberland. In 1739 he made a

survey of the Orkney islands. He subsequently settled in London as an optician, and obtained a high reputation for his skill in constructing telescopes. He died on the 15th June, 1768, aged 58. He had experienced the patronage of James, thirteenth Earl of Morton, and he evinced his gratitude by bequeathing a thousand pounds to Lady Mary Douglas (afterwards Countess of Aboyne), the daughter of his benefactor.

[376] Boswell refers to the Dowager Lady Colville, relict of Alexander, the eighth Baron. She was daughter of Alexander, sixth Earl of Kellie, and sister of the Hon. Captain Andrew Erskine.

[377] Thomas Alexander, sixth Earl of Kellie, an eminent musician and noted humorist. Died 9th October, 1781.

[378] David Dalrymple, son of Henry Dalrymple of Drummore, passed advocate in 1743, and was raised to the bench as Lord Westhall, 10th July, 1777. He died 26th April, 1784, in his 65th year.

[379] The parish of Carsphairn, in the Presbytery of Kirkcudbright, became vacant in May 1780, by the death of the Rev. John Campbell. The presentee, Mr. Affleck, was probably a son of John Affleck, of Whitepark, in the same county. His settlement was successfully resisted.

[380] The Rev. James Brown merits more than a passing notice. Youngest son of the Rev. John Brown, minister of Abercorn, he was born in that parish in 1721. Licensed by the Presbytery of Perth in 1745, he was in 1747 ordained minister of Melrose. In 1767 was translated to Edinburgh. At Melrose he gave an impulse to the linen manufactures of the place; he afterwards became a zealous promoter of the national charities. On his recommendation, Scripture Paraphrases were added to the Psalmody of the Church. He died on May, 1786.

[381] Lieut.-General Alexander Leslie was second son of Alexander, fifth Earl of Leven. In active service during the American war, he distinguished himself at the battle of Guildford, on the 15th March, 1781. His only child, Mary-Ann Leslie, married 15th June, 1787, John Rutherford, Esq., of Edgerstown.

[382] Sir James Johnstone, Bart., of Westerhall, was a lieutenant-colonel in the army and member of Parliament. In 1792 he laid claim to the marquisate of Annandale. He died unmarried in 1794.

[383] Mr. Robert Keith was ambassador at Vienna in 1749, and in 1758 was transferred to St. Petersburg. He died at Edinburgh in 1774.

[384] Miss Jenny Keith. The younger sister, Anne, latterly called Mrs. Murray Keith, was an intimate friend of Sir Walter Scott; she is the prototype of Mrs. Bethune Baliol, in the introduction to the "Chronicles of the Canongate." She died in 1818, aged 82.

[385] Thomas Barnard, D.D.

Milton Keynes UK
Ingram Content Group UK Ltd.
UKHW040044180324
439604UK00006B/982